BMW
E30 - 3 Series
Restoration Bible

By Andrew Everett

www.brooklands-books.com

BMW E30 - 3 Series Restoration Bible

Published by

BROOKLANDS BOOKS LTD.
P.O. BOX 146, COBHAM,
SURREY, KT11 1LG. UK
sales@brooklands-books.com

ISBN 9781855206786

BMW30R

Printed and bound in China

ACKNOWLEDGMENTS

Writing a book like this is the most long winded thing I've ever done, and has taken a year of my life. Originally it was planned as a restoration guide but it sprouted from there and has covered a great deal more; it is at its best when combined with a Bentley Publishing workshop manual (see details on page 170 and 175), probably the best manual on the market anywhere. Inspiration has come from many places but the guy who spent days taking digital pictures and really started the ball rolling is my good pal Alf Dickhaut from Germany, an M Power specialist who also distributes stainless steel brake hoses. When he should really have been with his better (and prettier) half Sandra, he spent time in a cold workshop taking many of these photos - about 130 in all. Thanks Alf. Next up comes Paul Wager from Total BMW Magazine who took the rust pictures of a particularly nasty 325i amongst others - thanks to him and the magazine for all their help. Brendan Purcell from the BMW Car Club's Irish section donated lots of 318iS knowledge including the sections of timing chain replacement which saved me a lot of grief. He also wrote the foreword which sums up the E30 nicely. Next we have almost the entire crew from www.e30zone.co.uk for various pearls of wisdom and yet more inspiration - Ian Haynes, Ant Woodjetts, Adam Patchton and just about everyone else there I think. Peter Walsh from PMW in West London gave hours of time with questions about E30's and the M3 in particular. Neil Waterhouse of All Gears in Worksop allowed me a week of workshop space and the use of facilities to build a 2.8 litre engine. Julian Smith helped with this engine (and the section on 2.7 builds) by telling me about shortening the pistons, thus saving me grief later. Then we have BMW (GB) who allowed us to use so many technical drawings and illustrations plus access to the electronic parts catalogue (E PC or ETK) to answer many of the questions. Thanks also to Bridgegate BMW, my local BMW main dealer in Chesterfield. In particular the guys in the parts department who answered many annoying questions - thanks to all the guys there for all the hassle, Dean, Rob, John, Adrian and Mike in particular. Because these guys were there in the eighties when the E30 was a new car, they remember an awful lot and old habits die hard! Last but certainly not least is the Brooklands Books team who of course made all this possible by agreeing to publish what seemed an unknown quantity - I think the term 'leap of faith' sums it up. Many hours (days!) was spent poring over the manuscript and they really are a pleasure to work with. Other helpers include Phil Crouch for technical advice and of course photographer Craig Pusey who donated some of his excellent photographs from various Total BMW and BMW Car magazine shoots. Thanks also to photographer Matt Harvey, plus Richard Dobney at BMW GB for the loan of his photos taken at the E30 press launch in 1983. Thankyou all.

Andrew Everett

Foreword

It is amazing to think that time has passed by and that the second BMW "3 Series" has achieved such status that it warrants this special book on its 21st anniversary. Maybe it is due to the sheer longevity of its design, its ability to satisfy the keen driver or its iconic status - but, whatever it is, there is no doubt that the E30 is one car from the past that will stay with us into the future. It is a pending classic and prices for well kept models have started to escalate; furthermore, there is a core of well cared for cars out there requiring basic attention by their dedicated owners.

As a result, there has never been a better time for a book of this sort. By focusing on the common faults which crop up repeatedly and by giving detailed, simple instructions regarding repairs, this book will be uniquely invaluable for owners who wish to try their hand at their own maintenance, especially those who may previously have been prevented from doing so by a lack of technical know-how or specific knowledge.

When Andrew invited me to provide an input to the preparation of this book, I immediately agreed as I am all too aware of the many people who are looking for simple advice to fault find and repair their cars through my involvement in forums, my own website and BMW clubs. I feel this book is an excellent reference for those people who are deeply passionate about these cars, now three generations old.

Being a fellow E30 owner, I am well aware of the devotion they continue to instill in the face of modern machinery. All of the models have the essence of character, put the driver first, have great depth to their performance, are well styled, classy, are robust, surprisingly cheap to run and quite easy to work on. They have all the qualities I like in a car; so much so, I do not envisage a day that I will be without my own car.

I'll end with this note: when you are out driving next, look around for cars from the '80s. The E30 is one of the very few models of that decade which can be seen every day on our roads - and there is no better statement than that.

Brendan Purcell

The Press Launch Team March 1983

CONTENTS

Brooklands Books

ROAD TEST SERIES
Abarth Gold Portfolio 1950-1971
Alfa Romeo Giulietta Gold Portfolio 1954-1965
Alfa Romeo Giulia Berlina Lim. Edit. Extra 1962-76
Alfa Romeo Giulia Coupes Lim. Edit. Ultra 1973-76
Alfa Romeo Alfasud 1972-1984
Alfa Romeo Alfetta Gold Portfolio 1972-1987
Alfa Romeo Spider Ultimate Portfolio 1966-1994
Alfa Romeo Spider & GTV Perf. Port. 1995-2005
Allard Limited Edition Ultra
Alpine Renault Ultimate Portfolio 1958-1995
Alvis Gold Portfolio 1919-1967
AMC Rambler Limited Edition Extra 1956-1969
AMX & Javelin Gold Portfolio 1968-1974
Armstrong Siddeley Gold Portfolio 1945-1960
Aston Martin Gold Portfolio 1921-1947
Aston Martin Ultimate Portfolio 1948-1968
Aston Martin Ultimate Portfolio 1968-1980
Aston Martin Ultimate Portfolio 1981-1993
Aston Martin Ultimate Portfolio 1994-2006
Audi Quattro Gold Portfolio 1980-1991
Audi Quattro Takes On The Competition
Audi TT Performance Portfolio 1998-2006
Austin-Healey 100 & 100/6 Gold Port. 1952-1959
Austin-Healey 3000 Ultimate Portfolio 1959-1967
Austin-Healey Sprite Gold Portfolio 1958-1971
Bentley & Rolls-Royce Portfolio 1990-2002
Berkeley Sportscars Limited Edition
BMW 6 & 8 Cyl. Cars Limited Edition 1935-1960
BMW 700 Limited Edition 1959-1965
BMW 1600 Collection No. 1 1966-1981
BMW 2002 Ultimate Portfolio 1968-1976
BMW 6 Cylinder Coupes & Saloons Gold P. 1969-1976
BMW 316, 318, 320 (4 cyl.) Gold Port. 1975-1990
BMW 320, 323, 325 (6 cyl.) Gold Port. 1977-1990
BMW 3 Series Gold Portfolio 1991-1997
BMW M3 Ultimate Portfolio 1986-2006
BMW M5 Gold Portfolio 1980-2003
BMW 5 Series Gold Portfolio 1988-1995
BMW 6 Series Ultimate Portfolio 1976-1989
BMW 7 Series Performance Portfolio 1977-1986
BMW 7 Series Performance Portfolio 1986-1993
BMW 8 Series Performance Portfolio
BMW X5 Limited Edition Extra 1999-2006
BMW Alpina Performance Portfolio 1967-1987
BMW Alpina Performance Portfolio 1988-1998
BMW Z3, M Coupe & M Roadster Gold Port. 1996-02
Borgward Isabella Limited Edition
Bristol Cars Portfolio
Buick Performance Portfolio 1947-1962
Buick Muscle Portfolio 1963-1973
Buick Riviera Performance Portfolio 1963-1978
Cadillac Performance Portfolio 1948-1958
Cadillac Performance Portfolio 1959-1966
Cadillac Eldorado Performance Portfolio 1967-1978
Cadillac Allante Limited Edition Extra
Impala & SS Muscle Portfolio 1958-1972
Corvair Performance Portfolio 1959-1969
El Camino & SS Muscle Portfolio 1959-1987
Chevy II & Nova SS Gold Portfolio 1962-1974
Chevelle & SS Gold Portfolio 1964-1972
Camaro Muscle Portfolio 1967-1973
Blazer & Jimmy Limited Edition Extra 1969-1982
Blazer & Jimmy Limited Edition Extra 1983-1994
Camaro Performance Portfolio 1993-2000
Chevrolet Corvette Gold Portfolio 1953-1962
Chevrolet Corvette Sting Ray Gold Port. 1963-1967
Chevrolet Corvette Gold Portfolio 1968-1977
High Performance Corvettes 1983-1989
Chrysler Imperial Gold Portfolio 1951-1975
Valiant 1960-1962
PT Cruiser Performance Portfolio
Citroen Traction Avant Limited Edition Premier
Citroen 2CV Ultimate Portfolio 1948-1990
Citroen DS & ID 1955-1975
Citroen DS & ID Gold Portfolio 1955-1975
Citroen SM Limited Edition Extra 1970-1975
Shelby Cobra Gold Portfolio 1962-1969
Crosley & Crosley Specials Limited Edition
Cunningham Automobiles 1951-1955
Datsun Roadsters Performance Portfolio 1960-71
Datsun 240Z & 260Z Gold Portfolio 1970-1978
DeLorean Gold Portfolio 1977-1995
De Soto Limited Edition 1952-1960
Dodge Limited Edition 1949-1959
Dodge Dart Limited Edition Extra 1960-1976
Dodge Muscle Portfolio 1964-1971
Charger Muscle Portfolio 1966-1974
ERA Gold Portfolio 1934-1994
Facel Vega Limited Edition Extra 1954-1964
Ferrari Limited Edition 1947-1957
Ferrari Dino Limited Edition Extra 1965-1974
Ferrari 308 & Mondial Ultimate Portfolio 1975-85
Ferrari 328 348 Mondial Ultimate Portfolio 1986-94
Ferrari F355 & 360 Gold Portfolio 1995-2004
Fiat 600 & 850 Gold Portfolio 1955-1972
Fiat Dino Limited Edition
Fiat 124 Spider Performance Portfolio 1966-1985
Fiat X1/9 Gold Portfolio 1973-1989
Ford Consul, Zephyr, Zodiac Mk. I & II 1950-1962
Ford Zephyr, Zodiac, Executive Mk. III & IV 1962-1971
High Performance Capris Gold Portfolio 1969-1987
Capri Muscle Portfolio 1974-1987
High Performance Fiestas 1979-1991
Ford Escort RS & Mexico Limited Edition 1970-1979
High Performance Escorts Mk. II 1975-1980
High Performance Escorts 1980-1985
High Performance Escorts 1985-1990
Ford Thunderbird Performance Portfolio 1955-1957
Ford Thunderbird Performance Portfolio 1958-1963
Ford Thunderbird Performance Portfolio 1964-1976
Ford Fairlane Performance Portfolio 1955-1970
Ford Ranchero Muscle Portfolio 1957-1979
Edsel Limited Edition 1957-1960
Ford Galaxie & LTD Gold Portfolio 1960-1976
Falcon Performance Portfolio 1960-1970
Ford GT40 & GT Ultimate Portfolio 1964-2006
Ford Torino Performance Portfolio 1968-1974
Ford Bronco 4x4 Performance Portfolio 1966-1977
Ford Bronco 1978-1988
Shelby Mustang Ultimate Portfolio 1965-1970
Mustang Muscle Portfolio 1967-1973
High Performance Mustang IIs 1974-1978
Mustang 5.0L Muscle Portfolio 1982-1993
Mustang 5.0L Takes On The Competition
Ginetta Cars Limited Edition Ultra 1958-2007
Goggomobil Limited Edition
Honda S500 • S600 • S800 Limited Edition 1962-1970
Honda CRX 1983-1987
Honda S2000 Performance Portfolio 1999-2008
Hudson Performance Portfolio 1946-1957
International Scout Gold Portfolio 1961-1980
Isetta Gold Portfolio 1953-1964
ISO & Bizzarrini Limited Edition Ultra 1962-1974
Jaguar and SS Gold Portfolio 1931-1951
Jaguar XK120 • 140 • 150 Gold Portfolio 1948-1960
Jaguar C-Type & D-Type Gold Portfolio 1951-1960
Jaguar E-Type Ultimate Portfolio 1961-1975
Jaguar XJ6 Series I & II Gold Portfolio 1968-1979
Jaguar XJ6 Series III Perf. Portfolio 1979-1986
Jaguar XJS Gold Portfolio 1975-1988
Jaguar XJ-S V12 Ultimate Portfolio 1988-1996
Jaguar XK8 & XKR Performance Portfolio 1996-2005
Jeep CJ-5 Limited Edition 1960-1975
Jeep CJ-5 & CJ-7 4x4 Perf. Portfolio 1976-1986
Jeep Wagoneer Performance Portfolio 1963-1991
Jeep J-Series Pickups 1970-1982
Jeepster & Commando Limited Edition 1967-1973
Jeep Cherokee & Comanche Pickups P. P. 1984-91
Jeep Wrangler 4x4 Performance Portfolio 1987-99
Jeep Cherokee & Grand Cherokee 4x4 P. P. 1992-98
Jensen Interceptor Ultimate Portfolio 1966-1992
Jensen - Healey Limited Edition 1972-1976
Kaiser - Frazer Limited Edition 1946-1955
Lagonda Gold Portfolio 1919-1964
Lancia Aurelia & Flaminia Gold Portfolio 1950-1970
Lancia Fulvia Gold Portfolio 1963-1976
Lancia Beta Gold Portfolio 1972-1984
Lancia Stratos Limited Edition Extra
Lancia Delta & integrale Ultimate Portfolio
Land Rover Series I, II & IIA Gold Portfolio 1948-71
Land Rover Series III 4x4 Perf. Portfolio 1971-1985
Land Rover 90 110 Defender Gold Portfolio 1983-94
Land Rover Discovery Perf. Port. 1989-2000
Lamborghini Performance Portfolio 1964-1976
Lamborghini Performance Portfolio 1977-1989
Lamborghini Gold Portfolio 1990-2004
Lincoln Gold Portfolio 1949-1960
Lincoln Continental Performance Portfolio 1961-1969
Lincoln Continental 1969-1976
Lotus Sports Racers Portfolio - covering 1951-1965
Lotus Seven Gold Portfolio 1957-1973
Lotus Elite Limited Edition 1957-1964
Lotus Elan Ultimate Portfolio 1962-1974
Lotus Elan & SE 1989-1992
Lotus Europa Gold Portfolio 1966-1975
Lotus Elite & Eclat 1974-1982
Lotus Elise & Exige Gold Portfolio 1995-2005
Marcos Coupés & Spyders Gold Portfolio 1960-1997
Maserati Cars Performance Portfolio 1957-1970
Maserati Cars Performance Portfolio 1971-1982
Maserati Cars Performance Portfolio 1982-1998
Maserati Cars Ultimate Portfolio 1999-2007
Matra Limited Edition 1965-1983
Mazda Miata MX-5 Performance Portfolio 1989-1997
Mazda Miata MX-5 Performance Portfolio 1998-2005
Mazda Miata MX-5 Takes On The Competition
McLaren F1 • GTR • LM Sportscar Perf. Portfolio
Mercedes 190 & 300 SL 1954-1963
Mercedes S & 600 Limited Edition Extra 1965-1972
Mercedes S Class 1972-1979
Mercedes S Class Limited Edition Extra 1980-1991
Mercedes 230 • 250 • 280SL Gold Portfolio 1963-1971
Mercedes-Benz SLs & SLCs Ultimate Port. 1971-89
Mercedes SLs Performance Portfolio 1989-1994
Mercedes G-Wagen Gold Portfolio 1981-2005
Mercedes 190 Limited Edition Extra 1983-1993
Mercedes CLK & SLK Limited Edition 1996-2000
Mercedes AMG Gold Portfolio 1983-1999
Mercedes AMG Ultimate Portfolio 2000-2006
Mercury Gold Portfolio 1947-1966
Mercury Comet & Cyclone Lim. Edit. Extra 1960-75
Cougar Muscle Portfolio 1967-1973
Messerschmitt Gold Portfolio 1954-1964
MG Gold Portfolio 1929-1939
MG TA & TC Gold Portfolio 1936-1949
MG TD & TF Gold Portfolio 1949-1955
MGA & Twin Cam Gold Portfolio 1955-1962
MG Midget Gold Portfolio 1961-1979
MGB Roadsters 1962-1980
MGB MGC & V8 Gold Portfolio 1962-1980
MGC & MGB GT V8 Limited Edition
MGF & TF Performance Portfolio 1995-2005
Mini Gold Portfolio 1959-1969
Mini Gold Portfolio 1969-1980
Mini Gold Portfolio 1981-1997
High Performance Minis Gold Portfolio 1960-1973
Mini Cooper Gold Portfolio 1961-1971
Mini Moke Ultimate Portfolio 1964-1994
Mini Performance Portfolio 2001-2006
Starion & Conquest Performance Portfolio 1982-1990
Mitsubishi 3000GT & Dodge Stealth P.P. 1990-1999
Morgan Three-Wheelers Ultimate Portfolio 1909-1952
Morgan Four-Wheelers Ultimate Portfolio 1936-1967
Morgan Ultimate Portfolio 1968-1990
Morgan Ultimate Portfolio 1991-2009
Nash Limited Edition Extra 1949-1957
Nash-Austin Metropolitan Gold Portfolio 1954-1962
NSU Ro80 Limited Edition
NSX Performance Portfolio 1989-1999
Oldsmobile Limited Edition Premier 1948-1963
Oldsmobile Muscle Portfolio 1964-1971
Cutlass & 4-4-2 Muscle Portfolio 1964-1974
Opel GT Ultimate Portfolio 1968-1973
Opel Manta Limited Edition 1970-1975
Pantera Ultimate Portfolio 1970-1995
Panther Gold Portfolio 1972-1990
Plymouth Limited Edition 1950-1960
Plymouth Fury Limited Edition Extra 1956-1976
Barracuda Muscle Portfolio 1964-1974
Plymouth Muscle Portfolio 1964-1971
High Performance Firebirds 1982-1988
Firebird & Trans Am Performance Portfolio 1993-00
Pontiac Fiero Performance Portfolio 1984-1988
Porsche Sports Racing Cars UP 1952-1968
Porsche 917 • 935 • 956 • 962 Gold Portfolio
Porsche 912 Limited Edition Extra
Porsche 365 Ultimate Portfolio 1952-1965
Porsche 911 1965-1969
Porsche 911 1973-1977
Porsche 911 SC & Turbo Gold Portfolio 1978-1983
Porsche 911 Carrera & Turbo Gold Port. 1984-1989
Porsche 911 Ultimate Portfolio 1990-1997
Porsche 911 Takes On The Competition 1990-1997
Porsche 911 Ultimate Portfolio 1998-2004
Porsche 914 Ultimate Portfolio
Porsche 924 Gold Portfolio 1975-1988
Porsche 928 Gold Portfolio 1977-1995
Porsche 928 Takes On The Competition
Porsche 944 Ultimate Portfolio
Porsche 968 Limited Edition Extra
Porsche Boxster Ultimate Portfolio 1996-2004
Railton & Brough Superior Gold Portfolio 1933-1950
Range Rover Gold Portfolio 1970-1985
Range Rover Gold Portfolio 1985-1995
Range Rover Performance Portfolio 1995-2001
Range Rover Takes on the Competition
Riley Gold Portfolio 1924-1939
Rolls-Royce Silver Clould & Bentley S Ultimate Port.
Rolls-Royce Silver Shadow Ultimate Port. 1965-80
Rover P4 1949-1959
Rover 2000 & 2200 1963-1977
Studebaker Ultimate Portfolio 1946-1966
Studebaker Hawks & Larks Lim. Edit. Premier 1956-66
Avanti Limited Edition Extra 1962-1991
Subaru Impreza Turbo Limited Edition Extra 1994-00
Subaru Impreza WRX Performance Port. 2001-2005
Sunbeam Alpine Limited Edition Extra 1959-1968
Sunbeam Tiger Limited Edition Extra 1964-1967
Suzuki SJ Gold Portfolio 1971-1997
Vitara, Sidekick & Geo Tracker Perf. Port. 1988-1997
Toyota Land Cruiser Gold Portfolio 1956-1987
Toyota Land Cruiser 1988-1997
Toyota Supra Performance Portfolio 1982-1998
Toyota MR2 Ultimate Portfolio 1984-2006
Toyota MR2 Takes On The Competition
Triumph TR2 & TR3 Gold Portfolio 1952-1961
Triumph TR4, TR5, TR250 1961-1968
Triumph TR6 Gold Portfolio 1969-1976
Triumph Herald 1959-1971
Triumph Vitesse 1962-1971
Triumph Spitfire Gold Portfolio 1962-1980
Triumph 2000, 2.5, 2500 1963-1977
Triumph GT6 Gold Portfolio 1966-1974
Triumph Stag Gold Portfolio 1970-1977
TVR Limited Edition Ultra 1958-1985
TVR Performance Portfolio 1986-1994
TVR Performance Portfolio 1995-2000
TVR Performance Portfolio 2000-2005
VW Beetle Gold Portfolio 1935-1967
VW Beetle Gold Portfolio 1968-1991
VW Bus Camper Van Perf. Portfolio 1954-1967
VW Bus Camper Van Perf. Portfolio 1968-1979
VW Bus Camper Van Perf. Portfolio 1979-1991
VW Karmann Ghia Gold Portfolio 1955-1974
VW Scirocco 1974-1981
VW Golf GTI Limited Edition Extra 1976-1991
VW Corrado Limited Edition Premier 1989-1995
Volvo PV444 & PV544 Perf. Portfolio 1945-1965
Volvo 120 Amazon Ultimate Portfolio
Volvo 1800 Ultimate Portfolio 1960-1973
Volvo 140 & 160 Series Gold Portfolio 1966-1975
Forty Years of Selling Volvo
Westfield Performance Portfolio 1982-2004

RACING & THE LAND SPEED RECORD
The Land Speed Record 1898-1919
The Land Speed Record 1920-1929
The Land Speed Record 1930-1939
The Land Speed Record 1940-1962
The Land Speed Record 1963-1999
Can-Am Racing 1966-1969
Can-Am Racing 1970-1974
Can-Am Racing Cars 1966-1974
The Carrera Panamericana Mexico - 1950-1954
Le Mans - The Bentley & Alfa Years - 1923-1939
Le Mans - The Jaguar Years - 1949-1957
Le Mans - The Ferrari Years - 1958-1965
Le Mans - The Ford & Matra Years - 1966-1974
Le Mans - The Porsche Years - 1975-1982
Le Mans - The Porsche & Jaguar Years - 1983-91
Le Mans - The Porsche & Peugeot Years - 1992-99
Mille Miglia - The Alfa & Ferrari Years - 1927-1951
Mille Miglia - The Ferrari & Mercedes Years - 1952-57
Targa Florio - The Porsche & Ferrari Years - 1955-1964
Targa Florio - The Porsche Years - 1965-1973

RESTORATION & GUIDE SERIES
BMW 2002 - A Comprehensive Guide
BMW 02 Restoration Guide
BMW E30 - 3 Series Restoration Bible
Classic Camaro Restoration
Engine Swapping Tips & Techniques
Ferrari Life Buyer's Portfolio
Land Rover Restoration Portfolio
PC on Land Rover Series I Restoration
Lotus Elan Restoration Guide
MG T Series Restoration Guide
MGA Restoration Guide
PC on Midget/Sprite Restoration
PC on MGB Restoration
Mustang Restoration Tips & Techniques
Practical Gas Flow
Restoring Sprites & Midgets an Enthusiast's Guide
SU Carburetters Tuning Tips & Techniques
PC on Sunbeam Rapier Restoration
The Great Classic Muscle Cars Compared
Weber Carburettors Tuning Tips and Techniques

MILITARY VEHICLES
Complete WW2 Military Jeep Manual
Dodge WW2 Military Portfolio 1940-1945
German Military Equipment WW2
Hail To The Jeep
Combat Land Rover Portfolio No. 1
Land Rover Military Portfolio
Military & Civilian Amphibians 1940-1990
Off Road Jeeps Civilian & Military 1944-1971
US Military Vehicles 1941-1945
Standard Military Motor Vehicles-TM9-2800 (WW2)
VW Kubelwagen Military Portfolio 1940-1990
WW2 Allied Vehicles Military Portfolio 1939-1945
WW2 Jeep Military Portfolio 1941-1945

ROAD & TRACK SERIES
Road & Track on Aston Martin 1962-1990
Road & Track on Austin Healey 1953-1970
Road & Track on BMW Cars 1966-1974
Road & Track BMW M Series Portfolio 1979-2002
R & T BMW Z3, M Coupe & M Roadster Port. 96-02
R & T Camaro & Firebird Portfolio 1993-2002
Road & Track on Corvette 1968-1982
Road & Track on Corvette 1982-1986
Road & Track on Corvette 1986-1990
Road & Track Corvette Portfolio 1997-2002
Road & Track Dodge Viper Portfolio 1992-2002
Road & Track on Ferrari 1975-1981
Road & Track on Ferrari 1984-1988
Road & Track Ferrari V-12 Portfolio 1992-2002
Road & Track Ferrari F355 360 F430 Portfolio 95-06
Road & Track on Fiat Sports Cars 1968-1987
Road & Track on Jaguar 1950-1960
Road & Track on Jaguar 1961-1968
Road & Track on Jaguar 1968-1974
Road & Track on Jaguar 1974-1982
Road & Track on Jaguar 1983-1989
R & T Jaguar XJ-S - XK8 - XKR Portfolio 1975-2003
Road & Track MX-5 Miata Portfolio 1989-2002
Road & Track on Mercedes 1952-1962
Road & Track on Mercedes 1963-1970
Road & Track on Mercedes 1971-1979
R & T Mercedes SL - SLK - CLK Portfolio 1990-2003
Road & Track on MG Sports Cars 1949-1961
Road & Track on MG Sports Cars 1962-1980
Road & Track Mustang Portfolio 1994-2002
Road & Track Nissan 300ZX & 350Z Portfolio 1984-03
Road & Track on Porsche 1951-1967
Road & Track on Porsche 1972-1975
Road & Track on Porsche 1975-1978
Road & Track on Porsche 1979-1982
Road & Track on Porsche 1985-1988
Road & Track Porsche 928 Portfolio 1977-1994
Road & Track Porsche 911 Portfolio 1990-1997
R & T on Rolls Royce & Bentley 1950-1965
R & T on Rolls Royce & Bentley 1966-1984
R & T on Toyota Sports & GT Cars 1966-1984
R & T on Triumph Sports Cars 1967-1974
R & T on Triumph Sports Cars 1974-1982
Road & Track on Volkswagen 1951-1968
Road & Track on Volkswagen 1968-1978
Road & Track on Volvo 1957-1974
Road & Track on Volvo 1977-1994
Road & Track - Best of PS
Road & Track - Peter Egan Side Glances 1983-92
Road & Track - Peter Egan Side Glances 1992-97
Road & Track - Peter Egan Side Glances 1998-02
Road & Track - Peter Egan Side Glances 2002-06

CAR AND DRIVER SERIES
Car and Driver on BMW 1957-1977
Car and Driver on Corvette 1978-1982
Car and Driver on Corvette 1983-1988
Car and Driver on Ferrari 1955-1962
Car and Driver on Ferrari 1963-1975
Car and Driver on Porsche 1955-1962
Car and Driver on Porsche 1963-1970
Car and Driver on Porsche 1970-1976
Car and Driver on Porsche 1977-1981
Car and Driver on Porsche 1982-1986

HOT ROD 'ENGINE' SERIES
Chevy 265 & 283
Chevy 302 & 327
Chevy 348 & 409
Chevy 396 & 427
Chevy 454 thru 512
Chevy Monster Big Blocks
Chrysler Hemi
Chrysler 273, 318, 340 & 360
Chrysler 361, 383, 400, 413, 426 & 440
Ford 289, 302, Boss 302 & 351W
Ford 351C & Boss 351
Ford Small Block
Ford Big Block

MOTORCYCLES
To see our range of over 70 titles visit www.brooklands-books.com

15/02Z91982

INTRODUCTION

Every once in a while, a manufacturer produces a car which is a sure fire classic. To be a classic, a car has to be an indelible part of a generation - the Morris Minor, the early Minis, a vinyl roofed Mark 3 Cortina or in the case of the eighties, the E30 BMW 3 Series. Why the E30? It's simple.

Before the seventies, BMW was a very upmarket, 'old money' maker of very expensive cars whose appeal wasn't immediately obvious. In a style conscious middle class Britain, anything with a vinyl roof, a bit of wood and leather trim was considered upmarket - the Cortina Ghia was a case in point. The fact that it wasn't actually that good didn't deter buyers.

By the eighties though, a new breed of young and upwardly mobile go-getters were appearing, Thatcher's children or 'Yuppies' to coin a well worn phrase. They were looking for something new with a prestige badge, expensive enough to dissuade the 'value-for-money' seekers but not so expensive as to be out of reach. Helped along by BMW's ad executives, the E30 was just the right car at the right time and definitely a car of its time. Wealthy housewives, city boys on their way to their first 911 Turbo, Sloane Rangers and the plain old style conscious all bought E30's. This really was the beginning of BMW's crusade to capture this market and today, the 3 Series is still the car in its segment to own. The E30 enjoyed an exceptional twelve year production run which was only bettered by the 6 Series Coupe.

Ten years after the last 316i Touring rolled off the line, the E30 is now hovering on the edge of classic status but it still has a foot firmly in banger territory. Despite building a well over 2.3 million cars, old and neglected E30's which are still saveable are now ending up in scrap yards for want of a bit of loving care - which is where you come in.

E30's are still a very DIY fixable car, the parts are plentiful and cheap new or used and a really nice one is still a distinctive car that has worn its years well. Workshop manuals don't tell you everything and so the aim of this book is to help you get the best from your E30, both in terms of preservation and restoration - use it with a Bentley manual and you'll be unstoppable.

A secondary aim is to make the cars go faster, something owners have been doing for twenty years. Now that the E30 is a cheap old car, the bits are old and cheap too and building something with 200+bhp, with sorted handling and brakes, is an inexpensive recipe for a bundle of laughs – a description you cannot really give to a modern E46, as wonderful and accomplished as they are.

The new BMW 3 Series; it's much better, thank you
When the E30 was launched in March 1983 there wasn't really a lot of opposition. BMWs were more expensive in real terms twenty years ago than they are today and some price comparisons will seem startling. Bear in mind also that a base price E30 came with no extras – steel wheels, no sunroof or air conditioning, wind-up windows and non-metallic paint jobs. If you thought the base model was expensive, try adding a few options.

BMW 316	£6250 (5 speed £6775)
Ford Sierra 1.6L	£5743
MG Maestro 1600	£6245
Alfa Romeo Giulietta 1.6	£6350
Ford Escort XR3i	£6151
VW Golf GTi 1800	£6808

Opel Manta 1.8S	£5655
BMW 320i	£8595
Ford Sierra 2.0 Ghia	£8017
Fiat Supermirafiori 2000	£5244
Austin Ambassador 2.0HL	£6551
BMW 323i	£9655
Ford Capri 2.8 Injection	£8125
Saab 900 Turbo 3 door	£10,995
Porsche 924	£10,524

Compared to the opposition, at first glance the E30 did not look overpriced but, as I said, the options could add up. To make an E30 half decent you would need electric front windows, alloy wheels, a sunroof, power steering and a radio. That lot alone would add almost £1400 to the total cost and suddenly an £8000 plus 316 was looking a bit steep – especially with the clock in place of the rev counter that some wag claimed was to measure the acceleration! But the buyers just did not care and as a result there are precious few base model cars about. Helped along by some low-key but very effective marketing, BMW then never stooped to the depths of TV advertising as they could sell every car the factory could make, and then some. Discounts were absolutely forbidden and it is thought that in the boom years many cars were sold without the buyer bothering to take a test drive – that is what iconic status does.

By 1987 the price of a fully loaded 325i Sport with every option box ticked, leather, air conditioning, cruise control, electric sunroof, Blaupunkt New York with amplifier and ABS, was nudging £24,000. Back in March 1983 that price was just £1000 short of a Ferrari 308GTB. Spurred on by its unstoppable race success, the M3 was the city boy's favourite but, like the 316, it came with no extras whatsoever. Improve the specification of a 1987 Evolution, with a base price of £27,381, by adding every available extra and you would be paying over £33,000.

The E30 soon gained a hierarchy of models upon which

M3's are now appreciating in value - but only excellent examples in original condition

you were judged, although nobody thought the driver of a red 316 with steel wheels was a loser; just someone on the way up the ladder. Imitations of BMW alloy wheels popped up, along with some then-fashionable body kits from Zender and Richard Grant – happy days indeed. Yet when the British economy collapsed and cars like Porsche 911s became all but un-saleable, the E30 was still sold in increasing numbers. Although the cars had become a statement of how well you had done, they were not too flash or conspicuous, although for a few years key damage and stolen badges were rife.

When the E36 arrived in 1991, the E30 appeared to be on the way down, although the Convertible and Touring models lingered on for another couple of years. The early examples were not as rustproof as they might have been and ten years on, as the E30 began its descent into banger territory, there seemed to be an unending supply of scruffy examples.

The E30 22 years on
Compared to most others, the E30 was a well-made car. However, it must be stressed that nothing lasts forever and that model was never as rugged as the bigger BMWs. So even if you go for one of the last 1993/4 cars, it will still need careful maintenance and the odd repair carried out. These cars are now at the age where the attention outlined in a later chapter will steer them in the right direction. A weekend of fettling and rust-proofing will work wonders but if what you want is a car where all you have to do is fill the tank with petrol and take it to the garage once a year an E30 is the wrong car and you should be looking at an E36 instead.

Original specifications
Unlike 99% of car manufacturers, BMW took the time to record details of every car they made. Not only will BMW in Munich have a record of what car you have, but in most countries like Germany and Britain the importers and dealers will have an accurate record too. By quoting the chassis number (or the original registration number in the UK), you can access the information. This is useful to have before travelling many miles to look at a car. Is it Henna red or Zinnober red? Did it have a limited slip diff, brown or green tint glass? Maybe that cheap 325i in the paper is a Sport and the owner doesn't know.

Where did they go?
As the twentieth and twenty-first birthday of the E30 has come and gone, the search for the first E30s is slowly growing as hardcore E30 enthusiasts try to locate the originals from 1982. As these cars slowly become recognised classics, it is inevitable that the very early Y registration models will have added kudos. There are still some out there, but not that many and few that are not

Where many E30s ended up ....

E30's make good budget club series racers

rusty wrecks. The first RHD cars off the line in November 1982 were six-cylinder 320i and 323i models followed in January 1983 by the 316. The very first examples of each model didn't always come to the UK though; the 320i chassis numbers begin with 743, the 323i with 753 and the 316 with 733.

At present, we have details of only a few of the very first batch of cars and so far only one is known to exist. Of the 320i models, the first RHD car was 7435000 built in July 1982 as a pre-production prototype and registered by BMW GB as TRD 413Y. This Sapphire blue car was probably used as a technical training vehicle as it was registered in January 1983 and subsequently written off, either in an accident or sent back to Munich to be scrapped. The next car is 7435001 and this is the second RHD 320i to come to Britain. Built in November 1982, it is also the first of the series production RHD 320i – traditionally BMW chassis numbers started with '001'. Registered as YSS 999Y in Aberdeenshire, it was a black car that was last used on the road on or before June 1st 1996 and was recently found rusting away in a damp lock up, sadly way beyond any hope of restoration.

As for the 323i, despite its RHD status chassis number 7535000 did not come to Britain but was probably registered by BMW and used as either a test or press car. 7535001, the first of the series production 323i cars, having been built in November 1982, came here in January 1983 and was registered the same month to BMW GB as TRD 410Y. Baltic blue in colour, it was used last on or before August 31st 1994.

What about the 'TRX' cars? For the launch in March 1983, BMW GB registered a series of eleven cars with number plates ranging from TRX 881Y to TRX 891Y. As yet, none of these cars has come to light and it is doubtful that any still exist – the last of these cars to be taxed was TRX 889Y, which expired in January 2002.

For the four-cylinder cars, a pair of two-door, blue 316 models were registered as TRX 892Y and TRX 894Y, the former last being taxed in 2001 and it's not known if these cars went to the press launch in Spain, although nobody at the launch remembers them. The 316 had a slightly later start to life and although they were launched along with the six-cylinder cars in March 1983, production didn't begin until January 1983 for the RHD cars. Again, pre-production car 7335000 didn't come to Britain but the first series production 316 did. Chassis number 7335001 is an Opal Green metallic 316 built in January 1983 but not registered until June 1983. Registered as PSP 310Y in Scotland, the last road tax expired on December 1st 1997.

One lucky survivor was UBL 44Y, chassis number 179, which was registered by BMW GB in February 1983 and lent to *MOTOR* magazine as a long-term test car. After this the car was sold to BMW Dealer Grassicks in Perth where it underwent a couple of personal number plate changes. Now in the hands of a BMW enthusiast in Scotland, UBL remains in concours condition and was featured in the September 2002 edition of *TOTAL BMW* magazine. Bracknell registration numbers were AN, BL, CF, DP, GM, JB, JH, JM, RD, RX and TF although thousands of cars were registered as employee cars before being sold on as used cars through authorised dealerships.

Once sold off by BMW GB, the press cars were scattered to the four winds as BMW dealers all over Britain took them. From here they just blended in with the other E30s, rusted and wore out along with the others and eventually ended up in scrap yards. Thanks to BMW's detailed records, I managed to get information on all the TRX cars. Now it's up to you to go and find them!

TRX 881Y: 323i, Henna Red, Anthracite cloth, chassis 7535036, built December 1982, registered January 17th 1983. Specification: Power steering, rear headrests,

Sport steering wheel, central locking, brown tint glass, electric windows, headlamp wash wipe, alloy wheels, electric sunroof and electric mirrors.

TRX 881Y: 323i, Henna red, Anthracite cloth, chassis 7535036, built December 1982, registered January 17th 1983. Spec: power steering, rear headrests, Sport steering wheel, central locking, brown tint glass, electric windows, headlamp wash wipe, alloy wheels, electric sunroof, electric mirrors.

TRX 882Y: 323i, Henna red, Anthracite cloth, chassis 7535033, built December 1982, registered January 17th 1983. Spec: identical to TRX 881Y but with front fog lamps. Road tested by *MOTOR* February 26th 1983 and used at E30 press launch Valencia.

TRX 883Y: 320i, Gloss black, Anthracite cloth, chassis 7435155 Built December 1982, registered January 10th 1983. Spec: Limited slip diff, manual sunroof, lockable glovebox, brown tint glass, steel wheels, manual windows. Road tested by *Autocar* February 26th 1983. Used at E30 press launch, Valencia.

TRX 884Y: 320i, Opal green met, Pine green cloth, chassis 7435116, Built December 1982, registered January 10th 1983. Spec: Limited slip diff, brown tint glass, manual sunroof, lockable glove box, steel wheels, manual windows. Road tested by *Drive & Trail* July 1983 and used at E30 press launch, Valencia.

The Press Launch March 1983

TRX 885Y: 320i, Polaris silver, Pacific blue cloth, chassis 7435130 Built December 1982, registered January 10th 1983. Spec: Limited slip diff, manual sunroof, manual windows, brown tint glass, lockable glove box, steel wheels. Used at E30 press launch, Valencia.

TRX 886Y: 323i, Henna Red, Anthracite cloth, chassis 7535029, built December 1982, registered January 10th 1983. Specification: as for TRX 881Y.

TRX 887Y: 323i, Opal green met. Pine green cloth, chassis 7535070, Built December 1982, registered January 10th 1983. Spec: Limited slip diff, alloy wheels, green tint glass, electric windows, manual sunroof, headlamp wash wipe, power steering, central locking, front fog lamps. Used at E30 press launch, Valencia.

TRX 888Y: 323i, Gloss black, Anthracite cloth, chassis 7535092, built December 1982, registered January 10th 1983. Spec: Recaro seats, central locking, brown tint glass, electric front windows, headlamp wash wipe, alloy wheels, electric sunroof. Used at E30 press launch, Valencia.

TRX 889Y: 323i, Opal green met, Pine green cloth, chassis 7535064, built December 1982, registered January 10th 1983. Spec: Limited slip diff, headlamp wash wipe, alloy wheels, electric sunroof, Sport steering wheel, central locking, brown tint glass, electric windows, front fog lamps. Used at E30 press launch, Valencia.

TRX 890Y: 323i, Baltic blue met, Pacific blue cloth, chassis 7535079, built December 1982, registered January 10th 1983. Spec: Limited slip diff, alloy wheels, green tint glass, electric windows, manual sunroof, headlamp wash wipe, power steering, central locking. Used at E30 press launch, Valencia.

TRX 891Y: 323i, Bronze, Nutria cloth, chassis 7535107, built December 1982, registered January 10th 1983. Spec: Limited slip diff, headlamp wash wipe, alloy wheels, electric sunroof, Sport steering wheel, central locking, brown tint glass, electric windows. Used at E30 press launch, Valencia.

Chapter 1

E30 - THE MODELS

316

This is, in E30 terms, the bottom of the barrel although it's a good car in its own right. Powered by the good old M10 engine, production started in January 1983 and ran right up to September 1988 with the last year's production being the facelift plastic bumper model. Available in two- and four-door versions, you might even find a rare Baur Cabriolet but they are not worth that much.

Advantages? Many! For a start, they are now very cheap. Fuel economy is pretty fair (you should get 25mpg) and when the carburettor is playing the game, performance is surprisingly good with crisp throttle response and good torque. It is also pretty reliable and mechanically unbreakable. The M10, given an oil change every 6000 miles, just goes on forever. The timing chain will begin to rattle at anything over 100,000 miles, but the simple expedient of fitting a stronger spring in the tensioner will keep that quiet for a bit longer. With only 90bhp available, the mechanical components are very understressed.

The disadvantages are that most 316s are poverty specification – wind up windows, no sunroof, no power steering – the early ones even had a clock replacing the rev counter in the instrument pod! The other disadvantage is the carburettor. Early cars up until September 1983 (British A registration) used a Solex Pierburg 2B4 series carburettor which was not too bad, although it was no prize. Later cars used the Pierburg 2BE, the E standing for electronic. If you think that an electronically controlled carburettor sounds like a disaster area you will not be disappointed because it truly is a terrible thing. However, they can be replaced by a Weber twin-choke carburettor. 316 Automatics were known to be absolute dogs with terrible driveability problems although a

Weber carburettor will sort much of them out. But when the original carburettor is working they are fine and are better to drive than a Weber equipped car.

Markets like Greece and Yugoslavia had a 316S which was a detuned 316 with a lower compression and a single-choke Pierburg 1B2 carburettor robbed from a 1500 VW Golf.

Look out for (if only to avoid) the really basic four-speed gearbox versions. These were never common but until around 1985/86 the five-speed gearbox was still an optional extra on these cars. However, do not discount a really tidy one because fitting the five-speed gearbox and prop-shaft takes just a day for a DIY mechanic.

316i

There are two versions of the 316i, the first one being the model from September 1987 until September 1988. Sold only in Europe and not Britain, this plastic bumper car was the M10 316 but with a Bosch LE Jetronic fuel injection system. It is a good car, but it was not to last because it was replaced in September 1988 by the next version with the M40 engine.

The M40 engine was, and is, a fickle beast. Given love and attention, it is not a bad engine but anything with rattling tappets and/or no service history is to be avoided at all costs unless all you want is a cheap banger. It certainly was not as good as the old M10 engine and the repair costs are horrendous.

As the M40 engined car got older the more equipment it acquired and late cars have power steering and central locking, with the later 316i Lux models being very well equipped. A Touring version was available later in its life

The Author at speed in a 1990 318i - Craig Pusey

A 318iS lower spoiler lip - Alf Dickhaut

and to be fair, the 316i doesn't give much away to the 318i and the automatic gearbox works well on these.

318i

The 318i started production along with the 316 in January 1983. Until September 1983 it was equipped with the old mechanical Bosch K Jetronic injection system and they were little flying machines capable of giving a Golf GTi a scare when fitted with the optional 4.1:1 final drive. BMW quoted 105bhp, but it is reckoned that a good one gave 110bhp. These cars were not sold in the UK until September 1983 with the advent of the four-door E30, by which time the old K Jetronic had been replaced with the economy-orientated Bosch LE system. It is felt that a lot of the 318i's sparkle was stubbed out by LE Jetronic, although quoted power remained the same it just didn't go as well. By 1985 BMW had fitted a lower final drive (4.1:1) that gave the 318i a bit more go. Again, look out for early four-speed cars.

By September 1987 and the advent of plastic bumpers, the 318i had gained the M40 engine. A Convertible and Touring estate joined later.

Sum up? The 318i is the 316, but better. Performance is a bit more peppy, the fuel consumption is often better and the insurance costs hardly any more. Like the 316, many older 318is were pretty sparse on the equipment and it falls to the later cars to have power steering (essential in my book) and central locking.

The 318iS

Towards the end of the eighties, BMW felt that they were missing out on the younger buyers who were turning to cars like the XR3i, Golf GTi and the Astra GTE. The E30 was becoming a bit too upmarket, and the M3 was very expensive. So, using an engine planned for the next generation 3 Series (the E36), BMW created the 318iS as an antidote to the smooth but breathless 320i.

The heart of the 318iS was the 16-valve, 1.8-litre M42 engine, itself a derivative of the M40 unit. Using twin overhead camshafts driven by a chain, the M42 also had

separate coils for each cylinder – in many ways, it was a junior version of the M3 engine and race versions used in the E36 racers gave up to 280bhp.

Early cars used the gearbox from the M40 318i, later ones a unique, close ratio Getrag 240 gearbox from the E34 518i. Suspension was Boge M Technic, with 325i type vented front and solid rear discs and either steel wheels with a special wheel trim or 14/15 inch BBS cross spoke alloy wheels were used. A deeper, colour-coded front spoiler lip identified the iS, along with a colour keyed rear spoiler. Although the distinctive front spoiler lip was optional in some markets, virtually all cars seem to have one. With sports seats and the M Tech 1 steering wheel, the 318iS looked and felt like a special car and they have a devoted following today. Problems include failing coils (which can often damage the ECU), a leaking profile gasket allowing oil and water to mix and noisy timing chains at high mileages. The model was only available as a two door, in Europe and America.

320i

The 320i would have been the poor relation of the E30 range had it not sold so well. It embodied everything that was good about BMWs with a superbly smooth engine, but today they are a bit unloved. The trouble is that the 325i costs very little more to fuel and insure, but is vastly quicker, having an extra 45bhp. For all that though, the 320i is a good car and a nice one is a lovely drive. The engine is a bit breathless low down, but at the top end they really sing although without the urgency of a 325i or a 318iS.

As soon as you get into the plastic bumper models there are still lots of good examples about, although many are a bit tired now. Again, there are two- and four-door versions as well as a Convertible and a Touring. Specific problems are few; the cracked cylinder head syndrome being the only real problem area.

320iS

Never sold outside Portugal or Italy, the 320iS was an

effort by BMW to fight, and beat, Alfa Romeo in the Italian under two-litre market. In Italy and Portugal, cars over two-litres were heavily taxed, leading to some rare specials, such as a turbocharged 2-litre V8 Ferrari GTB. Basis of the 320iS was the 325i, or in two-door form a 325i Sport with the M Tech body kit. Running gear was pure 325i, but the engine was a short stroke, 2-litre version of the 2.3-litre four-cylinder 16-valve M3 engine with 192bhp. It used an M3 five-speed sport gearbox (dogleg gear-change pattern) and a lower ratio final drive.

Quite few have now been exported out of Italy and a good one is well worth seeking. Not all cars came with the proper Bilstein M Tech suspension.

323i

The E30 323i had a lot to live up to – the E21 323i for example. The E21 was a real he-man BMW, all oversteer and white knuckles with a sparky 143bhp bite. The E30 version was initially a bit of a lemon with only 139bhp and the earliest production cars only just made that figure. From September 1983, the power was upped to a marginal 150bhp and two years later, the 323i was dead – replaced by the 325i.

The problem with the 323i is that they are now so old – at the time of writing anything between 19 and 22 years old, mostly with rust, oil leaks and a myriad of owners. Finding a good one is now almost impossible but if you find one that's half decent they are not bad – a 320i with a bit more grunt. Available in two- or four-door guise only, plus the odd Baur Cabriolet.

324d

The original 3 Series diesel created by the simple expedient of fitting a standard 316 with a 524td engine – but without the turbocharger. Performance is grim, but economy is good. Not sold in Britain, they are a fairly common sight in Germany, mostly with huge mileages. An interesting curiosity for a few hundred quid, but that's about all.

324td

This is better. By fitting the 524td turbocharged diesel engine into the E30, BMW built something that was the start of BMW's turbo diesel revolution. Again, they were never sold in Britain but in Europe they were a big success. Most are pretty worn out now, but importing a late 324td Touring would give you an interesting and practical car for not much money. These older diesels still used a mechanical diesel pump and they are generally pretty reliable although BMW mechanics in Britain will be puzzled.

1989 320i with an after-market front spoiler and de-chroming. In Germany this is called "Shadowline" - Alf Dickhaut

A 1988 320i with 15 inch "King" wheels - These were almost identical to Alpina wheels - Alf Dickhaut

323i standard interior from 1985 - Alf Dickhaut

324d only sold in Europe. They were popular as Taxis - Alf Dickhaut

UK Spec. First Generation 1987 325i Sport Dolphin Grey with Alpina 16 inch non-standard wheels - Craig Pusey

An original M Tech II bootspoiler - Alf Dickhaut

1984 323i Baur Cabriolet. This was an after market conversion based on any 2 door E30 - Craig Pusey
An early 325i Convertible. Much better than the Baur Cabriolet - Alf Dickhaut

325e

The first of the 325s, this was launched in Europe in 1984 but was never sold in Britain. An economy special, it was a 323i but with the engine, gearbox and final drive ratio from the 525e. With 125bhp and a red line of 4500rpm, it was low revving, tall geared, surprisingly accelerative and very driveable. But it had the same torque at around 3000rpm as a 3.5-litre and the engine gave quite a lot of push. They were also capable of well over 35mpg. But like the Eta concept, it failed and was quietly forgotten in favour of the 2.4-litre Turbo diesels because the 324td also offered 35 – 40mpg and diesel in Europe is much cheaper than petrol.

325i

Ah, now we are talking. With 171bhp, the 325i embarrassed a lot of bigger and more expensive BMWs and would give a 635CSi a good run for its money. Sport models in both metal and plastic bumper forms were proper hero chariots in their day, and a 325i is still a quick car in absolute terms today. Many have been thrashed to death though, and finding a decent one is becoming hard work. Specific problems include cracked cylinder heads, faulty ECUs on the metal bumper cars and the general air of tiredness in old age suffered by all cars.

The 325i Sport was a UK-only car with M Tech body kit and suspension, limited slip diff, close ratio gearbox (not dogleg), sports seats, M Tech steering wheel, black headlining and a de-chrome job. 15-inch BBS wheels were also standard. In Europe, a similar model was offered called the 325i M-package (M Paket in Germany) that was the same, but without the LSD, a commonly fitted optional extra. Plastic bumper sports often had Boge gas dampers, not Bilstein

Convertibles

There are two types of convertible – the Baur Cabriolet with the integral T bar roof, and the vastly more desirable full convertible built by BMW. The Baur was a conversion of a standard saloon, the convertible was a special model. If you can, avoid the electric hood as it is a disaster area. Performance of the 318i Convertible is not sparkling because the convertible is heavier than the ordinary saloon.

Tourings

These were built with all four engine sizes available between 1988 and 1994. The 325i came first, followed by the 320i and 318i and lastly the 316i. The last ever E30 was a 316i Touring built in February 1994. Because Tourings were bought new by a different kind of owner than, say, a 325i Sport many have survived better. It loses nothing in performance or handling to the saloon and although it is no Volvo Estate, they are surprisingly

A 325i Touring with 15" BBS Wheels - Alf Dickhaut

1990 325i SE with Hartge wheels. De-chromed with 318iS front spoiler lip - Craig Pusey

useful. For the little extra they cost, a Touring is a better bet than a four-door saloon.

Limited Editions

BMW has never been a company to do limited edition cars with bits tacked on. But they did produce a series of models such as the SE and a special version of the 1984 320i and 323i. These were all constructed and registered in late 1984 and around 300 were built, with the 320i being most popular. The specification included just one colour option which was Diamond Black with anthracite trim and the BMW 'Classic' stripe kit that the 635CSi and 735i SE had as standard. Other standard features included a manual sunroof, electric windows, 14-inch 'bottle-top' alloy wheels and M Technic Bilstein sports suspension. The first limited edition, the SE, appeared in mid 1986, for the British D registrations, and was available on the 320i and the 325i. SE cars had power steering, electric windows, 14-inch bottle-top alloy wheels, on board computer, rear blind, headlamp wash/wipe and an electric sunroof. 325i models added ABS braking but a month later this was standardised on the 325i. This SE package was continued unchanged into the late 1987 plastic bumper cars although 1990 model year cars were updated with colour coordinated mirrors and bumpers, a three-spoke leather steering wheel and other bits detailed later.

WHAT HAPPENED WHEN?

An exhaustive list of modifications and changeover /model launch dates are given elsewhere, but the life of the E30 could be divided into three main groups. Only one is a major facelift, and even then many of the changes and alterations BMW made are less than obvious. This is why, when ordering new bits or scrounging the breaker's yards for second-hand bits, never assume that a part from a 1987 model will fit a 1988 without question – very often it will not.

MODEL 1983

As launched in Britain in March 1983 and in Europe fractionally before, this was the original E30 of which precious few remain. 316, 318i, 320i and 323i, 4-doors from October 1983 plus the odd Baur Cabriolet. 195/60 tyres on six-cylinder cars, three-speed automatic transmissions on early cars, no plastic wheel trims on steel wheel cars. Speedometer reads up to 140mph only, three red lights for overdue service.

MODEL 1986

The first E30 upgrade, with most changes introduced in September 1985 after the August factory shut down. 195/65 tyres replace the 195/60s, revised final drive ratios, 325i replaces 323i, new front valance lower lip, larger front seats with new type seat upholstery ('Country' pattern), revised instruments with 150mph marked speedometer and only one red overdue service light. Steel wheel cars fitted with full size plastic wheel trims on six-cylinder cars. Analogue clock replaces digital. Full Convertible, SE and Sport introduced.

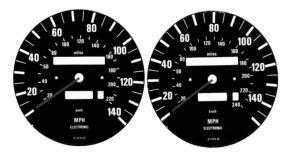

Early and late speedos; from September 1985 the speedo read to 150mph and 240km/h

MODEL 1988

The big one. Plastic bumpers, deeper front valance, deeper rear valance contoured around rear bumper, larger rear lamps, rear wheel-arches are set lower in the rear quarter panels (a feature introduced on the 1986 Convertible), new E32 7 Series style elliptical headlamps, Touring models introduced. M40 engines phased in, updated Motronic fitted to 325i, replacing LE Jetronic on 320i, new radiator design, new interior trim. 320i gains twin-tube gas dampers.

Standard M3 Engine bay - apart from cam cover colour they all look the same - Alf Dickhaut

One of the most successful racing saloons ever. An original works racing M3 is now very collectable - Craig Pusey

Experimental M3 instrument cluster. Note rev counter - Alf Dickhaut
1989 M3 tartan interior. All M3's had the bolster in centre of rear seat back, making the M3 a strict 4 seater - Alf Dickhaut

MODEL 1990

Minor revisions with new interior trim, new wheel trims, 318iS and Lux models launched with a slightly striped pattern trim. 'Smiley' headlamps with the semi circular cut outs in the reflector.

THE M3

Although all E30 M3s are pretty much the same, there are plenty of different models with a few subtle differences between each.

M3

This is the standard car where production began in September 1986. Leather or plain cloth trim (Houndstooth type check), 15-inch BBS cross-spoke wheels, black camshaft cover, 200bhp, fuel tanks with a total capacity of 70 litres with a 55-litre standard E30 tank plus an additional boot mounted 15-litre tank. 195bhp when fitted with catalyst, later cars with 215bhp and catalyst from September 1989. American market cars used a 4.1:1 final drive and a standard 535i (Getrag 265) overdrive gearbox with the 195bhp catalyst engine. Standard equipment on US cars included leather trim, electric windows and sunroof, air conditioning, radio and cruise control. They are identified by having orange marker lamps (reflectors) on the sides of the front bumper, a brake light in the rear screen and a mph speedometer, although Canadian cars use the standard kph unit. They both have a seat belt warning light in the check control panel. Both cars also use a standard E30 fuel tank with 55 litres and no additional tank. Numbers produced? 5187 cars were built up to August 1989 and a further 3544 catalyst cars up to May 1989. From here, the 215bhp catalysed version took over in September 1989 and 1914 such cars were assembled until December 1990. This later 215bhp catalysed engine is the same unit as the Cecotto limited edition. All M3s had ABS braking.

M3 Evolution

505 cars built from February to May 1987. Revised cylinder head but still 200bhp. Lightweight boot lid, (drilled holes), modified front bumper with steeply raked splitter extension, extra rear splitter under rear boot spoiler. Air scoops instead of front fog lamps, M3 badges on sill kick strips. The Evolution cylinder head is marked with an 'E' stamped at the back but this is very hard to spot with the manifolds in place.

M3 Evolution II

Based on the Evolution with 501 cars built from March to May 1988, although the plaque on the centre console says 500 cars. Only three colours available, Nogaro Silver, Macao Blue and Misano Red. Engine power was raised to 220bhp with 11:1 compression, revised cams, lightened flywheel and reprogrammed ECU. Camshaft cover and inlet plenum painted white with three colour (red, blue and dark blue) stripes. Taller 3.15:1 final drive ratio. Similar style front and rear spoilers, but made from thinner gauge plastics, thinner gauge glass used for rear screen and rear side glass, plus a top tint screen, standard electric sunroof in most markets. 16 x 7.5-inch BBS wheels. Interior trim is half leather with grey checked cloth and Motorsport three colour stripe in top corner, interior mirror with twin map lights, BMW Bavaria C electronic radio/cassette player.

M3 Sport Evolution

600 cars built between December 1989 and March 1990, only available in Gloss Black or Brilliant Red. Red cars had black bumper tape, black cars had red tape. Top tint screen on all cars. Satin, not gloss, finish for sills. 397 black cars, 201 red and 2 white cars for BMW dealers.

The 2.5-litre engine looks the same as the earlier 2.3 but has red plug lead caps. Inside, the bore was increased from 93.4 to 95mm and the crank stroke lengthened from 84mm to 87mm. Pistons oil cooled by jets at the base of the cylinders, 282 degree camshafts, larger inlet valves, sodium filled exhaust valves, 10.2:1 compression, catalytic converter.

Outside, the car used lightweight front and rear bumpers of a very similar design to standard 200bhp M3 ones, but with a three-position front splitter. Standard 63-litre E30 fuel tank with no additional tank, thinner rear screen and rear side glass and a three-position rear splitter on the rear boot spoiler. Front wings were different with larger wheel-arches (they are NOT wider). Wheels are 16 x 7.5-inch BBS but with Nogaro Silver centres. Front suspension lowered by 10mm.

The interior is also quite different with Recaro SR style bucket seats, suede covered M Tech II steering wheel and suede illuminated gearknob, no interior grab handles or map lights and red seat belts. A 'Sport Evolution 1990' dash plaque was fitted to the 51 official UK-supplied cars but were not always fitted to German or Italian market vehicles. Final details include a rubber sealing strip fitted between each front wing and the bonnet, sealing rings between the grille and headlamps and foam around the side grilles to seal them against the wings and front panel. The centre kidney grille has re-profiled vanes.

M3 Johnny Cecotto

480 cars built from April to June 1989, 215bhp engine with catalyst and with camshaft cover and inlet plenum painted to match car body colour – Nogaro Silver,

1989 M3 standard interior:
Note check tartan seat- Alf Dickhaut

In Alpine white, this M3 looks superb. The wheels are
E34 M5 with centres removed - Alf Dickhaut

Evo II engine bay in technicolor glory - Alf Dickhaut

An Evo sport front spoiler splitter - Alf Dickhaut

1989 M3 Johnny Cecotto in Macao Blue - Craig Pusey

A road going M3 Racer lookalike - Alf Dickhaut

*Did BMW ever make a better looking
car than this? - Alf Dickhaut*

*The M3 Convertible doesn't have the "race car" feel of
the saloon, but is a great "feelgood" car - Alf Dickhaut*

Macao Blue or Misano Red on all cars. 7.5 x 16-inch BBS wheels with black centres, Evolution front and rear spoilers. Special interior with light silver grey dashboard and centre console, silver grey headlining, half leather seats with striped cloth inserts, standard computer and illuminated gear knob. Numbered console plaque with engraved Johnny Cecotto signature. Options included full black leather, either Bison/Buffalo or Nappa and Silver (well, light grey) Nappa leather, although this is very rare.

M3 Europa Meister
The full name for this one is M3 Europa Meister '88 Celebration Edition. Introduced to celebrate the M3 winning the 1988 ETCC (European Touring Cars), BMW built 150 based on the standard 195bhp catalysed M3 between October and November 1988. Macau Blue with full grey leather trim and a console plaque with the signature of Roberto Ravaglia, plus cruise control and 15" wheels. But please do not confuse this car with the.......

M3 Roberto Ravaglia Edition
The 'Ravioli' was the UK market edition of the Johnny Cecotto car. They are one and the same car except that they are painted Misano Red and have the Ravaglia dash plaque which is not numbered. BMW themselves are not one hundred per cent sure how many they built, but it is around 25. This model too, has a catalyst.

The M3 Convertible
Built from a standard 316i – 325i Convertible shell, with a few minor changes, the M3 Convertible was built by BMW Motorsport, unlike the other M3 saloons. Production began in May 1988 with the 200bhp non-catalyst engine but by October the 195bhp catalysed engine was being used. Production ended in May 1989 but the car came back in March 1990 with the 215bhp catalyst engine that was by then being fitted as standard to the regular M3. All cars used the dreaded electro/hydraulic hood and the second batch of cars from 1990 and 1991 used the M Tech ll steering wheel. The Evo front spoiler was used, as was the headlamp wash/wipe system on most cars along with a glove box that locked with the central locking system. UK market cars used a stitched leather centre console. All cars had leather trim with the Motorsport tri-colour stripes in the top left corner and stitched leather door trims are also used. There were no Evolution convertibles, and just 786 were made. One last point – the sills are deeper and as such, M3 saloon front wings, rear wings and plastic sill covers do not fit.

M3 USA
The American market M3 was very similar to the European car but had a number of differences. They all used a 535i overdrive gearbox with the conventional

gear-change pattern and used a 4.1:1 ratio limited slip differential. The engine was a catalysed 195bhp version, and production ran from March 1987 until December 1990. Other distinguishing features include side marking lights in the outer edges of the front bumper, black intake grilles instead of the towing eye covers and a third brake light. Canadian models had heated seats as standard and all USA cars were loaded with all the extras such as leather trim, electric windows and sunroof, air conditioning and computer.

Options and standard equipment

Apart from the convertible, the standard M3 was a basic machine – no radio on most cars, no sunroof, manual windows, etc. Options included manual or electric sunroofs, electric windows, on-board computer, air conditioning, various BMW Bavaria, Becker or Blaupunkt radios, leather trim, heated front seats, headlamp wash/wipe, vacuum headlamp aim, top tint screen and electronic damper control.

OFF THE SHELF MODIFIED E30S

ALPINA

It was with the E30 that Alpina really increased their volumes and made their mark in the UK. 1983 saw the launch of the E30 in most markets and in Britain, Frank Sytner's concern in Nottingham took over the Alpina franchise from TWR and began to really push it through his BMW dealership. Basically, Alpina went from oddball to royalty overnight. The Alpina E30 story is a fairly complex one because even back then, Alpina and BMW were hand-in-hand and a lot of developments seen in production BMWs (the 4.6 litre X5 being one) came from Alpina.

C1 2.3

The old E21 323i was always a bit of a wild child, all oversteer and, all too often, accident-prone as well. Alpina took the original 323i under its wing and turned it

An original Alpina decal set. Expensive and many companies could reproduce them.

A four door Alpina C1 2.3

An Alpina C1 2.3. Bodykit is the BMW "Aero" kit from 1984, stripes are reproduction.

into the car it should have been, with 170bhp and a sorted chassis.

With the E30, the E21's often-nasty traits had been tamed but the introduction of Bosch LE Jetronic to replace the E21s mechanical K Jetronic system lost the 323i 4bhp and a bit of bite. The stage was therefore set for a return of the C1 2.3. When it appeared at the end of 1983 though, its pants had been ever so slightly been pulled down because BMW had upped power from 139 to 150bhp by changing the camshaft to something with a more aggressive profile. This meant a mere 20bhp increase for the C1 as opposed to a more creditable 31bhp. Basis of the C1 2.3 was a two- or four-door 323i from the factory. German market cars were built at the Alpina factory at Buchloe, but French cars were often assembled from 323i base cars by Garage Du Bac and British cars built by Sytner. Standard specification on all base cars to be converted included a limited slip differential, Bilstein dampers and a manual gearbox – either the standard overdrive unit with a 3.45:1 final drive or the close ratio sport gearbox with the 3.25:1 differential (some overdrive cars used the 3.25:1 though!).

Power steering was not standard and strictly speaking was not on the options list. The 323i was shorn of its engine, to be replaced by a complete Buchloe-built unit with a special gas-flowed Alpina head with reshaped, fully hemispherical combustion chambers, a set of forged Mahle pistons to match the reshaped combustion chambers, that raised the compression ratio from 9.8:1 to 10:1, and a 268-degree camshaft. The ECU, being an LE Jetronic type with analogue mapping was not 'rechippable' and the entire fuelling system was unaltered, save possibly for slightly raised fuel pressure. Cars built other than at the Alpina factory, according to their parts list, had the standard cast iron exhaust manifold. My own C1 did have this feature, and the road test cars from Sytners also used the standard 323i exhaust manifold. All cars used a big bore exhaust system designed by Alpina and made by Boysen with the Alpina script stamped into the silencers. A satin black finish camshaft cover was fitted to all cars. Standard gearboxes, clutches and limited slip differentials were used, and the suspension was reworked with slightly stiffer Bilstein dampers, which were modified from the 'yellow' units used on a 323i with sports suspension. Springs were stiffer and were of the variable rate type whilst anti roll bars were standard 323i. Wheels were the 7 x 16-inch 20-spoke Alpina rims with lockable centre caps and 195/50 Pirelli P7 tyres.

The specification of the car depended on what options you wanted. A base 323i could come in Gazelle Beige with no sunroof, wind-up windows and Alpina C1s have been built from these, although all cars had BMW sports seats. Common options were electric windows, manual or electric sunroof, headlamp wash/wipe, bronze or green tint glass, opening rear side windows, on-board computer and leather trim. All C1s came with the Alpina front spoiler, most had the Alpina rubber rear spoiler, all had a numbered plaque with a build number on the centre console, the four-spoke Alpina steering wheel (made by Momo), Alpina lettered instruments plus badges on the grille and

1989 Alpina C2 2.7 Touring. An ideal way to frighten your labrador! - Craig Pusey

boot lid. Many cars had the lurid side stripes, many did not. Another option was Alpina Recaro seats, as opposed to BMW sports seats which were made by BMW under licence from Recaro. The Alpina seats were trimmed with the trademark green, silver and blue stripes.

As a car, the C1 was moderately successful, but at £16,000 without options it was very pricey and it didn't offer vastly more than a factory 150bhp 323i with sports suspension and LSD. The performance was harder to extract and the ride rock hard. Late C1s used colour-coded door mirrors. With cars converted outside the factory the build plaque stated E30 – 0057 as opposed to C1 2.3 0057. Later cars converted by Alpina agents like Hammer BMW in Monchen Gladbach also said this. Only Buchloe built cars gave an exact Alpina model type.

C1 2.5
This was a weird one and quite rare with just 51 left-hand drive cars built between October 1986 and July 1988. In effect, it was a conversion on a standard 325i with the typical Alpina gas-flowed cylinder head, Alpina 268 degree camshaft plus exhaust and reprogrammed engine management. It gave 190bhp at 5800rpm and 235Nm of torque at 5000rpm. It also used Bosch Motronic engine management. In all other respects, it was a typical Alpina with the Bilstein/Alpina suspension, 25% limited slip differential and the spoilers, badges, stripes and steering wheel. Although it was a bolt-on conversion in Britain (and not all cars had Alpina wheels), it was both a Buchloe factory car in Germany or a dealer conversion.

C2 2.5
According to Alpina, the C2 2.5 appeared as a factory built car in July 1985. It used the longer stroke 76.8mm crank from the outgoing 323i in the 525e block, giving 2554cc, the gas-flowed head and 268 degree camshaft from the C1 2.3 and a special hybrid version of the Bosch LE Jetronic fuel injection from the 323i.

However, British magazines were road testing the C2 2.5 in February 1985 as a Sytner conversion to a 323i. They were quoting a 75mm stroke crank and a capacity of 2494cc which is exactly that of the 325i which did not officially exist at that time – the first 325s were built three or four months later which asks the question – did Alpina develop the 325i engine for BMW? It was certainly an outstanding engine and one typical of Alpina's talent.

Even cars built as late as September 1987 (the metal bumper) still used LE Jetronic, which suggests that a 320i was used as the base car, but for the last few cars Motronic was used. No cold start injector was used with either system.

C2 2.7

Like the C2 2.5, Sytner famously built the first C2 2.7 before Buchloe completed their first customer cars, although it really must be clarified that Alpina did all of the development work. It just so happens that Sytners assembled the first customer cars in February 1986.

Basis of the C2 2.7's engine was the good old 2.7 litre 525e engine, right? Wrong! Alpina voiced concerns about the suitability of the 81mm stroke grey cast iron crank to withstand serious abuse and many engine builders have broken 525e cranks at over 6500rpm – they were just not designed for this. Instead, Alpina took a standard 325i block (the same as a 525e incidentally) with its 84mm bore and used a modified 324td turbo diesel crank. The reason for this is because the diesel crank was made from forged steel and was a lot stronger than the cast iron Eta crank. With the excess metal machined from the heavy balance weights, the Alpina 2.7 crank is a thing of beauty. A cylinder head was gas-flowed and ported from a stock '885' casting from a 325i but the good old Alpina 268 degree camshaft was retained as were Mahle forged, domed high compression pistons. With reprogrammed Bosch Motronic, the tubular exhaust manifold and the usual meticulous assembly at Buchloe, the engine gave a very real 210bhp at a low 5800rpm and 267Nm of torque at 4500rpm. On the road, the C2 2.7 remains the ultimate E30 'all rounder'. It needs less than 6000rpm to achieve full power, has prodigious torque, yet remains as driveable and economical as a standard 325i. A fine achievement.

Early chrome bumper cars, like the others, could be built on a two- or four-door base but the C2 2.7 was built also as a Convertible or a Touring. Later two-door cars could also be built from a 325i Sport with the M Tech body kit. It was also built as a four-wheel drive.

B3 2.7

The C2 2.7 didn't sell as well as was hoped in Germany as it was felt that the 'C' designation was somewhat below the 'B' cars. So, from September 1987 in European markets except Britain (and predominantly Germany) it was fitted with a catalyst and renamed the B3 2.7. This model used a standard 325i camshaft as did the C2 2.7 when fitted with a catalyst. Power dropped 6bhp but apart from that, it was just a catalysed C2 2.7. This time, you could have two- or four-door saloons, a four-wheel-drive 325ix based saloon or Touring, a Convertible and a two-wheel-drive Touring.

B6 2.8

Launched in November 1983 in all left-hand drive markets, the B6 2.8 was a C1 2.3 but with a modified 2.8-litre M30 'big six' engine giving 210bhp. 259 cars were built, making it a reasonably good seller for Alpina. Unlike the regular 2.8 unit found in the 528i, the Alpina 2.8 used Bosch Motronic from the 3.2 and 3.5 litre M30. As a point of interest, the 'Britain only' E28 based B2.8 did not use this engine- it was a standard 528i with an Alpina exhaust system.

The B6 2.8 engine gave 210bhp over the regular unit's 184bhp (itself very creditable – a Ford 2.8 injection engine struggled to give 150bhp) with a hotter camshaft, gas-flowed head and a 9.8:1 compression ratio. It used standard 2.8 injectors and air flow meter but the Alpina exhaust and tubular manifold – a truly great engine that revs sweetly. Alpina kept the air box and air flow meter on the original (inlet) side of the engine by repositioning the throttle body on the other side of the M30's inlet manifold. Transmission was the standard 528i unit, but the Sport close ratio unit available as an option on the 528i could also be specified. Final drive was the standard 3.45:1 323i ratio in an E28 based 'big' differential with this gearbox or a 2.93:1 differential from the 525e with the Sport gearbox – both units were 25% limited slip as standard.

Suspension was as per usual but with re-valved Bilstein dampers, stronger springs but standard 323i anti-roll bars, 18.5mm front and 14.5mm rear. Brakes were

Alpina B3 2.7 Allrad. 210bhp with 4-wheel drive
- Craig Pusey

1985 Alpina B6 2.8 - This is the only
RHD version ever made - Craig Pusey

upgraded using calipers from a production Mercedes W124 but with Alpina's own mounting brackets and 296mm discs. With or without ABS they gave impressive bite. Wheels can be either 7x16 all round or (very rarely) with 8-inch wide rears although the cars I've seen used 7-inch wide rims front and rear. Alpina Recaro seats were a very common option to the point of being standard equipment as were goodies like the long-range (extra 40 litres) fuel tank in the boot and the digital display for the temperatures for various fluids mounted in the centre air vent hole. Production of the B6 2.8 ended in July 1986. The problem was the C2 2.7 – it gave just as much power as the B6 2.8 but because it used a regular M20 engine as a starting point it was a lot easier and cheaper to convert. Just one right hand drive car was made which lives in England.

B6 3.5

Appearing in August 1984, the B6 3.5 was a bit of a monster that we never saw in Britain. With the B6 2.8 as a base, Alpina simply dropped in the 261bhp engine from the E28 based B10, lit the fuse and stood well back. This car was, and is, an absolute monster. It's so quick and responsive as to chew the tails of modern day Porsches and would slaughter an E30 M3 – in fact, it would give a modern M3 a fright. 219 cars were built between August 1984 and December 1990 although the later cars from August 1986 had catalysts. Two- or four-door saloons were available and the B6 3.5 remains one of Alpina's hairiest moments – a true hero's car. Although Alpina produced almost all of them, Alpina dealers such as Hammer BMW in Monchen Gladbach, Germany built a few as conversions – one such car exists in Britain.

B6 3.5S

Purists groaned out loud when Alpina launched this car. Based on the legendary E30 M3, Alpina created a classic when it removed the standard S14 16-valve food mixer and dropped in the 254bhp catalysed 3.5 from the B10 5

Series. It's like the B6 3.5 only better. Handling is sharper, and with those Alpina pin stripes the box arched Alpina looks like the frisky bulldog it is. Probably the best E30 Alpina ever made, it could be argued that the B6 3.5S is the best E30 ever. With solid power and torque, it will not crucify a Sport Evo on road and track but do not let anyone tell you the handling is compromised. Alpina do not make bad handling cars, period. Although the B6 3.5S does have a touch more understeer in extreme conditions, it's not really noticeable and in most situations the sheer 'go' of the thing will haul you clear of the pack. This is a lovely, lovely old car – and one possibly only bettered by the Hartge H35S.

62 cars were made between November 1987 and December 1990 with some cars being based on Evo models – it's not 100% certain if any Evo Sport cars were converted but it's unlikely.

HARTGE

H23

Hartge were also on the ball in 1983 and launched their first modified E30, the H23 in late that year. The H23 was a modified 323i in much the same mould as the Alpina C1 2.3. Hartge dragged 170bhp from the 2.3 litre engine by similar methods to Alpina – a much better camshaft, gas-flowed cylinder head and forged pistons to raise the compression to 10:1. Hartge used a tubular exhaust manifold mated to their own bigger bore system and the manifold typically used 40mm bore pipes. It also used a special cast alloy camshaft cover. The engine was coded MB9E.

A 3.25:1 final drive ratio was used on all cars and wheels were 7.6 x 16-inch Hartge 11 spoke alloys with 195/50 front tyres and 225/45 rears. Suspension was by Bilstein with special valves by Hartge plus Hartge's own springs.

Alpina B6 3.5. A sadly neglected example spotted in Germany - Alf Dickhaut

1989 Alpina B6 3.5S. Based on the M3, Alpina replaced the S14 engine with a 260 bhp 3.5 6 cyl. engine - Craig Pusey

Items like a 40% lock-up limited-slip differential and stronger anti-roll bars were extras but all cars had the polished front strut brace and Hartge badging. Inside, Hartge badges on the instruments and a four spoke Hartge Momo steering wheel were fitted along with a footrest on LHD cars and a 280kph speedometer. Many cars also had Hartge body kit parts such as front and rear spoilers and side skirts. Unlike Alpina, Hartge were willing to sell complete parts kits and engines separately. For example, Hartge offered an H23 engine conversion consisting of a cylinder head, camshaft, camshaft cover and exhaust. H23 brakes were standard but with special Hartge pads.

H26 (323i)

This conversion took the 323i one step further and it realised 190bhp. The car is almost exactly as per H23 but with a capacity increase. Available as a conversion on a new 323i, there was a surcharge for the new, unused 323i engine. Basis of the MB10E engine was a 525e cylinder block that was fitted with the 323i crankshaft and connecting rods plus special pistons. Like the Alpina C2 2.5, this gave a capacity of 2554 cc. It used a 10:1 compression ratio and either a 3.45:1 or a 3.25:1 final drive with limited-slip differential. Hartge anti-roll bars were standard on the H26.

H26 (325i)

Based on a 325i, the conversion is similar to the H23 – wheels, suspension, steering wheel and instruments, badges and engine work. This time though, Hartge did not touch the cylinder head but fitted a hotter camshaft, the Hartge exhaust manifold and exhaust system, plus a reprogrammed ECU and the Hartge camshaft cover. Power was raised from the standard 171bhp to 190bhp. Engine code MB16E, final drive ratio 3.64:1. Tyre sizes 195/50 front and rear.

H27

Like the Alpina C2 2.7, Hartge also did a 2.7 engine conversion although it is not known if the diesel crank was used, or the standard 2.7 Eta unit. To be fair, the Eta crank is safe to around 6250rpm and nobody complains about Hartge engines. Power was quoted at 210bhp with a 10.2:1 compression ratio. The rest of the car was the typical Hartge conversion although this time the tyre sizes were 205/50. Engine code MB18E.

H27 SP

Beating Alpina to the post, Hartge developed a special induction system for the M20 engine with a lovely Ferrari-esque inlet manifold giving each cylinder its own throttle butterfly. Power was 220bhp at 6400rpm. No specific engine code.

1990 Hartge H26. A very effective conversion based on the 325i - Craig Pusey

H28

Like the Alpina B6 2.8, Hartge also developed a 2.8 M30 engined car but it wasn't a huge success. The 2.7 was a cheaper solution that was just as effective. I've never even seen one.

H35

Another lunatic creation, this was the standard bodied E30 with a 250bhp modified 3.5 litre M30. Not quite as powerful as the Alpina B6 3.5 but very sorted with typical Hartge suspension and 296mm brakes.

H35-24

One for the certified insane, this was the standard bodied E30 but with a 3.6 litre M5 engine complete with 286bhp. Very fast, probably too fast and a bit scary but the M3 based version was a lot better. Lots of special bits mean that every time you crack the custom-made sump on a speed bump, it is going to be expensive. It's a great car, but the Alpina B6 3.5S is more sensible with just as much real-world performance.

AC SCHNITZER

AC Schnitzer made some nice E30 conversions. The S3 was originally available as a modified 323i which gave 167bhp at 6000rpm but when the 150bhp 323i arrived at the end of 1983 it became a bit redundant. Another version was based on the 325i with 190bhp but the biggie was the S3 2.7. This was built along the same lines as the Alpina and Hartge 2.7 conversions and it gave 210bhp. This was also available with a catalyst. The conversion utilised a special Schnitzer Racing suspension kit that was set up at the Nurburgring, a 25% lock up limited-slip differential (standard BMW) and those lovely Schnitzer wheels – these were of the 16-inch Type 1 variety. The S3 also came in Germany with the full aerodynamic body kit which is particularly good looking.

The S3 was always available in the full range of body

styles, two- and four-door saloons, Convertibles and Tourings. Although Schnitzer did parts for the E30 M3, their main M3 conversion package was the superb S3 Sport 2.5

In Britain, Schnitzer parts and conversions were from 1989 distributed and fitted by Rossiters in Norfolk and although BMW (GB) now own the Schnitzer franchise, Rossiters are still a good source for Schnitzer parts and know all about the older cars like the E30 and the M3. Based on a standard 2.3 litre car, the Sport 2.5 was a viable alternative to the rather overpriced 2.5 Sport Evolution. At the heart of the engine, the crank was replaced by a special Schnitzer billet steel crank with 83mm stroke, which was even shorter than the standard 84mm stroke 2.3 crank. The bores were considerably enlarged to give a final capacity of 2431cc. Needless to say, the cylinder head was modified as well. Completing the conversion was the usual Schnitzer – Bilstein chassis upgrade and 17-inch split-rim alloy wheels.

In Britain, Schnitzer conversions are rare – only three 325i's, including one Touring, were converted to the S3 2.7 specification and no 2.5 litre M3 conversions were done, although one might have crept in as an import. Schnitzer's forte was suspension and it is thought that their suspension kits were the best, particularly for the M3. Other Schnitzer goodies included the single wiper that did not lift off at speed and the Sport mirrors.

Options and standard equipment.
Apart from the Convertible, the standard M3 was a basic machine – no radio on most cars, no sunroof, manual windows etc. Options included manual or electric sunroofs, electric windows, on board computer, air conditioning, various BMW Bavaria, Becker or Blaupunkt radios, leather trim, heated front seats, headlamp wash wipe, vacuum headlamp aim, top tint screen and electronic damper control.

The E21, predecessor to the E30 and the first 3 Series

HISTORY OF THE E30

The E30 in Europe
November 1982: E30 production begins, 323i first followed by 320i, 318i and 316. 323i and 320i use new Bosch LE Jetronic with overrun fuel cut off, 318i used Golf GTi type Bosch K Jetronic and 316 uses a carburettor. Two doors only at first although four-door prototype cars were present at the original launch. 175/70 tyres for four-cylinder cars and 195/60 for sixes. Rear discs on 323i, vented front discs on 320i and 323i.

March 1983: The E30 is launched in Britain, 316, 320i and 323i, manual and automatic.

August 1983: European 318i now has Bosch LE Jetronic. Four-door cars introduced in Europe, first Baur Cabriolets imported.

October 1983: Four-door versions of all models become available in Britain. 318i introduced in Britain with Bosch LE Jetronic. Four-speed automatics replace three-speed versions on 320i and 323i. The power of the 323i is boosted to 150bhp. Rear floor pan lowered to improve rear legroom.

January 1984: Baur Cabriolet launched, available on all cars 316 to 323i.

September 1984: Four-speed ZF automatic gearbox replaces three-speed on 316 and 318i.

October 1984: Four-speed heater fan replaces three-speed, "CHECK" replaces triangle on dash for check control system. Rear seat backs sculpted inwards to improve rear legroom. LE Jetronic fuel cut off lowered from 1200 to 1000rpm.

October 1985: Model 1986: 325i replaces 323i. 195/60

Press launch, Valencia 1983

tyres replaced by 195/65, speedometer recalibrated to 150mph, service lights revised – now just one red light and not three, revised final drive ratios, analogue clock replaces digital, revised front seats and interior trim with 'Country' fabric, 320i power raised to 129bhp, new front lower spoiler, standard rear centre armrest on 320i and 325i.

April 1986: 325i Convertible launched.

August 1986: Standard ABS on 325i, full plastic wheel trims on steel wheel cars (all models)

September 1986: 320i and 325i SE launched – bottle top alloy wheels, front fog lamps, power steering, electric windows (rears too on four-door cars), computer, headlamp wash/wipe, rear blind, electric sunroof. 325i Sport also launched with M Tech body kit, LSD, close ratio gearbox, Bilstein M tech suspension, de-chromed, BMW sport seats, M Technic 1 steering wheel, 15-inch BBS cross spoke alloy wheels. 316 has standard rev counter to replace the clock plus an analogue clock as for the rest of E30 range. 316 now has standard five-speed gearbox and glove box torch. ABS offered as option on 316 and 318i. Central locking now standard on all E30s.

September 1987: Major facelift on E30 saloons. Strut mounted plastic bumpers, deeper front and rear valances, lowered rear wheel arches, de-chromed side window surrounds, larger rear lamps, improved headlamps, black only side mouldings, black only screen rubbers, variable ratio steering racks (PAS and manual), 64-litre fuel tank, twin-tube gas dampers on 320i, M40 engine replaces M10 on 318i, 320i gains Motronic engine management. SE models identifiable by colour coded bumpers and door mirrors. Standard equipment on all cars now includes tinted glass and central locking. Revised automatic gearboxes.

September 1988: 316i with M40 engine replaces 316; power steering and electric front windows standard. 'Smiley' headlamps with cut outs from E34 introduced. 325i Touring models introduced.

February 1990: Lux models launched, based on 316i and 318i. 62-litre fuel tank, full de-chrome, 320i type trim and carpets, alloy wheels, manual sunroof, boot spoiler, 3 spoke steering wheel, outside temperature display. 320i and 325i SE upgraded with 7 Series pinstripe trim, leather look handbrake gaiter, 6.5 x 14-inch BBS cross-spoke alloys, electric sunroof, computer, sports three spoke steering wheel, electric rear windows on four-door cars.

April/May 1990: 318iS launched, based on 318i but with 136bhp 16-valve 1.8 engine, close-ratio gearbox, M Technic suspension, 14-inch steel wheels with special wheel trims with options of 14- or 15-inch BBS alloy wheels, BMW sport seats, M Technic 1 steering wheel, full de-chrome (shadow line), colour-coded bumpers and mirrors, power steering, no cost option metallic paint, tinted glass, central locking, electric front windows, tartan check cloth trim, extended front spoiler lip, rear boot spoiler.

December 1990: 318i Convertible launched.

April 1991: 318i Design Convertible launched, M Technic body kit.

THE E30 IN AMERICA

May 1983: 318i launched, 1766cc M10 engine with Federal specification Bosch LE Jetronic, impact bumpers, standard bottle top alloy wheels, electric windows. Power 101bhp, five-speed manual or three-speed automatic transmission.

A 325e snapped in a wintery Hamburg.
Clean examples are getting harder to find

15 inch BBS Cross Spoke Alloy Wheel

June 1984: 325e launched, as 318i but with 121bhp 2.7 litre Eta engine. Central locking, sunroof, bottle top alloy wheels, 3-spoke leather steering wheel, Recaro type seats, computer, check control system.

May 1986: 325es launched. M Technic suspension, front and rear spoilers, power sunroof, cruise control, air conditioning, M tech steering wheel, ABS brakes, front fog lamps, limited-slip differential. 318i also discontinued, replaced by 325, basically a 325e but with standard trim.

February 1987: 325i launched, 325e but with European 325i engine (catalyst equipped), 168bhp. Leather trim including sports seats, automatic climate control and 14-inch BBS cross-spoke alloy wheels. 325i Convertible also launched with bottle top wheels. First US specification M3 launched with lower final drive and convention-al H pattern gearbox, 192bhp, leather trim, electric sun-roof, climate control air conditioning.

February 1988: 325iX four-wheel drive launched. 325 and 325e now use the 'Super Eta' engine which is the existing Eta but with the 885 cylinder head from the 325i, albeit with the Eta camshaft. E30 range face-lifted with new impact bumpers and general changes to mirror late 1987 European facelift. Bigger fuel tank (16.5 US gallons), body colour mirrors, de-chromed side window surrounds.

August 1990: The 318iS is launched in the U.S, virtually same as the European version but with air bag and leather trim plus extra cooling slot in front panel. Four-door M42-engined version is just called 318i and the two-door is called the 318iC with standard suspension and trim.

THE MAIN E30 COLOURS AND PAINT CODES FOR ALL CARS WORLDWIDE.

1982 – 1985 cars:

Henna Red	052	(a bright, orangy red)
Alpine White I	146	
Lapis Blue	173	(dark non-metallic blue)
Opal Green	171	(light metallic green)
Sapphire Blue	149	(light metallic blue)
Baltic Blue	178	(medium metallic blue-grey)
Cosmos Blue	185	(medium to dark metallic blue)
Black	668	(continued for all E30)
Polaris Silver	060	(until around 1990)
Pasta Green	194	(non-metallic khaki green)
Planaten Green	188	(medium metallic green)
Basalt Blue	180	(non-metallic pale blue-grey)
Gazelle Beige	128	(light beige)
Bronzit	421	(light champagne gold, continued until around 1988)
Bronzit Beige	139	(darker brownish gold)
Graphite	087	(older colour used on very early E30)
Burgundy Red	199	(dark metallic red)
Safari Beige	147	(darker beige)

1985 onwards:

Arctic Blue	045	(lighter metallic blue-grey)
Zinnober Red	138	(blood red, continued until around 1990)
Karmin Red	172	(light, slightly purple maroon/red)
Dolphin Grey	184	(medium to dark metallic grey)
Diamond Black	181	(metallic black)
Alpine White II	218	(continued all though E30 production)
Saturn Blue	176	(replaced Lapis blue, slightly brighter blue)
Zobel Brown	190	(very rare, dark metallic browny grey)

Plus Cosmos Blue, Black, Polaris Silver, Bronzit, Burgundy Red.

Plastic bumper cars:

Lachs Silver	203	(silvery grey)
Cirrus Blue	189	(light metallic blue-grey)
Royal Blue	198	(dark metallic blue with purple tint)
Luxor Beige	219	(metallic light brown/mink)
Diamond Black	181	(metallic black introduced 1986)
Dolphin Grey	184	(metallic grey introduced late 1986)
Atlantis Blue	207	(dark non metallic blue)
Mineral Blue	231	(solid blue with green tint)
Malachite Green	205	(similar to Agate green)

Plus Alpine White, Zinnober Red, Gloss Black 668.

Late cars (approx. 1990 on)

Brilliant Red	308	(bright red)
Laser Blue	294	(fairly dark metallic blue with green tint)
Sterling Silver	244	(similar to Polaris)
Boston Green	275	(mainly late Tourings)
Mauritius Blue	287	(deep metallic blue, late Touring and Convertible 318i)
Granite Silver	237	(light metallic grey, similar to Lachs)
Calypso Red	252	(metallic wine red)
Vulcan Grey	329	(dark, non metallic grey)

Plus Gloss Black, Diamond Black, Alpine White II.

M3

Nogaro Silver	243	(Evo II and Ravaglia, Cecotto plus Evo Sport wheels)
Macao Blue	250	(dark metallic blue-purple, also 325i Motorsport convertible)
Misano Red	236	(Evo II and Ravaglia)
Mugello Red	274	
Gloss Black	668	(Evo Sport only)

Plus Diamond Black, Brilliant Red, Lachs Silver, Alpine White, Zinnober Red, Henna Red until 1987, Polaris Silver, Sterling Silver, Granite Silver, Dolphin Grey.

ORIGINAL PRICES AND STANDARD EQUIPMENT:

MARCH 1983:

316	£6,775
316 Auto	£7,515
320i	£8,595
320i Auto	£9,445
323i	£9,655
323i Auto	£10,535

Standard equipment: Electric door mirrors, digital clock, driver seat height adjust, front head rests, heated rear window, laminated screen, locking fuel cap (except when central locking is fitted) rear centre armrest on 323i, rear seat belts.

Optional equipment: Headlamp wash/wipe £217, Rear head rests £77, Power steering £405, three spoke sports steering wheel £83, manual sunroof £391, limited slip differential £277 (£294 on 323i), electric windows £274, green or brown tint glass £91, central locking £145, alloy wheels £417 – £525, leather upholstery £646, Bilstein sports suspension £120, ABS brakes £972, air conditioning £1,108.

Luxury pack with electric sunroof, electric front and rear windows, central locking and alloy wheels £1268 (£1573 on four-door 9/83)

JULY 1985:

316	£7,595
316 4 door	£8,020
316 Auto 2 door	£8,355
316 Auto 4 door	£8,780
318i 2 door	£8,520
318i 4 door	£8,945
318i 2 door Auto	£9,150
318i 4 door Auto	£9,575
320i 2 door	£9,595
320i 4 door	£10,020
320i 2 door Auto	£10,355
320i 4 door Auto	£10,780
323i 2 door	£10,895
323i 4 door	£11,320
323i 2 door Auto	£11,655
323i 4 door Auto	£12,080
Alpina C1 2.3	£15,995
Alpina C2 2.5	£17,245

Standard equipment: As for March 1983.

Optional equipment: As for 1983 but central locking £163 (£216 on 4 door), headlamp wash/wipe £244, tinted glass £102, manual sunroof £440, electric sunroof £558, electric windows £309 (2 door) £579 (4 door), seat heating £191, cruise control £275, limited slip differential £312, power steering £457, ABS brakes £1031, alloy wheels £492, Blaupunkt dealer fit radio £220. Metallic paint £276, dogleg sports gearbox £420, interior adjustable headlamps £54.

MAY 1990

316i 4 door	£11,245
316i 4 door	£12,510
316i Lux 2 door	£13,500
316i Lux 4 door	£14,025
318i 2 door	£13,275
318i 4 door	£13,800
318i Lux 2 door	£14,500
318i Lux 4 door	£15,025
318i Touring	£14,560
318iS 2 door	£14,750
320i 2 door	£14,985
320i 4 door	£15,510
320i SE 2 door	£16,900
320i SE 4 door	£17,700
320i Convertible	£19,245
320i Touring	£17,330
325i 2 door	£17,975
325i 4 door	£18,500
325i SE 2 door	£19,900
325i SE 4 door	£20,690
325i Convertible	£22,235
325i Touring	£20,430
325i Sport 2 door	£21,490
M3	£26,100

Standard equipment - base models: Central locking, green tint glass, headlamp levelling, electric front windows, power steering.

Standard equipment, 316i/318i Lux models: De-chromed, three-spoke leather steering wheel (not M Tech), rear spoiler, 14-inch alloy wheels (bottle top or BBS pattern), manual sunroof, rear head rests, clock with outside temperature display (poor man's OBC!), front fog lamps, 320i/325i 62-litre fuel tank. (55 on standard car).

Standard equipment, 318iS: Front and rear disc brakes (vented fronts), de-chromed, sports seats with check tartan pattern cloth, colour coded door mirrors, rear spoiler, M Technic 1 steering wheel, M Technic sports suspension, leather gear knob and gaiter.

Standard equipment 320i: Rear centre armrest, opening rear side windows on two-door, check control system between sun visors, front fog lights, velour carpets.

Standard equipment 325i: As 320i but with ABS brakes, boot spoiler and sports suspension.

Standard equipment, SE: Rear electric windows (four-door), leather gear knob, de-chromed, 3 spoke leather steering wheel, 14-inch bottle top alloy wheels, rear spoiler and Touring style sill covers, colour coded mirrors, electric sunroof, rear head rests, on board computer, interior light delay, headlight wash wipe.

Standard equipment, Convertible: As for 320i but with: rear electric windows, three-spoke leather steering wheel, 14-inch bottle top alloy wheels, anti theft system. 325i Convertible has sports seats, ABS brakes.

Standard equipment, Touring: De-chromed, three-spoke leather steering wheel, 14-inch bottle top alloy wheels, headlight wash/wipe. 318i Touring has de-chrome only.

Standard equipment, 325i Sport: As for 325i but de-chromed, M Technic 2 steering wheel, M Technic Bilstein sports suspension, limited slip differential, 15-inch BBS alloy cross-spoke wheels, M Technic body kit, black (anthracite) headlining, close ratio gearbox with standard H pattern gearshift, sports seats, map reading lights.

Standard equipment, M3: Catalytic converter, ABS brakes, de-chromed, M Technic 1 steering wheel, limited slip differential, special suspension, sports seats, heated mirrors, door locks and washer jets.

Optional equipment: On-board computer £363, clock and outside temp display £95, cruise control £348, metallic paint £375, catalytic converter £350, leather trim £901, ABS brakes £690, four-speed automatic £885, four-speed switchable sports/economy auto (6 cylinder only) £1400, de-chrome £241, 3 spoke leather steering wheel £133, M Technic 1 steering wheel £186, 318iS type front spoiler £160 (£277 when combined with boot spoiler), 15-inch BBS alloy wheels £1074, limited slip differential £396, rear electric windows £350, M Technic sports suspension £208, manual sunroof £571, electric sunroof £745, air conditioning £1371, sport seats £473, heated seats £243, rear head rests £112, BMW anti theft system £397, front fog lights £149, headlamp wash/wipe £310, heated mirrors, drivers door lock and washer jets £89, map reading lights £62, manual rear window blind £104. Baur conversion to any 2 door model £4470.

Oddballs: 316i Touring, £13,840, 318i Touring £15,840, 325i Touring £21,950, 318i Convertible £18,265, 320i Convertible £20,820, 325i Convertible £23,950. **(All May 1992)** 325iX 4wd £18,345 (July 1987, LHD only).

Chapter 2

BUYING AN E30

WHAT TO LOOK FOR

The E30 was always hailed as being a premium quality product, but in cold reality it was never as well built as the bigger BMWs. Early E30s could often be looking pretty tatty at eight years old – stone chips, rusting back arches, rusting lower front wing sections, threadbare driver's seat, etc. The thing to remember is that the E30 is now an old car and your chances of finding one that's absolutely mint are getting smaller by the day. The last Touring was built in early 1994, the first 323i being built in September 1982. If you feel the urge to go out and find a 1982 or early 1983 car, bear in mid that it's going to be a restoration project. Unless you found one of the early press launch cars, a Y registered E30 will not be a valued collectors item, just an interesting curiosity at club gatherings. In Britain, there are only a tiny handful (i.e two or three) early 1983 cars in mint, collectors condition – the rest all went west or survive in a perilous state. The first ever right-hand drive 320i was recently found but sadly was way beyond help, having rusted into the ground in a damp lock up.

Some E30s are being viewed as worthwhile for some light restoration – i.e new bolt on wings, maybe a rear wheel-arch replacement, seat re-trimming etc. These cars are going to be the 318iS, 325i Sport and, of course, the various Alpina cars. Cars like these will always have a value to enthusiasts, so before committing six months of your life to welding a beige 1985 316 back together, step back and think again. You can buy a really decent, 'regular' E30 for practically peanuts these days. The chrome bumper cars are very overlooked. Because there are so many scruffy, rusty old heaps about, it is reasonable to automatically assume that the one advertised twenty miles from you will also be scrap, but you would be surprised at how many decent ones there are left – lower mileage cars that were looked after.

WHERE TO BUY

The best place to look for mint examples is in the specialist BMW magazines and also in BMW Club magazines too. Some are overpriced, but at the end of the day a car is worth what someone will pay for it. Apart from

UBL 44Y, The only remaining BMW press car from 1983

the 318iS, 325i Sport and the Alpinas, regular E30s are still not hugely desirable so when a 1989 316i is priced close to that of a 1992 E36 model, you have to stop and think unless it is a particularly superb, low mileage car.

Extras are vital – I would not want an E30 without power steering, central locking is nice to have and a sunroof is very good news. All E30s after 1989 have power steering and central locking and cars without it are a bit sparse. They are also very hard to sell on again because even at the banger end of the market, punters want all the toys they can get.

Typical worn seat bolsters

The original colour sticker - the small number on the left is the paint code

Cheaper E30s are still prolific in publications like *Loot*, *Ad Mag* and the *Auto Trader* but my own favourite place to buy a cheap E30 is at a car auction although prices here seem to be climbing. You have got to know exactly what you are doing and to make it worthwhile, you have got to buy it cheap because more often than not, they are in the auction for a reason. If it is from a big car dealer chain as a part exchange, chances are it will be okay though. As an example of what to pay, assume the 1990 320i you're looking at is a decent, clean looking thing with a long MOT. Out of a paper, you would be paying £1000 so you want to be paying £500 or less. Do the usual checks on oil and coolant condition, but you will find that all E30s in auctions are sold as seen. That means that every problem the car has is now yours, bought and paid for. If you're new to car auctions, try not to look like a novice. I know a car auctioneer or two and they can spot one a mile off. To avoid getting singled out and stitched up, do not walk around with one of those newsagent used car price guides and when you are bidding, do not have hordes of family members around. When you bid, be on your own. Do not wave your arm about when bidding either. Raise your hand to attract the auctioneer's attention – he will not forget you. Just nod to increase your bid, or shake your head to duck out. Do not get carried away. Set your limit, and walk away when it's broken because there are plenty of other E30s about.

Older, scruffier cars can often sell for under £100 and they are ideal for spares. A scruffy old 325i with no MOT is worthless junk to the serious car dealers, but you can strip it and sell the parts and turn that £100 into £500 in short order. But a rusty high mileage 316 four-door with no extras is worth the value of the battery, the petrol in the tank and not an awful lot more.

It takes real skill to let a car rust like this - but a new wing is cheap.

BODY

E30s were better at rust resistance than most of the opposition, but anything made of steel will eventually corrode. Later plastic bumper models are just as prone as the older cars, and they can rust in a few extra places too. The trick with old cars (not just E30s) is to avoid anything which is terminally rotten and many outwardly decent looking E30s can easily consume ten expensive hours of a welder's labour. However, as this book gets older, so will the E30, and of course one day a scruffy E30 will stop being a worthless old nail and become a restoration project.

Starting at the front, E30 bonnets never seem to rust. Stone chips that can fester are common on banger examples but serious rusting through is something I have not yet seen. Front bumpers are seemingly always scraped on the corners on plastic bumper cars, and the chrome bumpers on earlier cars do not seem to rust like those on the E28 5 Series although the rear ones always seem to have a bend in the middle and the chrome does wear off on the corners. The front valance under the bumper lasts well on the older cars, but on any E30 the corners of the valance by the wheels rusts – the plastic bumper cars seem more prone to this.

Front wings can get edgy around the wheel arches down in the mud flap area, and really grim cars will be rotting in the arches themselves. Later cars rot in the area between the mud flap and the door, and paintwork pimples in that area are common. New wings are still available from BMW, but unless the car is a cheap banger, avoid the pattern wings as they just do not look right or fit properly. BMW wings are not that expensive anyway.

Because plastic arch liners were fitted under the front wheel arches, the inner wing structure tends not to rot but avoid any car that's had them removed – normally because it has been excessively lowered and the tyres touch the arches. One bad winter with no arch liners and it can get a bit ropey in there.

Under the bonnet, look for rust around the battery tray and fuse box. This area is double skinned, and having rebuilt a rusted Alpina C1 2.3 (due to no arch liners!), I can tell you that rot there is a problem. The bulkhead area behind the battery has a rubberised sound-deadening pad and it is great for harbouring moisture. It's probably too much to ask to remove it but as soon as you own the car, remove the battery and the sound deadener (this is held on with a couple of twist clips) and give the area a good going over with a wire brush and anti rust treatment. If it has gone through, cutting the rot out and welding a new piece of metal in is not a nightmare but you want to know just how far that rot goes.

Check strut top, inner wing for cracks - especially the M3

On the M3, check for rust around the screen rubber.
Late E30's rot between the wing and plastic vent grille
An example of bad cosmetic rust - another door is the
only permanent answer

The scuttle can be a problem area. On the M3, the screen is bonded in and many cars suffered here. The older chrome bumper cars were normally quite good, but for some unfathomable reason the later plastic bumper cars rot out in the corners, just above where the wings fit. A good body shop can pop the screen out and weld a new section into the scuttle, but on the M3 it nearly always means a new scuttle from BMW. On the M3 though, a

Touring tailgates can rust here ....

in here ....
and here ....

new scuttle is a desirable thing to have because sooner or later, they will all rust there. On new scuttles, which are only available from BMW, the chassis number is stamped in the horizontal part of the guttering, and not in the vertical part like an original car. When ordering a new scuttle from BMW, you have to present the dealer with the logbook (registration document) to prove that you own that car to avoid giving a stolen car another identity.

Doors do not really rust, but when they do it's normally in the top front corner under the door mirror, or in the bottom corners. Either way, a good second-hand door is the best option and cheap with it.

Sills? Being at the bottom of the car, they have been exposed to road salt, grit and stones for at least a decade. Peeling underseal leads to water getting underneath and causing rust, that soon spreads. The front and rear jacking points are the most vulnerable areas and the sill overlap joints just under the door edge is noted for cosmetic rust. More importantly, look at the jacking pad underneath front floor – if that is rotten and about to fall off, it is a carpets out job to repair it.

Whilst you are under there, check the condition of the steel brake pipes. Most E30s are ready for a new front to back pipe by now as they rust where the pipe threads over the rear axle carrier. When the pipe does burst, the car will not fail to stop but it will lose all its fluid quite quickly.

Sunroof panels can also rot in the front corners, but it is not a massive job to fit a good used one. When the roof skin bubbles up around the sunroof, that's a more involved repair and the car would have to be something special to warrant the trouble.

Back wheel arches are a sore point. Nobody ever bothers to clean out the arch lip and over the years wet mud lodges there and festers away. By the time rust is coming through, it's too late and the car will need a new inner and outer arch section to make a lasting repair. We cut the lower back quarter panel off of our guinea pig 325i (a 1986 example) to show just what is hiding behind those bubbling rear arches. Be very suspicious of a car with chrome arches as you just know that they are hiding something nasty. Look inside the arches too – on the fuel filler side a metal cover fits over the fuel filler neck and it can really rot. It is a cheap bolt-on part still available new from BMW though. More importantly, check the area inside the arch that forms the end of the sill, just next to the subframe mounting.

Look underneath at the chassis legs where the coil springs sit – any rot around that area is an MOT fail and it is a sod to get to if you have to weld in new metal.

At the rear, look at the metal around the boot rubber seal, especially around the rear lamps. Older cars can often rust badly here and you need to lift the rubber seal away to check the seal mounting flange. Boot lids do not really rust, but check the inside of the boot lid. E30s suffer from condensation and they can often look a bit grim. More importantly though, you really need to remove the boot carpet mat, and then pull back the side carpet trims. It's a bit tough and can require some brute force, but doing this will reveal the condition of the rear shock absorber mounting turrets. The worst you want is some minor rust stains – you can thoroughly clean the inner arch from outside with the wheel removed, remove lifting underseal and treat any rust. But if it's exploding in rust, just walk away because you just know that when attacked with a screwdriver it will fall to bits. Cars from the Northern climates, like Scotland, can be really prone to this (and all the other rusty bits too).

At the end of the day, it's down to you what you think is acceptable. If you are paying top dollar for a car to keep it needs to be pretty close to perfect. If it is a cheap banger you want it needs to be structurally sound and vaguely capable of passing another MOT without the local mobile welder requiring a banker's reference. If you're buying something for restoration (an M3 or an old Alpina for example), you need to know exactly what you are taking on. Too many E30s have appeared to need 'a couple of back wheel arches and a front wing' yet reveal a lot more rot once you start digging.

In the case of a rusty Alpina that's got rot everywhere you look, the quickest solution would be to go out and find another E30 the same colour with a much better body. But in the case of old chrome bumper examples, that is often a tall order.

ENGINE
There are so many different types of E30 engine, but we'll start at the bottom with the M10. A good tough little motor, it suffers from noisy timing chains, worn camshafts and rockers. Even in an advanced state of wear it will plod on, consuming more and more oil and when the time comes, they are cheap to replace and there are plenty around. An oil change, adjustment of the tappets and a few washers packed in behind the timing chain tensioner spring can work wonders. This is not the best solution of course, and a guide to replacing the timing chain is detailed elsewhere here. The big killer of old engines is infrequent oil changes and on old E30s, it is common so remove the oil filler cap to find black gunge there. This is a result of short journeys and infrequent oil changes. Forget any notions of using a flushing oil because all it will do is dislodge bits of crud which might block an oil way. Just keep the engine oil changed and

Check spare wheel well for rust

All E30s can get damp and rusty in here. Cars built before April 1983 did not have the plastic vent shown here

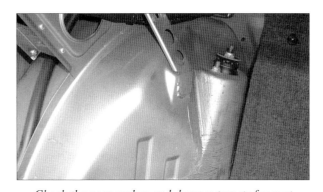

Check the rear arches and damper turrets for rust

A 325i engine bay. On Tourings the battery is in the top corner

leave it at that. As for general engine wear, it is surprisingly rare to find an E30 that burns oil and smokes. Some old engines might puff out a bit of blue oil smoke on start up from cold but that's all it should do. I have had 318i models that have covered over 200,000 miles and use no oil at all so the old quip of 'what do you expect' from the vendor should be ignored when the thing is making smoke signals.

With the engine warmed up to full operating temperature, you should drive the car in third gear up to 4500rpm, back off for about four or five seconds and then accelerate again. If it puffs out a big cloud of blue smoke, look elsewhere. Yes, you could buy the car anyway and remove the cylinder head and replace the valve stem seals, but by the time they are burning oil like that the valve guides will be knackered. On M10 engines the oil light can sometimes take a few seconds to go out in the morning from a cold start. This is normally due to the pressure relief valve in the pump sticking. It can go the other way though. I once had a very early 316 whose engine was a real peach but the oil light would take over ten seconds to go out. When the next owner went to fix the problem, it was found that the pressure relief valve had jammed shut and the resulting high oil pressure had blown the oil seal from the oil pipe where it fits into the block. It was leaking oil badly internally, but the jammed pressure relief valve was producing just enough oil pressure.

Exhaust manifolds are known to crack on the M10 and, like any other old BMW engine, the exhaust manifold studs can unwind and drop out. This causes the relevant gasket to blow, but you need to exercise extreme caution when fitting a new stud. Some owners (myself shamefully included) have wound a new stud in, tightened it a bit too much and stripped the thread in the cylinder head. A disaster.

On both 316 and 318i cars, they should start readily from cold, although cars that have been fitted with the Weber

replacement carburettors can be a bit reluctant and need a good battery to spin them over – the Weber replacement carburettors were never of the same high quality as the regular Webers fitted to production Fords for example and they seem prone to blocking jets. Like any other BMW engine, a good strong antifreeze mix for the coolant is essential to avoid cylinder head corrosion. Given proper maintenance, the M10 will just go on forever as I have proved to myself a few times. Oil leaks include a front crankshaft oil seal (easy), the rocker cover gasket and the oil pressure switch at the back of the engine by the distributor. This last one can dump a surprising amount of oil because it is screwed into the main oil pressure gallery.

Now for the M20 engines. This range of engines covered the 320i, 323i, 325e and 325i and BMW made millions of them. Just about everything that has been said about the M10 holds true for this engine – regular oil and coolant changes, plus this time there is a cam-belt to think about too. 25,000 miles is a very safe change period but make 35,000 the absolute danger point and 30,000 a good average. If the belt breaks on an M20, it will not just bend a few valves but it will smash the valve up against the rocker and break the rocker shafts out of the head – the cylinder head is then good for nothing but scrap. The bottom end of the M20 is good for 200,000 miles and even engines at that mileage that have not been too well cared for will still show signs of the original cylinder honing marks. The big problem with the M20, like the M60 before it (E21 320 and 323i) is the dreaded cracked cylinder head. Therefore, if the car you are looking at has any trace of oil in the water or water in the oil, ignore the hopeful owner's assurance that it just needs a new head gasket. Some heads were cast with a water jacket that wasn't quite thick enough, a condition that was impossible for any manufacturer to check.

An excellent shot of an old 325i head sawn in two shows the thickness on the cylinder head and where it cracks. Proper welding needs to fully penetrate this part of the head.

The M20 head cracks here

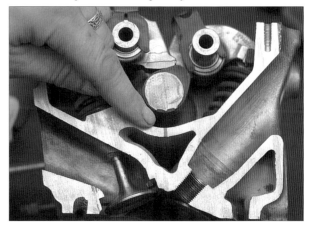

Some heads crack, others do not, and it is just a lottery. Late 1991 cars are just as likely to suffer as older ones, 325is are as likely as any – in fact, the 325i head is more prone if anything. Bad signs include a brown mayonnaise sludge on the inside of the oil filler cap and on bad ones, put your finger inside and see what is on the inside of the camshaft cover. If it's more horrid brown sludge, that engine has got problems. By the time oil is getting into the water, it means that the gunge is already inside the radiator and the heater matrix. When repair time comes, you will have to replace all the heater hoses as the oil contamination will have ruined them. They will look fine until the engine get just a fraction over normal running temperature in a traffic jam and one explodes.

Six-cylinder exhaust manifolds are not especially prone to cracking but if they do, it is as big a problem to replace as the other BMW manifolds because the engine is tilted over – not much fun at all.

Unlike the M10 which can leak oil without any detriment, apart from your drive, oil leaks on the M20 need sorting. The common ones are again the oil pressure switch, the sump gasket can weep and so can the camshaft cover gasket. The really painful ones are the oil seals for the camshaft, auxiliary shaft and the front crankshaft oil seal. They might not leak a lot of oil, but what they do leak tends to get onto the camshaft belt, which is really bad news. The oil seals themselves are not expensive from BMW but replacing them is very labour intensive.

Should the M20 engine you are looking out sound a bit tappety, always assume that there is a worn camshaft lobe. A rhythmic 'tap tap tap' sound indicates a worn camshaft lobe and it's not something you can adjust away. The 325e engine is particularly prone to this because of its extremely pointy lobe shape. It is often caused by poor maintenance leading to a blocked oil hole in the camshaft oil spray bar and with the hole unblocked, the camshaft will plod on until it gets remarkably noisy. Eventually though it will just break a rocker.

M40 engines? Basically, unless you buy a cheap banger, do not buy an M40 engined car with noisy tappets. Using oil like Castrol Magnatec can do a lot to quieten down an M40 that is a bit marginal but really harsh ones are just to be avoided. Camshaft belts should be replaced no longer than every 25,000 miles, 20,000 miles if the belt wasn't tensioned with the proper BMW tensioner. Obviously you need to find out when the camshaft belt was last replaced and most owners of less than prime examples will deny all knowledge of it. If that's the case, make a belt change your number one priority. All old E30s will need a set of new under-bonnet fuel hoses but the M40 seems quite prone to smelly, leaking fuel hoses where they run under the inlet manifold as well as leaky injectors.

Going back to the M40 tappet situation, bear in mind that these engines use hydraulic tappets. Most of them will have a little rattle as the engine fires up from cold but it should only last a second or two before running quietly. You might hear a couple of tappets having an intermittent rattle as the engine warms up. These tappets are on the way out and you should get a new set fitted – expensive if you have to get someone else to do it. Also, forget about any additives as they often just make it worse, as they did on the only M40 engine car I ever owned. Just use a 10/40-grade oil and be done with it. Oil leaks from the crank front oil seal are quite well known so only ever buy a dry one.

The M42 engine on the 318iS was rather more robust than the M40 that spawned it and although it used a standard M40 1800 block, it used a forged steel crank, lighter con rods and forged pistons. For a start the top end lubrication is a lot better and secondly it has a double row (duplex) chain to drive the camshafts and not a rubber toothed belt. The only real problem these engines suffered from was with what is known as the profile gasket. This sits at the front of the engine between the cylinder block and the head and seals off the water jacket that runs through that area. When it fails you will get water in the oil and this was a well-known problem. Most were repaired under warranty and as it was done since around 1994, all the better because it will use the later E36 type gasket. Once the engine has been repaired with this later gasket, the chances of the same thing happening again are pretty slim. Heads can crack from an exhaust valve seat access into a waterway - a car that starts on three cylinders is a giveaway.

Hydraulic tappets are a lot better on the M42, but be aware that it's much like M3 engine inasmuch that the top end can sound slightly busy without being obviously noisy. A 'jangly' noise at idle is often a tired timing chain tensioner so a new one will improve things. Bear in mind though that by 140,000/150,000 miles, the M42 likes to have a new timing chain and a rattle at around 3-4000rpm is a sure sign of a tired one. We will show later on how to replace a chain but the parts are expensive and a low mileage engine from an E36 Coupé or a Z3 is often more cost effective. The spark plugs on the 318iS have their own coil, so misfires are often down to a failing coil unit. A good 318iS though is a joy and is to be recommended far above a plain 318i.

Now for the good old S14 engine as fitted to the 320iS and the M3. Based on a modified M10 block (they are not interchangeable by the way), the S14 is a proper competition engine that happened to find its way into a road going production car. Despite its racing pedigree, a good one will rack up 150,000 miles plus and I have seen them with 200,000 miles on the clock and still going, albeit a bit weary. Timing chains tend to be a bit noisy at idle, but the noise should disappear when revved to 1500rpm and above. Not that you should put up with a noisy chain at all though, because an hour spent fitting an E36 chain tensioner will eliminate the noise. Tappets on the S14 are not hydraulic, but shimmed buckets, and the top end can sound busy, again without being obviously noisy. Because it is an M10 derived engine, the comments about oil leaks apply. Camshaft covers rarely leak oil but front crank oil seals can, but it is a simple job to replace one. Water pumps seem to last forever and most cars will still be on the original one. They look similar to an M10 pump but they are not the same. Replacement is easy and a new pump from BMW is surprisingly inexpensive. As for oil, the S14 doesn't like super thin synthetics. Use synthetic 10w 40 as a minimum, but 5w/30 is just too thin. Castrol Magnatec is a superb choice and will withstand almost anything. If you want to do track days and regularly use 7500rpm, you might feel happier using a synthetic – it's up to you.

Particular S14 problems centre on inlet manifold air leaks, especially around the rubber mounting blocks. With the engine running, spray carburettor cleaner around the blocks; any change in engine note indicates an air leak. A high idle speed that will not come down is due to a blown resistor in the ECU caused by using a big power pack to jump-start a dead car.

GEARBOX

On the manual transmission E30, gearbox failures are very rare, if not virtually unheard of. ZF made a small handful of gearboxes for these cars but Getrag built the vast majority and they really know how to assemble a gearbox. Signs of failure are noise in all gears except fourth (lay-shaft bearings) and crunching into gears. Even so, these units will go on and on in a poor state and failure is normally due to neglect, leading to a substantial drop in the oil level. Used gearboxes are also very cheap – right now you can buy a second-hand one for around £50 for most models, although specialist breakers will charge more. The rare and expensive gearboxes are the 'dogleg' units used in some 323i and to be honest they are not that clever anyway. Most are 20 years and 150,000 miles old do not forget. The M3 gearbox is a big Getrag 265 unit and, US models apart, they are all the 'dogleg' gear-change pattern where first gear is across to the left and back. This unit was shared with the E28 M535 when equipped with this unit and the pre-1982 635CSi unit will also fit. Most of these gearboxes have had a hard life though and noisy lay-shaft bearings (also denoted by a rattle at idle that goes when the clutch pedal

is depressed) are becoming a known problem. In these cases, it's best to get your own gearbox rebuilt by a specialist rather than try an unknown quantity. But few gearbox specialists have the correct tool for pulling off fifth gear. Most gearboxes have their fifth gears located on the shaft by a woodruff key or by splines. These gearboxes have the fifth gear pressed on and use the most incredible interference fit to transmit drive; 35 tons of pressure is needed to shift them. Should you find an old E28 5 Series (1981 to 1988) in a scrap yard with a 'dogleg' gearbox, removed it because it is the same as the M3. The Getrag 265 were an option on the 528i and 535i/M535i but because it is from a ratty old 5 Series, most non-BMW breakers will not know what it is. I have paid £50 for them and they are worth seven or eight times that much.

Sloppy gearlevers are a common problem and most older, higher mileage cars will need a gear linkage rebuild. This is dirty, frustrating work even if the parts needed do not cost that much. So if the gearlever feels like a spoon in a bowl of porridge, to fix it is a £150 job at a specialist.

Now for the automatics. Very early E30s used the three-speed ZF 3HP 22 automatic gearbox robbed from the last E21 318i and the E28 520i and they are not so bad as old automatics go. Under-geared at higher speeds, they are nothing special at all and to be honest, you are not likely to see one now. Towards the end of 1983 BMW started fitting the ZF 4HP22 four-speed automatic gearbox which was rather better. For a start it had a proper top gear, which allowed much easier cruising; at over 53mph the torque converter would lock up to create a solid drive. So when the car is up to working temperature, cruise along in top gear on the flat at 50mph and wait for what feels like an extra gear change at between 50 and 56mph. In effect, it is like a fifth gear. If it does not change it is not the end of the world as long as the other gears engage (count the gearshifts!) but it is a bargaining tool.

The big no-no on these units is long periods of idling in park or neutral. When they get old the ZF auto boxes develop a cross leak of pressurised oil from the oil pump which partially engages the forward clutch. Revving the engine in P or N will quickly destroy the gearbox so remember the rule of thumb with these – as soon as the engine starts, put it into D or R. At traffic lights or even in traffic jams, no matter how bad, leave it in drive because although it seems wrong, it is much healthier for the gearbox.

Problems with auto boxes are myriad although the smaller units fitted to the E30 are really tough – 200,000 miles is normal. Problems include lack of drive in either forward or reverse until revved (valve block), failure to change from first to second for about a half a mile (sticking governor), pulling away in second gear (also sticking governor) and failure of reverse gear after a long run which comes back after cooling down (valve block). What feels like a slipping clutch when on the move (i.e. the revs take a while to drop back in fourth gear) is the torque converter about to fail. A gearbox that hangs on to first gear and will not engage top is often a kick-down cable that is too tight. If the gears engage correctly when the cable is removed from the throttle lever (just a few seconds work) that is the problem.

Now we get onto the EH automatic transmission, the EH standing for Electro-Hydraulic. It is an automatic gearbox with its own ECU in the boot that talks to the engine ECU and also takes a signal from the throttle position switch on the throttle housing. These are ninety-nine times out of a hundred really reliable. But when they do play up and the 'trans programme' light comes up, expect the worst. The ECU is in the boot on the opposite side to the fuel filler and because the typical E30 boot can get a bit damp, they can fail. Also, the electric solenoids inside the gearbox (you can see and replace them with the bottom pans removed) can play up but this is not something for DIY. Instead, it is a job for a proper automatic transmission specialist with the correct diagnostic equipment with which he can interrogate the ECU and locate the fault. Given 30,000-mile oil and strainer changes, these gearboxes just go on forever and do not seem to suffer the problems that early 7 Series four-speed auto boxes did.

DRIVELINE
All E30s, apart from a batch of 325e automatics use a two-piece prop-shaft with a rear and centre universal joint plus a rubber coupling at the front between the gearbox and the prop-shaft – this can also be called Guibo or Donut. Some 325e autos used a universal joint at the front instead of the rubber coupling as did some automatic 525e models. Problem areas are the rubber coupling which can emit a knocking vibration when pulling away and a failed centre bearing causes vibration on the move. In both cases the bits themselves are cheap enough but it is labour intensive – exhaust off, heat shields off and about two or three hours labour to replace both. Even if you only need a front coupling, you may as well replace the centre bearing whilst it is in bits although some mechanics can replace a failed front coupling without even disconnecting the centre prop-shaft bearing or taking the prop-shaft off.

Differentials are very tough, but the small type as found on all cars except the late 323i, 325i. 325e and M3 (inc. 320iS) doesn't wear quite as well as the big type. Clonking when throttling on and off, plus a 'zizzing' noise at speed are all signs of a dodgy differential. Even so, like the gearboxes, the noisy E30 differentials will go on and on forever as long as it has oil. Stuffing the area under the rear seat base with household loft insulation and adding carpet under the boot mat cuts out a lot of the noise coming into the car should it really annoy you. Even so, a good used one is cheap enough, unless it is an limited-slip differential in which case it is not.

An audible hum that gets pretty loud the faster the car goes might well be a wheel bearing. If the noise goes away, or gets much louder, when going round a corner suspect a failing front wheel bearing. Such is the longevity of these cars that most are still on their original wheel bearings. A noisy rear wheel bearing is harder to spot but

This is the official BMW Dealer sticker

Prüfen	Austausch
Check	Replacement
Contrôle	Echange
Contrôle	Sustituciôn
Controllo	Sostituzione

km: 98674
Dat.: 7 10 02
km:
Dat.:

11 31 1 739 073

A full toolkit - no plug spanners on the diesel and the M3 plug spanner is slimmer and extends

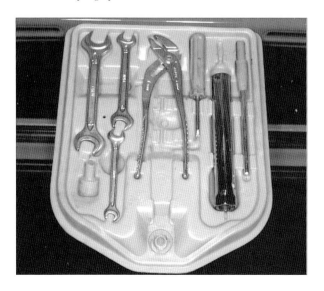

Check front chassis rails for kinks and repairs

A tired but original M3 ideal for restoration

M3s still race at the 24 hours race at the Nurburgring

it will cost about the same to replace as a second-hand differential so budget accordingly.

SUSPENSION

Most E30s have done over 100,000 miles now and most need suspension attention. Front dampers on cars without M Technic suspension (Bilstein) are going to be pretty tired by now. A feeling of the car rear wheel steering and uneasy on the back end is a sign of knackered rear axle beam bushes and a clunk on acceleration and deceleration confirms this. Budget around £150 for this job and it is not a DIY proposition. A rattle over bumps from the rear shelf area is a failed rear damper mounting or two but they are cheap and simple to replace.

A wandering feel from the front could be worn out dampers, a dodgy ball joint (listen for rattle over bumps) or it could be collapsed rear mounting bushes for the front wishbones. Replacing both wishbones with the bushes is DIY, but budget £100 for the parts. It is often difficult to check for ailments with the vendor hovering over you, but check the condition of the front strut bodies. It's not uncommon for them to rot out where the springs seat and some shocking bodges have been seen.

GENERAL

It's a bit much asking for a fully stamped service book on cars as old as this, but a car that still has the original handbooks in the white plastic BMW wallet gives me a good feeling. Chrome bumper cars (those up to about 1988) had a maroon coloured handbook with the car details on the first page and the service history at the back. Later cars used a thinner silver handbook and a separate silver service book which is much more likely to go missing in action. The original white BMW torch in the glove box and a full toolkit in the boot is another good sign.

E30s are not colour sensitive, but some colours are bad for resale. Black, reds, Royal Blue and the various metallic silvers and greys are good, as are Malachite Green and Boston Green on Tourings. White is a bit neutral but the metallic browns and beiges, plus non-metallic dark blues, weren't known as 'Doom Blue' at BMW dealerships without good reason.

As a rule, the higher the specification, the more it is worth and the easier it is to resell. SE models of the later 320i and 325i are good news. The colour-coded bumpers look better, the trim is better and bits like the three-spoke leather steering wheel and the computer are just nice to have. A case in point is a 1986 Alpine White 316 four-door. Fitted with aftermarket BBS copy wheels, it really was immaculate but had no factory extras at all. Impossible to sell at any price it eventually donated its engine to a BMW 1800 saloon and that was the end of that.

CONVERTIBLES

One thing you may well have noticed is that the E30 was never as rust resistant as the 5 Series. The probable reason is that they were built in different factories – Dingolfing for the true mass production E30 and Regensburg for the 5 Series. Look very hard and you still might not find a 1989 E34 5 Series which is rusty but you will find plenty of 1989 E30 saloons which are blessed with scabby back wheel-arches and other rusty bits.

You'd never get BMW to admit this, but the Regensburg built cars like the 5 and 7 Series were better made than the E30s. Where exactly is this heading? Well, the E30 Convertibles were all built at Regensburg because they just got in the way at the regular E30 production facility. As a result they seem to last a lot better than the saloons but many have been butchered with nasty wheels, lowering springs and the kind of neglect that E30s suffer. As a result, there are not many really nice ones left but a tatty cheap one will make a worthwhile restoration project because values are on the up for nice examples.

The Motorsport Convertible is a rare and desirable thing identified mainly by Macau Blue paint and the bubble leather – this is leather whose surface is made of lots of tiny bubbles and yes, it is almost impossible to replicate or restore once it is damaged or worn out. These cars also had the dreaded electric hood.

BUYING M3s

It depends on what you want from an M3. As the cars get older, they attain classic status but there are still more than enough suspect examples. Some real tat was dragged in from Germany in the nineties when prices for decent British supplied cars were still high. As a rule, cars that have been in Britain from new command a premium when they have a proper, verifiable service history.

Most M3s have had an accident, be it a big one or a minor knock, because that is just the kind of car they are. It really depends on how well they have been repaired.

For doing track days, the slightly daft thing to do is to go out and buy the most expensive Sport Evo you can find, strap on all kind of bits and take it out for a few track days. Firstly you will not enjoy it any more than a well-worn 2.3 and secondly you run the very real risk of destroying what is now a rare car. And would you buy a Sport Evo with a history of track days? Maybe you would, but not for top money.

For this sort of thing, take your pick from the hundreds of cheap 2.3 cars that are about, bolt your roll cage and racing seat in and off you go – and should you go 'off', it is not the end of the world.

If you want an M3 to keep as a nice, semi-collectible road car then only a bog standard car with known history and provenance will do. Do not fret about the mileage either; a car with 120,000 miles but a couple of caring owners and a wad of bills and history is better than something with 80,000 miles but no history other than a forged service book. As soon as an M3 sports aftermarket wheels, big exhausts and the usual 'optical tuning' its value plummets.

But which is the best one to buy? This is one of those questions that is hard to answer. Sport Evos do command a premium over the 2.3 cars that is not always justified. They should be worth thirty per cent more than a mint 2.3 but not twice as much because they are certainly not twice as good. As for the Evo models, well, do not pay daft money for an Evo I because they were little better than the standard 200bhp car. The Evo II was more like it and many reckon a really prime example has the measure of a Sport Evo without the restrictive colour choice. Limited edition cars are worth more than a standard 2.3 but not vastly more. My choice would be a late 1990 2.3 with the 215bhp engine in properly maintained condition with extras like electric windows and sunroof. Leather trim is nice to have but leave it at that. Air conditioning rarely works on a car this old and the electronic adjustable damper set up (EDC) was money better spent on a good holiday when the cars were new. It is a waste of time but if it works properly then it is not a problem – just be aware of the cost of new bits when it goes wrong.

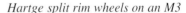

Hartge split rim wheels on an M3

CHASSIS AND OTHER ID NUMBERS

All E30s have both a VIN (Vehicle Identification Number) and numbers on the engine and gearbox. The VIN (often called a chassis number) is on an alloy stamped plate on the front panel above the headlight plastic cover. The VIN is also stamped in the body and can be found by the rubber seal on which the bonnet sits on the scuttle panel below the screen. If this number is wrong (i.e. does not match the number on the VIN plate or logbook) or is not there at all, you need to know why.

Preferably, just walk away because there is something not right about it. Only BMW supply replacement scuttle panels and they all have the chassis or VIN number stamped in when ordered from the dealer.

Engine numbers: these are stamped into the block. On the four-cylinder units the number is on a flat surface by the starter motor mounting top bolt, on the sixes it is underneath the alternator.

Chapter 3

KEEPING YOUR E30 ALIVE!

Weekend fettling makes an old 3 feel much newer, adding years to its life. So a couple of days a year spent inside and underneath an E30 will pay you back when the time comes to sell.

BODY:

The E30 is not really a rust bucket but the newest car is now 10 years old and the oldest is now 22 – by the time rust erupts it is all too late, so stop it now before it eats into the structure of the car. I have used Waxoyl in the past and it's good stuff but only on rust which is developing. Having said that, it will hold back quite bad corrosion but not forever. Job one is to jack the car up, remove the front wheels and then the under wing splash shields. E30 wings rust all around the edge of the wheelarch due to wet mud getting trapped behind the shield edge and also – particularly on later plastic bumper cars – the back of the wing where it meets the sill. Mud flaps make the problem worse and with the shields removed (about 10 minutes) it is only another ten small 9mm bolts to unbolt the whole wing. Even if you do not particularly want to go this far, clean out the arch edge with a wire brush as well as the rear lower corner and rustproof it thoroughly. Plastic bumper cars also rot on the rear edges of the front valance so do the same here. Whilst the arch liners are out, clean up the front jacking points as these are a common casualty.

The sills can rot badly and it is worth attacking the underseal with a sharp screwdriver to check. Remove any that is flaking, clean any rusty metal with a wire brush, prime and paint with black Hammerite. Also, clear out the sill drain holes and spray rust-proofing fluid into them.

Rear arch edges are now a common casualty but if they are not rotting, give them a really good clean out with a wire brush and paint (or spray) anti-rust fluid around. You can even paint grease there as it does not wash away easily. From inside the boot, remove the side carpet trims and spray plenty of anti-rust wax around the arches. Bonnets do not rot, but the scuttle area at the bottom screen corners certainly does. Later plastic bumper cars seem a lot more prone to this for some reason. The answer is to remove the plastic grilles and spray Waxoyl or similar up behind that area. To do this you will need to hire a compressor for a day and buy a proper air fed rustproofing gun with angled and flexible ends – they cost about £60 from someone like Brown Brothers or Machine Mart and you might as well rustproof the whole car. With 40psi, the stuff gets into all the nooks and crannies but with 90psi it turns into a mist that clings to everything and is therefore more effective. Heating the can of wax up in a bucket of boiling water helps enormously too.

Sunroofs need oiling and exercising and you will be surprised how sad and rusty the window mechanisms get inside the doors. Remove the door trims, carefully peel back the plastic door cover and spray the mechanisms with penetrating fluid. Work the windows up and down a few times and those sluggish electric windows can suddenly get a lot livelier. Lightly grease everything, including the felt window runners. Also spray the door lock mechanisms with penetrating fluid followed by spray grease.

Damp boot? Remove the entire contents – trim, spare wheel, everything. Remove the rear lights and either grease the seals or fit new ones; grease the new ones anyway as it is a superb water seal and better than silicon which eventually dries out. Rub grease into the boot seal to bring it back to life and adjust the boot striker plate to

Even the 6-cylinder engine is easy to service

tighten the boot lid down. Doing this will make the boot marginally harder to shut but the seal will soon adjust itself. Mind you, a new boot seal is not expensive.

Finally, go around all the panel edges, removing any small rust spots and treating them. Remove the battery (in the boot on the 325i) and clean the tray area, spraying Waxoyl or similar as you go. Rustproof the underside of this area too as it is a favourite rot spot and remove the sound deadening panel behind the battery (not 325i) and treat the metal work behind there too.

USING THE BMW JACK

The BMW (Bilstein Heber) jack as fitted in the boot is a masterful piece of work. You will find that once you have fitted it into the floor bracket and lifted the car, it does the job well enough. But when lowering the car, it mysteriously gets very close to the bodywork and threatens to dig into the paint, Next time you go to a breaker's yard look at all the small dents in doors and rear panels above the jacking points. The answer is a) do not use the BMW jack unless you absolutely have to and b) if you do, make sure the top of the jack is at least five inches away from the body to avoid problems. If it does get close, use a big hammer to belt the bottom of the jack inwards or place an old magazine or something between jack and body.

ENGINE

On all cars, draining the coolant and refilling with new antifreeze every year prevents corrosion and holds back what is already there. On the M10 engines there is no drain plug on the block so just remove the bottom radiator hose and let the coolant escape. If the coolant is rusty, flush it through with a hose; remove the heater hose on the back of the head and flush through there but you will need the ignition on and the heater set to hot. Most cars have a radiator drain plug and it is a good idea to remove it to flush any sediment from the base of the radiator. When refilling, add the antifreeze first but do it slowly,

pint by pint, allowing a couple of minutes between each pint. On the M10 cars add five pints of neat anti freeze followed by enough water to make up the 12-pint (7-litre) capacity with a 40/60 percent mix anti freeze to water. Using a pint milk bottle makes filling the system accurate and with less spillage that straight from a 5-litre container. On M40 engines do exactly the same but be aware that you should not overfill the system. The header (expansion) tank is built into the side of the radiator and even with the full 7-litre/12-pint capacity it should not exceed the full mark. It gives the false impression that the radiator is only half full.

As for the M20 engines on the 320i, 323i and 325i, it is similar but there is a bleed screw on top of the thermostat housing and a drain plug on the exhaust side of the block. Use a close fitting 8mm socket to undo it and poke the hole through with a paper clip if blocked. You will need 10.5 litres (19 pints) of coolant and 40 percent anti freeze which is about 4 litres or 7.5 pints. Do not just chuck it into the header tank though – you will get an air lock. Remove the top hose from the engine, slacken and refit the hose on the radiator so it is upright and pour the anti freeze in through there to fill the radiator, pint by pint, nice and slowly. Now remove the hose and refit it to the thermostat housing only and pour the water in though there – this will fill the block and cylinder head. When all the coolant is in, refit the hose, turn the heater to hot and start the engine. Open the bleed screw and get rid of all the air. As soon as the heater starts to pump out warm air, the system is bled. One last thing – on any E30 a set of new radiator hoses is an excellent idea, including the one on the back of the head to the heater.

As for oil changes, I have used Castrol GTX or Magnatec and you do not need anything else. BMW filters from the dealer are only about three or four pounds so there's no excuse for using a cheap and nasty pattern filter.

Tappets: set the M10 engines to 0.20mm (0.008 thou/inch) stone cold and the M20 sixes to 0.25mm or 0.010 thou/inch also cold, setting them to 9 thou will quieten them down. Adjust them with a 10mm spanner and four inches of metal coat-hanger wire but use the feeler gauge between the eccentric and the valve, not between the rocker and the cam. Are the spray bar oil hoses clear? Check by removing the coil lead and cranking the engine – every pair of camshaft lobes should have an oil supply. On the M10 all you can do is clear the holes with a paper clip because the spray bar is held down with the head bolts, but the M20 and M40 oil spray bars can be easily replaced with new ones. As I just said, on the M10 the head bolts hold it down, although these can be removed with a bit of applied bodging. The M40 has hydraulic tappets, which do not need adjustment, so if you have a top end rattle, bad luck.

Camshaft belts – only the M20 and M40 have them. Replacing the one on the M20 is a DIY job, but only if you are a very competent mechanic. The M40 is tricky without about £80 worth of special tools. There are no timing marks on the cam or cam sprocket, requiring a tool to hold the camshaft still, and to tension the belt requires another tool and the tension has to be one hundred per cent perfect and not set by eye. M10 chains rattle eventually and Euro Car Parts do a split link chain that is quite simple to fit, but the top camshaft wheel is also normally knackered. Split link chains require a chain link riveter that you can get from a bicycle shop.

CHANGING THE OIL

Quite a simple job really, but a couple of pointers. Firstly, the oil needs to be good and hot to drain properly. The ideal time to do this is after a good long run, twenty miles or more, when the oil is fully up to temperature. Use an old washing up bowl to catch the oil and spread plenty of old newspaper around it because the oil has a habit of getting where it shouldn't. It will also be hot enough to scald so you should wear some rubber gloves. The other thing is to always use a BMW oil filter. BMW reduced the prices of these consumables to the point where a genuine BMW filter is actually cheaper than most aftermarket ones. They can sometimes come with a new sump plug sealing washer but if it does not, buy one because they are only a few pence.

Six-cylinder cars with the alloy sump (and some of the others too) had a hollow sump plug – why I do not know. They were seemingly designed to break off in the sump when over tightened and for what they cost, a new one is not a bad idea at all, even if yours hasn't broken. It only takes a couple of over tightening episodes plus a brush with a road hump (look for a ground down flat bit on the plug) to cause a fracture. You might find that when you undo the sump plug, you leave half of it behind – do not panic. Wait until the oil has drained out, and then jack the front of the car up at an angle to stop what is left coming out when you remove the rest of the plug. Very often lightly hammering an old screwdriver into the hollow and turning anti clockwise will remove what is left. Also, hammering a spline drive or torx socket into the hollow will normally get them out, as can a suitable allen key. They are never that tight in the sump. In the past, I have had to resort to using an electric drill set on anti clockwise but this is tough on the wrists when the drill bit bites! Failing that, you will have to use an EasiOut but it rarely come to that.

On most cars the oil filter is very easy to get to, but the 325i can be a real cow. It is because the filter screws onto the oil cooler adaptor and it sits right under the exhaust manifold and you have to wait for the manifold to com-

Adjusting the tappets for valve clearances is important. Do it every 12,000 miles

pletely cool to get in there. The chain or strap filter wrenches are best, although the old trick of sticking a screwdriver through the middle works well enough. Cars with M10 and M20 engines used the screw-on disposable oil filter, but the M40 and M42 engines use a paper element in an integral alloy housing – not unlike ancient BMC cars like the Mini and 1100. You undo a single, 13mm bolt on top, lift off the cover, withdraw the filter element, clean up the bowl, fit the new one and put the lid back on. Remember to fill the housing with clean engine oil right to the top before fitting the lid and always fit a new rubber sealing ring – BMW filters always come with a new one in the packet.

CHANGING SPARK PLUGS

Again, pretty simple work but if they have been in there a while go carefully. If they are tight unwind them a turn or two, spray WD40 onto the thread – plenty of it – and wind the plug back in again. Work it backwards and forwards until it begins to ease up. If it's still tight, continue to unwind them but a quarter of a turn at a time, winding them back a quarter and them out again. It takes time to do this, but it's easier than removing the cylinder head to have the broken plug removed.

Where the plug leads run most cars have a plastic tube to keep things looking tidy. This is a great idea, but the plug leads will sweat inside there. I can remember a 728i with a seemingly incurable misfire caused by damp inside this tube. With the tube cracked open (it is a two-piece thing), we could clean the plug leads with thinners, clean out the tube, dry it all off and reassemble it – misfire gone. The plastic distributor cap covers on M10 and older M20 cars can do just the same thing.

TRANSMISSION

Nobody ever bothers to change the gearbox oil. Be different and drain both the gearbox and the differential oil. Refill with SAE 80 oil in the gearbox and SAE 90 in the differential until it runs out of the filler aperture. Did your car have a notchy gear-change when cold? Then refill with a synthetic gear oil. On automatics, remove and wash out the bottom pan after draining the oil, fit a new filter screen and O ring and refill with about three litres. To check the level, run the car in neutral or park and check that the level is in between the two blips on the dipstick. Do not run the engine for more than a couple of minutes in park or neutral – if you have to, jack the rear up and run in neutral with the handbrake off.

Differential oil rarely gets changed and by the time it has done 80,000 miles it really stinks. Changing it is cheap and easy but you MUST use the correct limited slip differential oil. If you do not the differential could be an unlimited slip type in less than 1000 miles. You have been warned!

Finally, replace the clutch fluid. It is easy: run a pipe from the bleed nipple into a jar filled with some old brake fluid, undo the bleed nipple and pump the old fluid out, filling with new as you go. It can make a heavy clutch a lot lighter.

SUSPENSION
It only needs a couple of suspension bushes to wear for an E30 to handle like a double bed. Favourite are the front wishbone rear bushes that bolt to the chassis either side of the gearbox. Standard bushes are okay but solid M3 ones press in and are much better. Rear axle bushes are another common problem and you cannot change them yourself. Rattling from the rear end is normally failed rear damper top mountings that are cheap and easy to replace.

UNDERNEATH THE CAR
Look at the metal brake pipes over the differential as they can rust horribly. You will need new ones from BMW ready made (they are not expensive) plus new flexible hoses as they all rust together. Look in the repairs sections for details of why you should pay someone else to do this job for you. Also, clean the fuel tank up and rust-proof it; remove the exhaust heat shield between the two halves and spray the rust-proofing gunk in there too. On the E30, the fuel and brake pipes run on the inside of the passenger side chassis rail and they need wire brushing and either greasing or spraying with anti rust fluid. Unplug the speed sensor from the differential, spray WD40 or similar in both the plug and socket and give the joint some exercise. This avoids problems with the speedometer and econometer. Cars with automatic transmission have steel pipes running to the gearbox oil cooler in the base of the radiator. If they are really rusty replace them, taking care when unscrewing from the radiator, but if they are not bad, rustproof them. You would

be surprised how fast a pinhole in one of these pipes can dump all the automatic gearbox oil and ruin the box.

REPLACING BRAKE PADS
All E30s including the M3 use floating calipers. This means that the calipers slide on steel pins and when they get sticky through lack of lubrication and then corrode, the callipers will stick, causing the pads to overheat along with the disc. This is noticeable from a bad shake or steering pull just after using the brakes. Very often this will also damage the piston seal in the caliper body and at this point, the caliper is scrap. Good clues to sticking callipers are pads that are significantly more worn on one side of the car and also when the wear difference between two pads in one caliper is pretty major. As a rule, the outer pad wears a bit more than the inner one because the caliper piston is acting directly on it but if one pad is little worn and the other is down to the metal, suspect that caliper. Reconditioned calipers are cheap enough anyway.

To change the pads is pretty easy and is detailed in a workshop manual. Just remember to clean everything up with a wire brush, particularly the areas where the brake pads slide. Use copper grease sparingly on the backs of the brake pads to avoid pad squeal and on the areas where the pads will slide.

VALVE CLEARANCES
On the engine, the valve clearances are set by shims and every 25,000 miles they need to be checked and adjusted. This requires the special BMW tool to depress the buckets and remove the existing shims. To do the job you need to remove the camshaft cover, clean all the oil off the cams and buckets with carburettor cleaner and let them dry. Start with the first tappet and have the camshaft lobe pointing upwards. Spray WD40 over the bucket and check the clearance. Write it down. Now do the other fifteen valves, writing them all down as you go. At the end of this, you will have a set of clearances that most probably will not be what the factory specifies. Now you have to put it right. Let us say that one valve clearance is 3 thou too tight. Take note of the number on the back of the shim, this is the thickness. You then need a shim 3 thou thinner. This job involves taking all the shims out, marking them so that you know exactly which valve they came from, doing the maths, ordering the new ones and refitting them. It is a big job, but if you can do it yourself you will save quite a lot. Before the camshaft cover goes back on, pour half a litre of engine oil over the cams so that they do not run dry on start up.

M3 SPECIFICS
Because the M3 is an E30, most of what's been said applied to these cars. However, there are a few pointers.

Engine oils

M3s do not need a very thin grade synthetic oil – a 10/40 is fine. A good mineral oil like Castrol GTX is also very good. You will find that by using a 5W/30 grade you will be forever adding oil as the car uses it and also the timing chain tensioner will be noisy if you still use the original E30 type.

Gearbox and final drive oil

Synthetic gear oils are always good to use but the Getrag 265 unit in the M3 really likes it. Lay-shaft rattle from a tired gearbox will not get any better but the gear change will. If you use the car for serious track use, synthetic oils will really improve the protection provided and keep the oil temperature down.

As for the diff, all E30s with a limited slip differential need specific LSD oil. Ordinary EP 80 or 90 gear oil will not do. Sure, it will lubricate the running parts but the clutch discs in the LSD unit will not like it much.

Inlet manifold blocks

The inlet manifold sits on rubber blocks on the M3. It is a good system but eventually they crack and will cause air leaks. If you suspect this, spray the rubber blocks with carburettor cleaner with the engine idling. If the engine tries to stall or speed up, you have found an air leak.

Brakes

The E30 M3 used discs that were specific to this car but they are not particularly expensive from BMW. The calipers are from the E28 5 Series (1981 to 1988) and again, reconditioned calipers are cheap – probably the same price as the new disc.

Beating the rust bug

The M logo on the M3 does not protect the M3 against the rust bug. Although they do not rust badly, there are certain places where they do go and these are not always visible. The scuttle panel under the screen is a typical case. M3 screens are bonded in and the bonding process means that any water that gets trapped in there, stays in there. Also, fitting the screen rubber trim often meant a small nick in the paint as it was fitted. Water lodged there means rust. If the car is still good in this area the way to prevent rust is to inject a lubricant like Tectyl or Waxoyl under the screen rubber. Releasing fluids just dry out so they will not do anything.

Front wheel arches do not rust but back arches that have been modified to clear big wheels are bad news. Hammering the arch lips up just cracks paint and under seal and the mud just gets in there and can't get out. Keeping the area clean and rustproofed is the only way

to stop this. And being an M3, repairing a rusty back arch will cost more than a standard E30.

The last bit is the outer plastic sill covers. No, these do not rust but if they have never been off before, now is the time to remove them and give the body underneath a good clean up. You will find some surface rust (or worse) but bite the bullet and do it. Even if you do not find anything nasty, clean and polish the area and spray on a coating of anti rust wax.

COMMON QUESTIONS AND ANSWERS – AND QUICK FIXES

Q: My 3 Series automatic will not start in park but it will in neutral. Sometimes there's a strange buzzing noise from in the glove box when it is in park. What is this?

A: Simple – the two screws holding the upper and lower quadrant assembly have worked loose and the inhibitor switch is not being activated. Remove the centre console and tighten the screws, having repositioned the quadrant upper half. The noise you hear is the inhibitor relay trying to activate.

Q: I can hear exhaust noise coming into the car. The manifold is not blowing anywhere though.

A: Some aftermarket down-pipes are noisy without actually blowing and this is due to the thickness of the steel. Remove the steering wheel centre badge or boss and pack the top of the hollow steering column with blu-tac. Nothing else works and it is an amazing cure.

Q: One of the electric windows has stopped working. What's the most common cause?

A: Nine times out of ten, it is a faulty switch. Substitute the switch from the working window and the window should work again. Take the old switch apart by prising the bottom out and cleaning the contacts inside with fine emery. They normally work again. If the motor is not working, check that there is power getting to it. If not, a fault in the plug connectors in the body is common, especially with the rear doors.

Q: The door lock on my 3 Series only goes straight onto the deadlock position which is straining the old key a bit. What is the cure?

A: Lack of lubrication in the lock is the problem, but you will have to remove the interior door trim, being careful with the top stainless trim, and douse the lock in penetrating fluid before giving it a few minutes of non-stop exercise.

Q: After a long fast drive, the coolant level warning light comes on. Yet when I pull over to check it and release the expansion tank cap the water is under pressure but as soon as the cap is off the water level returns to normal. What is causing this?

A: This could be the beginning of a crack in the head, but it could also be a blockage in the small hose (same diameter as fuel hose) that runs from the top of the radiator into the expansion bottle. With the engine up to temperature, remove the expansion bottle cap and see if water is coming out of this hose and into the tank. If not, or if it is only spitting water back in, that is the problem. Hot water rising to the top of the radiator has not got anywhere to go and the level in the expansion bottle is dropping as a result.

Q: My M40 engined 316i is using a lot of water. I fill the radiator to the top but a day later it has dropped back down to halfway. Why is this happening?

A: Because you're overfilling it! The clear white part on the side of the radiator is the expansion bottle and it does not indicate the coolant level inside the radiator. What the engine does not want it will just spit out so keep the level topped up to the max mark on the radiator.

Q: My 318iS is using water.

A: Could be a number of things. Oil mixing with water in the engine is probably a failed prolite gasket. An external leak at the front of the block is the same. If it starts on three cylinders before catching or running on all four, suspect a cracked head.

Q: The display on the OBC is very dim, is this a bulb?

A: Yes, But it's a swine to replace. Firstly, remove the radio, then look at the side of the OBC - you will see a small white square. Use long nose pliers and pull on the white bit and the bulb pack will slide out - on many cars though you will need to remove the OBC first.

Q: Do I really have to remove the gearbox first to remove the engine?

A: No! The manuals say you do, but they are wrong. On a 320i-325i Auto it's tight but they do come out the top as one unit - you might have to remove the PAS pump though.

Chapter 4

BODY RESTORATION

BODY RESTORATION

The subject of restoring an E30 bodyshell in 2004 is a thorny one. At present there are still more than enough good cars to make a major restoration a bit pointless but as time goes on and numbers drop, this will change. Restoring cars is never about monetary gain anyway, just the achievement of bringing something back from the dead. Some cars are never worth doing though. A terminally rotten car without a decent panel is just not worth the effort, no matter what model. If it is really that rare and desirable, then find a better shell to start with and rebuild it using that. Unlike the CS Coupés and '02 models, the E30 was made in huge numbers and after twenty years there are still plenty around.

Fortunately, the E30 is well catered for when it comes to body panels. BMW still stock just about everything for the E30 and if BMW made the part, it is going to fit properly. Three examples are front wings, bonnet and outer sills. Pattern front wings are normally a waste of time. Sure, if your E30 is just a cheap car that you want to keep on the road for the next couple of MOTs and you plan on being the last owners then go ahead, although I would go to a breaker and buy a good second-hand wing the same colour. Most of the pattern wings will fit after a fashion and line up okay after a bit of minor fettling and the majority are made of half decent thickness metal. However, some are just awful. BMW front wings are made on the original presses from BMW quality steel with BMW quality factory primer. They are a lot more expensive than a pattern wing but they are still inexpensive in absolute terms. They also fit properly and require the minimum of preparation before fitting and painting and will last as long as the original, whereas a pattern wing will not.

Bonnets? I have not seen a pattern E30 bonnet that fits properly. They never have quite the correct shape, do not have the strip of seam sealer where the skin wraps over the frame and never sound the same when closed. I would rather use a second-hand original bonnet than a new pattern item but new ones are still available from BMW.

Outer sills are where the game is won or lost with an E30. They all rust around the jacking points and most sill replacement jobs involve a pattern sill welded on, which looks absolutely terrible, being merely a repair as opposed to restoration. I once saw a black Alpina C1 2.3 four-door that had been absolutely ruined with cheap cover sills welded on. BMW outer sills are again a perfect fit and come with the proper joins plus the original type jacking point brackets. But there is a disadvantage we will come to later. The moral of all this? Even if you are nailing an old MOT failure back together, it is always quicker and easier to use the original BMW parts and do the job right, rather than trying to fit some dreadful bit of bent steel which will always look like a cheap and nasty repair. Above all, remember genuine BMW body parts for the E30 ARE NOT EXPENSIVE.

REMOVING BUMPERS

This is a job that causes a lot of head scratching. On the older metal bumper cars the front one is pretty easy and explains itself. On the rear one though, BMW added a couple of sneaky bits to confuse you. The rubber end caps by the wheel arches are removable by accessing the single 10mm bolt from under the wheel-arch. The rubber mouldings just pull off. The bumper is held on by two bolts and four nuts. The outer two secure the bumper corner pieces to the rear quarter panels from inside the boot by the wheel arch housing with a 10mm bolt each side. The centre bar is held on by four 13mm nuts. The top two are accessible from inside the boot, the other two are directly below it but under the boot floor. This means that you have to grovel underneath the car and undo the two rustiest 13mm nuts on the whole car.

On the plastic bumper cars, things are easier. On both ends, you remove the bumpers by removing the two big Allen or Torx bolts that you will see when you look at the underside of the bumper. The corners are secured by plastic sliding brackets that attach to the wings with 13mm bolts but these always seem to come undone okay. The bumper then sides off the mounting posts.

SILL REPLACEMENT

The only proper way to replace an E30 sill is to remove the front wing. Fortunately, this is a very, very easy job which will only take you about 40 minutes although I have removed wings in breakers yards with just a couple of spanners in under 20 minutes. Thankfully, BMW designed the E30 shell for easy accident repairs. It is necessary to remove the wings so that you can weld the sill on at the front and you need to do this right to seal the sill off effectively. Unlike cheap cover sills, the BMW E30 sill is a replacement that includes the rear inner sill but does not include the rear part of the sill, that is the bottom of the rear wing. The cover sill is just a bit of steel to weld over the top of an existing rusty sill.

This is where the sill to rear panel seam is.

When your BMW sill arrives, you will see exactly where to cut the old one and the best way of getting the old sill off is to use an electric drill with a spot weld cutter. This drills into the spot weld and when you have got them all done – a long and tedious task – you can use a flat blade bolster chisel to cut the sill off. You will need to use an angle grinder to clean up the mating surfaces.

Now, if the outer sill had rusted through, you can absolutely guarantee that the inner sill is suffering as well. BMW outer sills can come with, or without, the

BMW repair parts for body side. No 4 is the outer sill that incorporates part of the rear inner sill

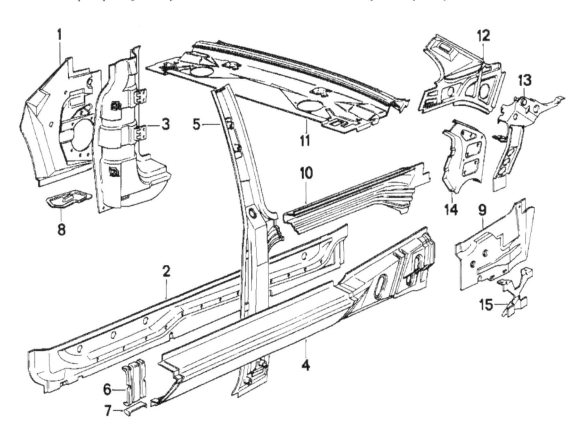

jacking points but BMW still supply the jacking points on their own. With the floor edge where the outer sill joins at the bottom cleaned up, you might well have to cut out rusty bits and weld in new edges although it's very rare to have to replace the whole lot. The inner sill membrane is shown on our guinea pig 325i with the rear wing cut away and this is what comes with the BMW outer sill. So, if you are doing a complete restoration on a car, the BMW sill is for you. You will still have to buy a pattern outer sill from somewhere else to get the rear part which lays on top of the BMW sill at the back to recreate the seam three quarters of the way along. If the rear inner sill is still in good condition, then use only the front part of the BMW sill. The trouble with fitting the complete BMW sill is that even with the bottom sill part of the rear wing cut away, it is very hard to cut the rear inner sill off. Me? Unless it was really awful, I would not remove it. It may just need a new lower lip welding on which is rather easier.

But what if you are not doing a major restoration but you want to replace the outer sill in a decent fashion? Use a pattern sill. Obviously you will need a decent quality one because the cheap sills are just rubbish. Very few, if any, pattern sills come with the seam and few come with the jacking points that you will have to buy from BMW. The big problem is welding the sill to the rear wing on two-door cars. It is not at all easy to get a good neat join so what a lot of owners have done is just to cut out the rotten parts of the sills and weld in new metal. This is probably the best way of doing this. You have to be absolutely ruthless in cutting out the rot but if it's rotten all the way along, then a new sill it is. The way to do this is to cut the old sill out and then cut the new sill and tuck the rear part under the old. When the welds are ground back, you can use plastic filler to make the area smooth before priming, painting and undersealing it.

As for the method of welding – well that is a tricky one. British MOT tests demand that any repair is seam-welded but that is not original. Originally it would be spot welded but very few home restorers have a spot welder. Instead, you can plug weld it. This means drilling holes in the lower lip of the new sill where it meets the floor edge and welding through to create a spot weld. These can then be ground flush with a grinder before being given a smear of plastic filler, rubbed down, primed and painted. It would be a very harsh and unrealistic MOT tester who failed the car.

FLOOR REPAIRS
E30 floor pans do not really rust, but the front corners by the jacking pads do. BMW welded the jacking pads onto the floor before undersealing the entire underneath and that worked okay for a few years. But moisture gets

Rusty inner sill - new ones are available.

everywhere and when it gets underneath the underseal, rust will follow. By the time the jacking pad is rusty, it is ready to fall off taking a few square inches of the front floor corner with it. To repair it properly means lifting the carpets and sound deadening and you will probably find it is a bit damp in there as well. On the passenger side, or driver's side on the M3 and LHD cars, the wiring loom runs along the inner sill that adds another complication. Again, you have got to be ruthless and cut all the rust out. Be vicious with the screwdriver and find all the rusty weak metal that is hiding under that shiny painted

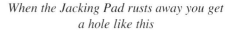

When the Jacking Pad rusts away you get a hole like this

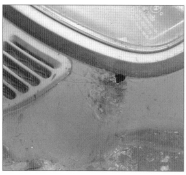

1/ Typical scuttle rust on a plastic bumper car. Removing the screen and new metal is the only answer

2/ Inner wing - most is protected by the arch liner, but there's a hole there!

3/ It's rare, but E30's can rust here

4/ The usual scabby rust caused by neglect - in fact this wing was a cheap replacement

5/ Front jacking pad completely rusted away

6/ This rust stems from the join between the sill and rear wing. It can be tidied up but will always come back

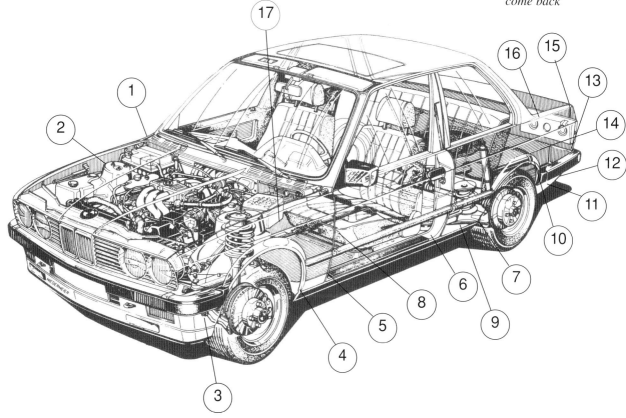

7/ This hole meant water had got into the sills as well. Metal near the rear axle beam mounts was rusty as well

8/ A split door is rare, but not unknown. A good welder could repair this

9/ With the lower rear wing removed. The inner sill is exposed. Even on this rusty car the inner sill is still sound.

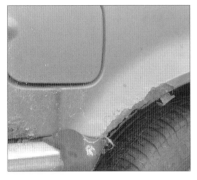

10/ Scabby rear arch is beyond saving

11/ Major rust in the rear quarter panel is only just repairable.

12/ Ropey rear valance: Repairable but this car needed a new rear arch as well

13/ This rust is the result of the bumper being clouted and the paint damage left to fester.

14/ Corrosion in the boot. It started where the fuel filler neck bolted on.

15/ Water logging under the rubber boot seal can cause rust - in bad cases a new rear panel is needed.

16/ Rust around aerial is common but easy to repair

17/ This was a 1986 325i with severe bulkhead rot - a write off

seam sealer. Get in there with a grinder fitted with a cup wire brush and clean it all back to bright metal, both inside the car and underneath. You do not need to fit a new jacking pad, you are probably better off without it as the factory only used it to transport new shells, but a new one is easy to fabricate from mild steel. If you do fit one though, be sure to seam weld it all the way around so that moisture cannot get in and rust it away again in a few years time.

With the carpet pulled up, look at the area of the bulkhead where the glove box hinges bolt on. If in doubt, remove the glove box and hinge completely and if you are really serious, take out the front seats and centre console and remove the carpet from the car. That way you can really get to grips with this job. I did the same to my 1986 325i, a tatty car bought purely to photograph for this book. With the carpets removed, what I found was a completely rotten bulkhead where the rust had spread up to the wiring loom hole where the loom passes through from the engine bay into the car. In fact, the loom was just hanging where all the metal had rusted clean away. Cars like this need to be special to warrant a proper repair job but to be honest this was an extremely bad car that had received some shoddy accident repair work on that front corner. Repair would involve removing the loom and an awful lot of trim, plus the dash as well. It was caused by moisture trapped between the sound-deadening mat in the engine bay/transmission tunnel area and the bulkhead. Water runs down the back and it never really dries out in a typical Northern European climate. On really bad cars like this one, the brake servo is not really attached to the bulkhead! During a complete rebuild or restoration, take the opportunity to remove this sound deadening completely and rustproof the metal behind. If you just want to keep the car good, heat up some Waxoyl until it's really thin and inject it behind the sound deadening.

Bulkhead rot this bad spells the end really

At the beginning I said that E30 floor pans do not really rust but sometimes they can go in places that are hard to spot. Look under the car and you will see an alloy exhaust heat shield between the tunnel and the chassis rail. I have seen cars where the floor has rusted right though above this exhaust shield and you cannot spot the rot until the shield is removed. This happens when a leak causes the sound deadening to get waterlogged and the warmth from the exhaust provides a breeding ground for ferrous oxide. So when doing a restoration, or even just replacing the exhaust down pipe, take time to drop the heat shield and clean up any corrosion.

FRONT INNER WING REPAIRS

If your E30 has had its inner wing plastic mud shields left in place, chances are it will not be too bad in there. They like to rust out in the corner where the inner wing joins the bulkhead but repairs are not complex, although they do need to be strongly seam welded. It is when the arch liners have been removed after a particularly shoddy accident repair, or because the car has been lowered so the tyres touch. Then, the inner wing 'rifle butt' reinforcing section can just rust away and cause massive problems to the restorer. BMW do sell all the inner wing parts to repair a bad one, but if your shell is rusty here, as well as everywhere else, you really need to be looking for another one. If that's not an option, such as with a chrome bumper car where almost all of them are rusty, then the bits are not expensive and the actual process of cutting the rust out and welding the new sections in is not complicated, just long winded and boring. When I did this job on my Alpina C1, I constantly trial-fitted the front wing to ensure that it was being welded in the right place. Get it wrong, and even a BMW front wing will not fit.

A complex area is rot in the battery tray and its opposite number under the fuse box. This area is double skinned

Rust here is rare, but hard to repair

and a proper repair means taking the front wing off. The fuse box area is a particular pain because the fuse box cannot be moved very easily. Doing it well involves removing the fuse box and the front wiring loom, a very big job. The second skin is visible under the arch.

REPAIRING DOORS
In a word or two, forget it. BMW made a couple of million E30s and the doors do not really rust, apart from going scabby on badly neglected cars. They can split and crack around the check strap area, although this is really rare, and that sort of damage could be repaired by seam welding. But if you're thinking about re-skinning, do yourself a big favour and buy a good used door – they will be around forever and it is just not worth going to the trouble of re-skinning a damaged door. Unlike BMW 2002 doors that are known for having rusty bottom sections, the E30 doors were so well protected with wax injection at the factory that I cannot ever see a time when good used doors will not be available. By the way, the M3 door is different because they do not have the rubber side mouldings of the normal E30s and therefore do not have the holes drilled in for the clips or the pressed-in channel that holds the rubber moulding. In these cases, and also on E30 Convertibles, a good second-hand door might be rare. If your budget will not stretch to a new door, then a new skin is the best answer, but do yourself a big favour and only use a BMW skin because they are guaranteed to be the only ones that fit correctly.

To fit a skin, you need to strip the door to a shell and then grind the edges all around until you break through the skin into the doorframe. Then you can just break off the inner edges of the skin and pull the main door skin off although there are odd spot welds to be dealt with. Before fitting the new skin, the edges of the doorframe need to be cleaned up to perfection. Try the door skin for size to make completely sure it is a one hundred per cent fit and then paint the bare metal edges. Lay a bead of seam sealer on the doorframe where the skin will be placed and fit the skin. Turn the door upside down so that it is resting on the skin and using a proper panel beating hammer and dolly, start to flatten the inner skin over the frame. It is a difficult job to get right and a body shop would not charge that much to do this if you are not confident. However, just removing the old skin is not too bad a job.

REAR ARCHES
Most E30s that have seen ten or more British winters will be showing signs of rust in the back arches. If all you have is a few rusty scabs on the inner lip, clean them back with a grinder before priming and repainting. Keeping the arches clean from mud and regular rust-proofing will keep them good but you only have to look at the photos of the 1986 wreck to see what can happen.

The arches on this car did not look too bad before I attacked them with a grinder, hammer and chisel but, as the pictures show, the inner arches had fallen apart. This leads to water getting into the sills and the rust had also infected the rear valance.

BMW do not make outer arch repair sections, but the rear inner arches are still available. With the old outer arch cut off (follow the line shown in the photo) it is a big job to cut the old inner arch out and weld in a new one. To make a lasting repair job, it is what you must do. If the outer arch lip is bubbling up, I can guarantee that the inner arch lip will be shot. Various after-market panel makers will supply E30 rear outer arch sections.

M3s are not as bad as the regular E30 because of the shape of the arches. But many cars had the inner arch lips beaten up or ground back to clear bigger wheels and that just ruins them. Repairs need considerable skill with a MIG welder to avoid distorting the rear wing and repair sections are not available for the outer arch.

Going back to the standard E30, do not be tempted to use the whole arch repair section because if you try to join the arch it will never look right. Instead cut the old arch back to the area where it curves into the rear wings and join it there. That is where seam welding can be ground back and finished with plastic filler. Needless to say, any repairs must be sealed from the elements to stop any future problems recurring. The best way of sealing a welded join is to paint the weld with primer, letting it dry and then use proper automotive seam sealer. The mistake normally made is just to leave the seam sealer exposed to the elements. Instead, you should paint over it, something like Hammerite is ideal, followed by a coating of anti-rust wax like Waxoyl. Do not be tempted to use a cheap household bath sealer because they can be quite corrosive and just will not withstand the elements.

Rusty rear arch has also affected the inner arch and rear valance too.

Be also aware that not all E30 rear arches are the same. Cars built from September 1987 with the plastic bumpers have wheel arches that are lower in the shell. Put another way, the distance from the bottom of the rear window to the arch is longer on these later cars. Also, all BMW convertibles, but not Baur cabriolets, had these lower rear arches from the very beginning so if you need to replace a rear arch on an any convertible, you need the later post-September 1987 (1988 – 1993) type arch repair sections.

REPLACING THE SCUTTLE

On the regular E30, replacing the entire scuttle is not often needed. If it has just rusted at the ends where the wings bolt on, cutting the rusty metal out and welding in a section of new steel will be fine, as long as you remember to rustproof the inside of the repair. You will also need to unbolt the front wings but this is simple enough.

On the M3, though, the rust is of a different nature because the screen is bonded in. They rot all along the scuttle under the rubber trim and by the time the rust is peeping out, it is all a bit too late. The only option is to have the screen removed by a professional, remove the front wings and weld in a new scuttle panel. These are still available from BMW but to order one, you need to show the BMW dealer a copy of your registration document. Once they have seen that and they are satisfied that you are the owner of that car, they will ask BMW in Munich to stamp your chassis number onto the new panel.

Is it necessary to remove the dash? Not always, but if the rust has spread into the dash rail then removing the dash will be required – thankfully it's not that big a job. At the end of the day, you need to remove the screen and have a good dig about in there to establish just how rusty it is. You might be lucky and catch it in time – with the screen out the rust can be cleaned up with a grinder (be sure to cover the interior trim, the dash top and also place sheets over the inside of the door glass) before priming and painting. You could even cut out the rusty sections and weld new metal in, but ultimately the only way to ensure an everlasting job is to fit a complete new scuttle and rustproof it thoroughly.

RUST AROUND THE SUNROOF

A rusty sunroof panel is not a major problem as there are still enough serviceable used ones about and the chances of finding one painted the same colour as your car are very good. M3s and regular E30s use the same panel but they are not the same as any other BMW. Although replacing them is simply a matter of screws and washers, in fact it can be a complete cow of a job and you need a lot of patience. Basically you need to slide the sunroof back and, using your fingers, pull the headlining panel in the sunroof down to unclip it. Now close the sunroof and slide the headlining panel back. You can now tilt the sunroof open and remove the small Torx screws that hold it on. Sometimes the job is easy; sometimes it is not.

Rust in the roof skin is a bit more involved. The patch-up job involves cutting the rusty bit out with an air saw (do not even think about using a hammer and chisel!), sliding a bit of fresh steel in and tack welding it in place. The MIG welder needs to be on a low setting because there is very great risk of distorting the roof. By doing this, the roof skin will not show any signs of rust for some time but you just know it will pop up again eventually, maybe even somewhere else.

The proper way of doing the job is to remove the headlining and for this the front screen needs to come out, along with the door seals, the sunroof handle trim and the grab handles. Carefully peel away the headlining from the edges and using a screwdriver, prise the headlining reinforcing bars from the inner roof rail. It is slow, tricky work and if the headlining is at all rough, think about having a new one made and fitted by a professional. This is not as expensive as you would think and a colour change to black on cars with a white headliner is worthwhile because it looks so much better.

To access the inside of the sunroof area remove the headlining as far back as you can and tape it out of the way. There is no point in completely removing it as it will make refitting about a hundred times harder and you would have to remove the rear screen as well.

With that done, you can see the rust in all its glory and it will not be a pretty sight. But at least now you can attack it with a wire cup brush in a grinder and find out just what is minor surface rust and what is rot. Repairs are pretty much as described earlier – do not be shy, cut it back to clean metal and do not attempt to seam weld it, as you will distort the roof. Some distortion is pretty much inevitable unless you are a very skilled welder (and if you are not, pay one) but in the normal rot spots at the front corners, you can blend repairs in with filler. Before the roof lining goes back in though, paint the inside areas with red oxide primer followed by seam sealer.

REAR PANEL REPLACEMENT

E30s rot around the rear number plate lights, along the seam where the rubber boot seal sits and around the rear lights. In most cases minor welding repairs are fine but often on the older pre-facelift cars and the M3s, a new rear panel is the best option. Water sits under the boot seal and can make a real mess of the seal and because it is double skinned it is hard to replace long sections. If the rear panel is really bad, and you plan to keep the car, fitting a new rear panel is often the best option.

BMW

316/318/323i *Type E30*

APR 83 – MAY 91

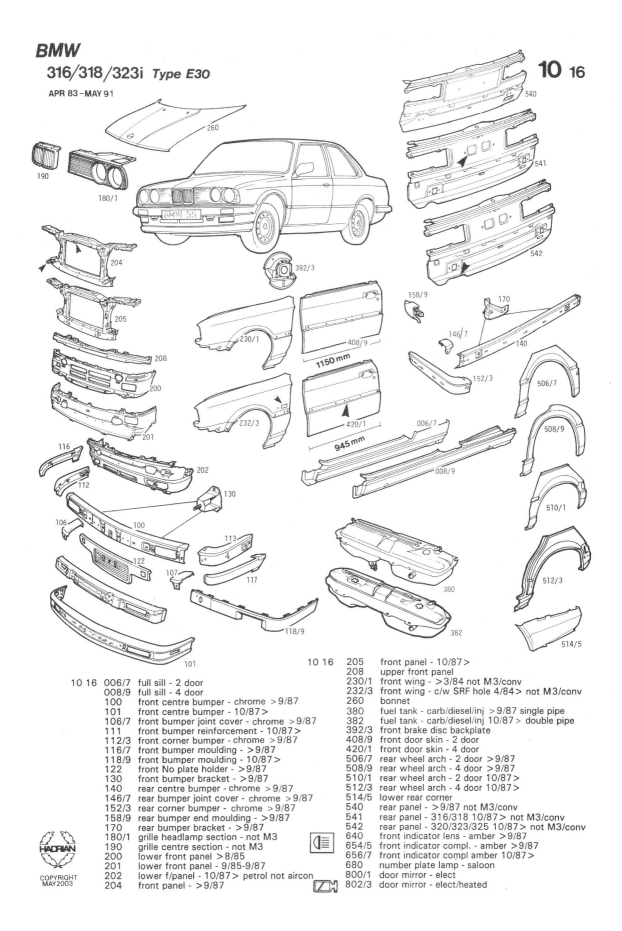

10 16	006/7	full sill - 2 door
	008/9	full sill - 4 door
	100	front centre bumper - chrome >9/87
	101	front centre bumper - 10/87>
	106/7	front bumper joint cover - chrome >9/87
	111	front bumper reinforcement - 10/87>
	112/3	front corner bumper - chrome >9/87
	116/7	front bumper moulding - >9/87
	118/9	front bumper moulding - 10/87>
	122	front No plate holder - >9/87
	130	front bumper bracket - >9/87
	140	rear centre bumper - chrome >9/87
	146/7	rear bumper joint cover - chrome >9/87
	152/3	rear corner bumper - chrome >9/87
	158/9	rear bumper end moulding - >9/87
	170	rear bumper bracket - >9/87
	180/1	grille headlamp section - not M3
	190	grille centre section - not M3
	200	lower front panel >8/85
	201	lower front panel - 9/85-9/87
	202	lower f/panel - 10/87> petrol not aircon
	204	front panel - >9/87

10 16	205	front panel - 10/87>
	208	upper front panel
	230/1	front wing - >3/84 not M3/conv
	232/3	front wing - c/w SRF hole 4/84> not M3/conv
	260	bonnet
	380	fuel tank - carb/diesel/inj >9/87 single pipe
	382	fuel tank - carb/diesel/inj 10/87> double pipe
	392/3	front brake disc backplate
	408/9	front door skin - 2 door
	420/1	front door skin - 4 door
	506/7	rear wheel arch - 2 door >9/87
	508/9	rear wheel arch - 4 door >9/87
	510/1	rear wheel arch - 2 door 10/87>
	512/3	rear wheel arch - 4 door 10/87>
	514/5	lower rear corner
	540	rear panel - >9/87 not M3/conv
	541	rear panel - 316/318 10/87> not M3/conv
	542	rear panel - 320/323/325 10/87> not M3/conv
	640	front indicator lens - amber >9/87
	654/5	front indicator compl. - amber >9/87
	656/7	front indicator compl amber 10/87>
	680	number plate lamp - saloon
	800/1	door mirror - elect
	802/3	door mirror - elect/heated

The actual process is not that hard. Use a hacksaw to cut the old panel off on the vertical joins but use a hammer and a very sharp bolster chisel to make the horizontal cut along the boot floor. A lot of grinding will be needed to clean up the joints and the genuine BMW panel is, of course, by far the best fit. Plug spot welding is best along the boot floor join but on the rear panel, proper seam sealing is absolutely essential.

As the rust pictures show, you can often find more rust below the rear bumper. On both the chrome bumper and plastic bumper cars rust can erupt and the rear valance on the sides forms part of a box section so it is not just there as decoration. BMW do not do a repair panel for the rear quarter valances so it is down to the pattern panel folks to supply something. However, the rear centre valance comes as part of the BMW rear panel.

FRONT PANEL REPLACEMENT
The front panel on the E30 is a bolt-on panel, which is held by a myriad of 8mm bolts. With the front bumper and grilles removed you will see all of them and even the ones that seem cunningly concealed do not hide for long.

M3 BODYWORK
There is nothing extra involved in an M3 as in terms of panel replacement they are the same as any other E30. Rear arches were often trimmed back for big wheels and this is difficult to put right. If you are lucky they have just been beaten up and can be folded back again, although some very skilled panel beating will be needed to make it all look original.

Be aware that the body panels on the M3 Convertible are unique to that car. The doors are a cross between those used for the E30 Convertible, with no rear frame, and the M3, with no swage line. The sills and front wings are also different to a standard M3. The boot lid is E30 Convertible.

BEST TOOLS
When doing a body restoration, the best tool you will have is a good old angle grinder. Use it with a cutting disc for cutting and a grinding disc for grinding – the discs are different for a reason. The wire cup brushes are very effective at removing paint from hard-to-get-at areas. The big thing with angle grinders is not to buy a cheap one. Purchase something expensive but good, like Black and Decker, Makita etc. because they just last for years.

The other really handy tool is the DA or Orbital sander. Nothing sands paint down better but unless you have a compressor, I would go for an electric one, as they are just as good. 40 grit discs will remove anything in its path whilst 1000 grit is good for final finishing.

If you have a decent compressor another really excellent tool is a mini sand blaster. These are about the size of a paint spray gun and are superb for getting rust out of awkward areas, such as around the jacking points. Unlike a wire brush in an electric drill, which will just polish the rust, the sand blaster, which uses a fine black grit, will really get rid of the rust. The only downside is that it gets everywhere including up your sleeves!

FINISHING AND RUSTPROOFING
I'm not going to go into the ins and outs of painting cars here, because you can either paint cars or you can't. If you are going to have the car painted at the body shop, do remove all the trim and bits you can, but do not get involved in preparation. If the paint shop prepared the car and there is a filler mark in the paint, it is their fault. Even if you flat the car down yourself, do the priming and deliver the car, make sure you ask the painter to do the final preparation – that way, any problems will be down to him and not you. Spend as long as it takes on getting panel gaps right. Make sure the panels sit properly and the doors, bonnet and boot close as they should. It is amazing how a weekend will disappear when you get really fussy, but it is time well spent.

The other big task is taking the shell back to bare metal. If the car has got basically a good finish, and you are doing a few repairs before a repaint, then do not bother because you are just making a hell of a lot of work for yourself. The only time you need to strip a panel to bare metal is when the paint has reacted, or if there are lots of scabs on a single panel (in which case buy a better one) or when the paint has blistered. This condition, as well as when paint reacts, are usually due to a previous nasty paint job and in these cases you do need to strip it back to the metal. Do not use the chemical strippers either because they make a horrible mess, you need water to wash it all off and it is just a nightmare. Instead, use a heat gun, but go carefully to avoid overheating the metal and warping it.

If you need a single panel painting such as a door, be aware that the new paint will not match the original and you will have a panel that sticks out like a sore thumb. This is why proper painters will insist on painting the whole side of the car or painting halfway into the wings and the other door before lacquering the three panels involved.

For small paint repair on non-metallic cars, use a BMW aerosol can but only on the edge of a panel, never smack bang in the middle. Preparation is the key to a decent job and if you think fresh paint will cover a blemish, think again because it will not. Use decent grey primer and 800 grit wet and dry to finish off and polish the edges of the repair with T-Cut or a similar cutting compound; this helps it to blend with the existing paint. What about repairing small areas of metallic paint? You might get away with small repairs, such as the edge of a wheel arch lip, but nine times out of ten it will not work.

Rust proofing is important. A product like Waxoyl is a good idea, but do not ever use it before the car is painted because it will react badly. Even if you have brushed some on in a hidden area, the heat in a paint oven will make it run. The best way to rustproof a car is to ignore the hand-held pumps you get with the rust proofing fluid and use instead an air fed gun with the proper probes and extensions. Heat the can of anti rust wax in a bucket of very hot water and inject it into the sills and box sections at about 60 or 70psi. This will turn the wax into a fog that will cover and cling to everything in its path. The object is not to have gallons of the stuff swilling about because it will stink forever, but coat everything with a fine film. On areas like inside the arches you can apply a couple of thicker coats – after a few days driving in dry weather dust will stick to it to form a highly effective sticky substance.

The sills and rear valances were painted in a tough, rubberised anti stone chip paint which BMW body shops will sell you. After this, the sills were always finished satin black. On the chrome bumper cars the valance under the rear bumper was painted body colour; plastic bumper cars had the rear valance body colour down to the swage line on the valance and satin black for the lower part. This included colour-coded cars like the 318iS. 325i Sport models had body coloured plastic combined bumpers/valances. The plastic sills on the M3 were a satin finish, not gloss, although many resprayed cars will have the wrong gloss finish

OPENING THE BONNET WITH BROKEN RELEASE CABLE

This might seem like the end of the world but really it's simple to sort out. Firstly you need to remove the right hand grille - that's right hand when you're standing in front of the car (passenger side on a UK or Australian car, driver's side on all others and M3's!). To do this, remove the two screws at the bottom of the grille first. Use some masking tape along the bonnet edge to avoid damaging the paint, insert a screwdriver between the bonnet and the grille and lift the handle up so as to force the inner part of the grille down and out of the clips - it will then be possible to wrangle the grille out. Now look in to the left of the headlamp assembly. You will see a pair of 10 mm bolts and these hold the bonnet release latch to the front panel. In between these two bolts is a small hole. Insert your flat blade screwdriver in here, wriggle it about a bit and the bonnet will pop open. On later cars (about mid-1987) BMW added a hole in the grille so you could do this without removing it.

Restoration Notes

Chapter 5

SUSPENSION AND STEERING

STEERING SHAFTS AND COUPLINGS
These shafts contain two universal joints and a rubber flexible disc coupling and most are getting a bit ragged now. Like a prop-shaft front coupling, the disc is made by SGF Jurid of nylon-reinforced rubber. Eventually the rubber perishes and can break, leading to very vague steering. Control is maintained, but only just. You have two options when this happens. The expensive one is a new shaft assembly from BMW. The cheap option, costing about six pints of beer and two hours work, is an SGF coupling repair kit containing a new rubber disc and four nuts and bolts. The repair disc differs from the original because it is fitted with steel sleeves for the bolts.

Taking off the shaft can be difficult. Remove the top and bottom pinch bolts and nuts, wedge an old screwdriver into the expansion slots in the top and bottom joint and give it a good hammering. This loosens the joint from the rack and the column. Now soak both joints in penetrating oil and go and make a cup of tea. After five or ten minutes go back and get the shaft off. Using a hammer and a long bar, drive the shaft down onto the rack but go carefully – hit it too hard and you might damage an expensive steering rack. Plenty of penetrating oil and moderate taps are all that is required. After a while, the shaft will drop away from the column. From underneath, tap the shaft back up off the rack and free.

What you have to do now is to either hacksaw or grind the rivets away that hold the two halves of the shaft to the rubber coupling. Once done, a hammer and a punch will make short work of the rivets, driving them out of the halves of the shafts. The nuts that come with the rubber disc are locking nuts used to assemble the shaft. When refitting, cleaning the internal splines with paraffin and an old toothbrush, along with the corresponding rack and column splines, will make life easier.

A word of warning if the universal joints on your shaft are knackered. There is not just one shaft, but a number of different types. There is a long one for non-power steering cars and a short one for cars with power steering. Left-hand drive cars like the M3 seem to have another length again and even the splines are different. So, it you want a good used shaft for your 1987 320i with power steering, go for a car the same type and build year.

STIFF STEERING
You may find that even with power steering, the steering on your E30 is really stiff and doesn't self centre very well. This is common on cars that have been stood for a couple of years without moving and the problem is the lower steering column bearing. The inner column tries to seize but luckily the cure is easy and doesn't involve any dismantling. Remove the lower dash cover to expose the steering column and then drill a nice big hole as close to the bottom as you can get - a hole about 5 or 6 mm is fine. The next thing is to inject plenty of penetrating fluid. This will run down the shaft into the bearing and free it up but it won't last forever because it evaporates. So follow it up with oil from an oil can and the steering should regain its proper light feel.

STEERING RACKS
The manual steering rack on the E30 is a tough old thing. They do not really go wrong and even if the inner track rod ball joints are worn out, the kiss of death for most steering racks, BMW designed theirs so that the joints can be unscrewed and replaced. To do this, undo the clip and pull back the rubber rack gaiter. Put the steering onto full lock so that the joint you want to remove is up against the rack housing, bend back the lock tabs and loosen the joint with a 32mm spanner. Now use a proper 'scissor' ball joint splitter to crack the joint at the strut end. Unscrew it, transfer the old outer joint if need be

(just a 13mm nut and bolt) and fit the new one. Because steering racks do differ slightly between chrome bumper and plastic bumper cars, order these bits quoting the chassis number. When reassembling, make a note of how many threads were wound in on the old track rod and make a corresponding paint mark on the new one. This will at least ensure that the new one is about right but the car will need to have the tracking (wheel alignment) set up properly.

When changing a power rack, the engine mounts need to be released and the engine lifted. When replacing a rack, the two retaining bolts can seize in the alloy rack body.

Power racks are a bit more involved. They too are reliable as power steering racks go but because they are more complex than a manual rack, they are more likely to go wrong. Leaks are the big thing with these. Many end up with rack gaiters full of oil and when they get to this stage they should be exchanged for a new or reconditioned rack. The other problem is what we jokingly call 'PPAS' or partial power assistance. This is when there is power steering when turning left, but heavy manual steering when turning right or vice-versa. Again, a new or reconditioned rack is the only answer; forget about overhauling the rack yourself. Steering racks did change in detail in 1987, so if buying another rack, get the right year. There are still plenty of good used ones about and the basic check is to make sure the gaiters are not full of oil.

SUSPENSION REPAIRS

Changing shock absorbers (dampers)

Firstly you need to establish what kind of dampers you have. If you have a 316i, chance is they are just standard Boge. If you have a 325i maybe it has M Tech suspension and in that case you need Bilstein dampers or Boge gas on 1989/1990 cars. How do you tell? Easy. Jack up one front corner of the car. Look inside the spring at the plastic cover over the damper rod. If it is a hard plastic sleeve with a rubber bump stop at the top that can easily be slid up and down the damper rod with your fingers, you have not got Bilstein suspension. If you can see a squashy plastic concertina cover that cannot be moved, you have Bilstein suspension. Metal bumper 325i Sports and all Alpinas have this kind of damper as standard, M3s do not.

Where to buy dampers? For a cooking car like a 316i, you can get them anywhere really. Boge are very good of course and Al-ko dampers are not bad either. If I had a 318iS, a 325i Sport or M3 I would buy from BMW to get exactly the right damper. Alpina cars like the C1 and C2 cars did use some slightly harder valve Bilsteins, but check the price before committing yourself as Alpina parts are definitely not cheap. For my money, I would fit 325i Sport Bilsteins as they soften the ride a touch without compromising the handling.

Changing the front dampers is quite simple, but a couple of pointers. Slacken (but do not remove!!) the top 19mm damper nut before you even jack up the car – with the strut off, it can be very difficult, if not impossible, without an air wrench. If the dampers are not going to be re-used, clamp them with some really strong vice grips if you have to. If you are going to re-use them try to grip the damper shaft as far to the top as you can. If a portion of the damper shaft marked by the vice grips has to go past the oil seal the damper will start leaking and fail very quickly.

Taking the front struts off is pretty easy, but you do need a proper ball joint splitter and not some cheap rubbishy thing. The forked type that you hammer in to split the joint are bad news because they will always split the rubber boot. They were developed for use on Minis and are not suitable for BMWs. A proper, heavy-duty ball joint splitter will be about 6 or 7 inches long, be pretty heavy and require a 22mm spanner to operate. The small ones you see for a few quid are completely useless.

So, with the top 19mm damper nut loosened, the next job is to remove the brake caliper – 13mm bolts with locknuts on the regular E30 but sleeved Allen bolts on the M3. Tie the caliper up out of the way to avoid stretching the rubber brake hose. Now you have the steering track rod end – a plain nut to remove and split the joint with your ball joint splitter. Spray plenty of releasing fluid on the nut and if the joint breaks before the nut is fully off, fit the ball joint splitter on upside down so that in effect may you are clamping. With that done, tackle the lower ball joint. Again, plenty of WD40 or similar and remove the nut slowly. It can be very hard work to get it off and it might break the joint because the nut is very tight. Put an axle stand under the ball joint and lower the car so the weight of that corner is on the ball joint. It should come off then. With the nut off, split the ball joint. On the M3, remove the three bolts that hold the strut to the lower ball joint mounting plate.

Lastly, the anti-roll bar link on the M3. There is a nut holding it to the strut body but you will need another spanner to hold the ball joint steady while you undo the nut – tedious work. Force the anti-roll bar up or down with a long bar to disconnect it. On all cars, remove the three top 13mm nuts and remove the strut.

Use coil spring compressors to fully compress the springs until they are loose in the strut and oil the threads to make the work a bit easier. Remove the 19mm top nut followed by the washer and the spring plate. Make notes of where everything went and in which order.

Getting the screw collar off the damper body to remove the inserts is difficult without a simple and cheap tool – Stilson grips. These apply more pressure to the collar the more you twist and for this job they are unbeatable. Forget about using anything else. You will need to clamp the strut body in a very substantial vice as these collars are very tight. What I have done is to remove the strut, take the spring off, and then put back the top mount and refit the strut to the car. Then you can really get a grip on the collar and take it off. Some are so badly rusted that they have to be removed with a chisel. When fitting the new dampers, do not forget to pour a little neat anti-freeze into the strut body before you insert the struts. This cools the damper and is often overlooked. Apply thread lock to the three lower strut bolts as well on M3 cars. Wash the grease out of the top strut mounting bearings with carburettor cleaner or brake cleaner, forcing new grease into the bearings.

On the rear springs, fitting new, shorter coils is hard. Refitting a standard spring can be a nightmare and sometimes you have to undo the axle mounts and drop the rear axle one side at a time to do it. Greasing the rubber spring gaskets makes it a lot easier, but two people are much better than one.

REAR SHOCK ABSORBERS
These are easy enough on the saloon and a clonking rattle from the rear end is a sign that the top mounts have failed - easy enough to replace. On the Touring models though, this job is a complete pain. The outer parts of the rear seat back need to be removed and this requires a bit of brute force and ignorance. Then you have to remove the rear side trims in the load area followed by the rear seat belt assembly - it really is utter joy. Needless to say the 13 mm nuts for the top mounts will delight you by dropping down into the confines of the body never to be seen again so order up some new ones and use grease on the socket to 'glue' the nuts in.

Front wishbones
What fun these are to repair. The E30 front wishbone pivots on a ball joint at the front and on a rubber bush at the back. When the ball joint fails, you might get a rattle over bad road surfaces but the car will wander on the road. New ball joints are available but they are a complete sod to fit – it just is not worth it so you should fit an exchange wishbone. The trouble is new wishbones from BMW, and anyone else, do not come with the rear rubber mounting. The rear rubber mounting is a circular bush pressed into a cast iron 'tennis racket' shaped bracket that bolts to the chassis leg with two bolts. If the bush is in good condition you can squeeze it off with a big ball joint splitter, using a 13mm nut or two to get it off the last inch. To refit the bush, lubricate it in washing up liquid (do NOT use oil or grease) and twist it on. It is hard work.

But it is likely that the bush will have seen better days and for what they cost, you should consider fitting a new one. It is just a case of mounting the tennis racket in the vice and cutting through the steel inner bush until it loosens and comes out. As a rule, cars like the 325i and the 320iS had stronger bushes. See under the modifying section about the three different types of E30 wishbone bush and what to fit. Needless to say, just press the new one in with the vice but do take care to line up the arrow on the new bush with the arrow on the tennis racket. To fit it, use washing up liquid (Fairy Liquid seems most effective) and twist the bush assembly onto the wishbone.

Getting the ball joints apart needs a word of caution. If you need to split the ball joints, do yourself a big favour and buy the most expensive ball joint splitter you can, the scissor type with a nice big 22mm bolt is the best. Avoid the fork type you hammer in as these destroy the ball joint rubbers which although not important when fitting new ball joints will still ruin the good ones you want to keep.

The main pivot pin on the wishbone is a three-inch long pin with a big 22mm nut. Be really careful with these and

Alloy and steel wishbones.
Replace like with like or in pairs

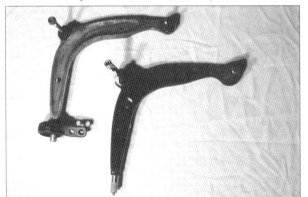

How to remove the "tennis racket" wishbone bush

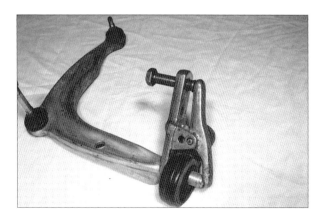

spray plenty of penetrating fluid. They have a nasty habit of releasing in the subframe when the nut is half undone and then they are a complete nightmare to remove. Putting the jack under the wishbone and supporting the weight of the front of the car is one possible solution but if the nut is really tight you are in trouble. The best idea is to spray it with penetrating fluid, undo the nut until it gets tight and tighten it again a turn. Undo it two turns, go back one turn, undo another two turns and so on. Keep spraying penetrating fluid on it and you should be okay. The trouble is that with the engine in there is no way of getting down on the nut to split it with a chisel although there is barely enough room to get on it with a special nut splitter.

A final word on ball joints. If the outer ball joint that connects to the strut has failed, again you need a complete wishbone. Standard bushes are part number 31 12 9058 815, the up-rated 325i type are 31 12 9058 931.

Rattling over bumps – M3

The M3 uses a 5 series type link between the anti-roll bar and the strut, rather than the solid rubber bushing of the standard E30. These used ball joints and they wear out and rattle. The links were used on the E34 5-Series, E36 3-Series and the E32 7-series, plus all of the 8-Series cars. They are cheap enough from aftermarket companies.

Rear axle bushes.

As for the various suspension bushes in the rear end, you cannot beat the standard factory rear subframe bushes. You could fit harder ones, but they transmit too much noise and vibration for a road car. Some people swear by them, but they were comparing this wonder bush against a tired old BMW bush that had been in the car for six years. Changing these bushes is not a DIY job unless you have the expensive special tool. This costs about the same as a BMW dealer or specialist will charge to supply and fit a pair of new ones so unless you own a number of E30s and are planning on owning loads more, it might not be worth it. Even with the special tool, it is often hard work. Where some inexperienced mechanic, BMW or otherwise, will come unstuck is with the mounting plate. This fits to the rear outer sill area with two Allen bolts. These never like to come undone, and you have to really clean them out inside and find an Allen key that's a good, tight 'hammer' fit. If it still rounds off, hammer a spline drive socket attachment in. The last resort is to drill them out. Forget about using a conventional Allen key because the bolts will just laugh at you.

Trailing arm bushes

Also at the rear end we have the trailing arm bushes. These do not really fall to bits in the way worn out rear subframe bushes can, but they can go soft with age.

Changing them is a tough but simple DIY task that is so much easier with the whole rear trailing arm removed. This involves undoing six Allen bolts that hold the inner CV joint to the differential and the best tool for this is a half-inch drive ratchet with an Allen key adaptor. Hammer the Allen key in good and hard, remove it and clean all the loosened dirt, and then hammer the Allen key back in again before unscrewing the bolt. Very late cars may use a torx bolt instead. Disconnect the handbrake cable and the brake fluid line before disconnecting the lower shock absorber bolt – but place a jack under the trailing arm and jack the arm up a couple of inches before you undo that bolt. Now it is just the two nuts and bolts holding the trailing arm to the subframe, plus the anti roll bar connection if the car has one. Pressing the bushes in and out can be done in the vice, using washing up liquid to lubricate.

Differential mounting bush

Also at the back, we have the differential mounting bush. This takes a good old hammering and the standard type can be replaced with the later, solid bush for vastly better differential location. The bush you want is fitted to the 3-litre Z3 and the M Roadster/Coupé and the BMW part number is 33 17 2228 425. I suppose this ought to come under the modifications section but it is just a good idea to fit one, even on a cooking 316i. All that axle movement in stop start-traffic can be drastically reduced with one of these bushes.

To replace the bush, jack up the rear of the car and place axle stands under the subframe bushes. Put the jack under the differential and raise it slightly. Now remove the bolt that goes through the differential mounting and let the jack down so that the differential drops enough to clear the boot floor mounting. Put under the differential a suitable container to catch axle oil and remove the bolts holding the alloy rear cover to the differential casing. The rear alloy cover will now come off and if you are really organised, you will have a new rear cover gasket as well. Part numbers are 33 11 210 428 for the six bolt differential and 33 11 210 405 for the eight bolt type.

To remove the old bush, cut the old rubber centre out and then cut through the steel outer ring until it drops out. Clean up the differential cover mounting surfaces and then press the new bush in with the vice. Reassembly as they say, is a reversal of dismantling but before you put the rear cover back on, make sure the oil refill plug comes undone okay. If might be an even better idea to do this before it all comes apart.

Front wheel bearings

Like most BMWs built in the last twenty or so years, the front wheel bearings are a complete unit with the hub.

You pull it off with strong tyre levers or a proper puller, throw it away and fit a new one. Very often the old hub will pull off and leave the inner bearing race behind but it is a case of big screwdrivers, a bit of applied violence and some shocking language to get it off. Simple subject and nothing more to be said.... but if your car has ABS, make sure you get the ABS version with the serrated ring. On cars without ABS, sometimes you will be supplied with a 'one size fits all' hub with the ABS ring. This may have to be chiselled off but it is dead easy. The other thing with these is not to add any more grease. You would not believe it, but packing the steel cover full of grease is the worst thing you could ever do for a wheel bearing. All that will happen is that the bearing will overheat and destroy itself in pretty short order. What I am saying is that the grease that is in the bearing itself is enough. But hang on, when you took the dust cover off, there was grease in it, right? Yes, and that was the grease that the bearings didn't want being spat out.

Rear wheel bearings

In two simple words...forget it. This is an absolute cow of a job. I would sooner pay someone with the special tools needed than spend a day swearing and getting nowhere. In the past, I have resorted to changing complete rear trailing arms because it's easier than changing a bearing. If you can borrow the special tools to do it, go ahead. If you cannot, do not attempt the job.

Changing drive shafts

This too can be a drama. With the big centre nut removed and the inner CV joint disconnected from the differential, spray plenty of WD40 in around where the nut fits and gently tap the end of the shaft with the nut refitted a few turns. It can go one of two ways. It will either come out singing and dancing, or will want to remain welded to the car forever. The danger here is that too much force will result in half the rear wheel bearing coming along for the ride, which is very, very boring. A three-legged puller is the best tool for the job, relying on persuasion as opposed to force.

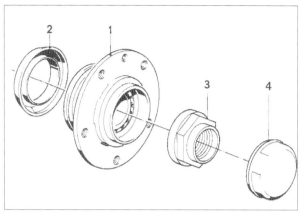

Front Hub. On all E30's, the hub contains the wheel bearing and is replaced as a complete unit. Again, ABS cars have a trigger ring which needs removing, on cars without ABS.

Rear hub and wheelbearing. The hub (1) is different on ABS cars.

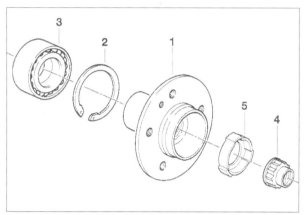

Restoration Notes

Chapter 6

BRAKES

BRAKES
The braking system on the E30 is pretty straightforward. 316, 316i, 318i and 320i cars without ABS use a disc front and drum rear set up, whilst all other cars use rear discs. 316, 316i and 318i cars used solid front discs with ventilated front discs for everything else. It is the usual split hydraulic system with the usual problems relating to old age but it is not hard to work on. Some cars will have ABS and that can be problematical in old age with many an owner driven to drink by the flashing orange ABS light on the dashboard.

Servicing and repairs
First things first – brake fluid should be changed every year. Brake fluid is hygroscopic which means it absorbs moisture. This can gather inside the fluid reservoir and once there is moisture in the fluid it will not show up until the brakes are used hard and get really hot. The water will boil and evaporate leaving air locks in the hydraulic circuit and not much of a reaction from the

If the master cylinder is leaking or faulty fit a new one: don't even consider a "repair"

brake pedal. Synthetic brake fluids will go a long way to curing this, but so will renewing the fluid every year with conventional mineral based fluids.

BLEEDING BRAKES
Bleeding the brakes is easy enough. My preferred method is to open all four bleed nipples (or three on some disc brake cars) and basically evacuate the system - a length of old small bore rubber hose (such as windscreen washer pipe) into an old jar. With all the old fluid out, remove the plastic reservoir from the brake master cylinder - it just pulls off. Wash this out in the sink until its really clean inside and out but let it dry thoroughly before refitting - it just pushes on. With that done, fill the reservoir with clean fluid and pump it through starting with the rear brakes first. To save time, have four old jars and open all the bleed nipples. This will quickly displace all the old fluid left in the system. Pressure bleeders that run from the air in a spare wheel are good but for the rear brakes inflate the spare wheel to 50 psi!

Old rusty calipers should be replaced. The left hand unit is the M3 caliper, shared with the 81-88 5 Series

When the time comes for new discs or pads do not just buy the cheapest you can find because most of the really cheap ones are poor quality and have no place on your car. Some of the cheap discs and pads really are utter rubbish, but the brakes are an area where you can cut costs without sacrificing quality. My own recommendations are Textar pads (as used by BMW) with BMW discs. E30 discs are so cheap to buy from BMW that it is a false economy to run the discs down to almost nothing. Anything that comes in a Lucas, Lockheed or Girling box is going to be decent quality too, but there is a lot of fake stuff going about so buy only from a reputable supplier. BMW are still the place to buy M3 discs, but this car used E28 Five series calipers and brake pads.

Calipers get old and rusty like any other, and when the pistons start to stick, they are just one step away from being thrown in the bin and replaced. At every pad change, push the piston out slightly by pumping the brake pedal twice (and no more) and spraying some WD40 or similar releasing fluid between the piston and the rubber dust seal using the long red probe. This will lubricate the piston seal slightly and can often bring a sticky caliper back to life. Sticking calipers can often be diagnosed on the road. All caliper pistons should retract slightly after use to provide a running clearance between the disc and the brake pads. If the caliper piston is sticking, the pad will tend to be held against the disc after use resulting in friction and overheating. The car may well want to pull to the left or right; you may get a terrible vibration through the steering wheel as the disc overheats. If you pull over and leave it for a few minutes, the car will drive okay until the next time you use the brakes. By the time they get this bad, the calipers are just about dead. The answer is a reconditioned caliper from one of the aftermarket suppliers. Yes, you could in theory buy a new seal kit and repair the old one but the consequences of getting it slightly wrong and having a terrible accident because your brakes failed does not bear thinking about. At the end of the day, brake parts do not cost much but your life – and that of others – depends on them.

E30 calipers have a habit of sticking also on their sliding pins. With the caliper unbolted, the two sliders into which the 13mm caliper bolts screw should move in and out easily. If they do not move easily, or are seized solid, you will need at least new pins; or maybe a new caliper mounting bracket – a good second-hand one is quite acceptable. Efforts at cleaning and lubricating seized ones do not seem to work very well. When you have got it all working okay, coat the pins with copper grease. Give the caliper mounting bracket a really good clean with a wire brush and clean with a file the areas where the brake pads fit, coating these areas lightly with copper grease too. Also coat the backs of the brake pads with copper grease to avoid brake squeal.

Sticking calipers can also cause steering wheel vibration under braking but by the time you have sorted out the calipers, the chances are the discs have warped. Also check that there is not any play in the steering rack or front suspension ball joints.

Removing the front discs should be easy...but the Allen key that holds the disc to the front hub can be a complete swine to get out. If the Allen bolt rounds off like they normally do, use a spline drive socket and hammer it good and hard into the bolt. This normally shifts them. If nothing seems to work and you are fitting new discs anyway, get your biggest hammer and give the inside of the disc a few really good whacks and it will come off, leaving the bolt behind. Now you can get a pair of strong self-locking grips on the job and have that bolt out in no time.

For the rear brakes, we have either rear drums, that are great fun, or discs that are quite simple and reliable. The rear brake shoes on the drum brakes cars are supposed to be self-adjusting, and when the car is relatively youthful, they are. But when the car is old and the brake bits inside are all rusty, the adjusters seize up. About the best advice here is to take notes of where the springs go, which way the shoes fit and then take it all apart cleaning and copper greasing it as you go. When fitting new shoes, you will need to wind the adjuster in fully, fit the drum and then apply the brakes and the handbrake to centralise the shoes. The brake pedal will have loads of travel, so remove the drums and click the adjuster round bit by bit until the drum just fits. Now apply the brakes and the handbrake again so that the self-adjuster can do its stuff.

New rear shoes rarely come with the handbrake lever so this will have to be removed from the old brake shoe and fitted to the new one. The secret of doing rear brakes is to take notes of where everything went and only do one side at a time – that way you can nip around to the other side to see what things look like!

One problem with getting the rear drums off is that the shoes have worn into the drum so that there is a sizeable lip around the outer edge. This makes getting the drums off a really difficult task and about all you can do is get them off enough to see the brake shoes. Then use a big screwdriver to lever the shoes back against the back plate whilst you use another screwdriver, or a tyre lever, to force the drum off. Once removed, either fit a pair of new drums, or use an angle grinder to grind off the lip. This will make refitting the drum a whole load easier. Sometimes, the drums will seize on the hubs. To sort this apply the handbrake with the rear wheels off and the drum retaining screw removed (one at a time), start the engine and drive the car. The hub will then spin inside the stationary brake drum.

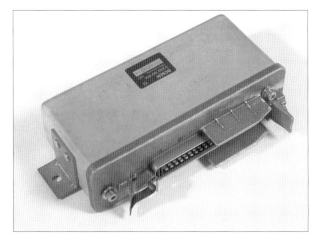

An early ABS control unit. Using a booster pack to jump start a dead car can damage it.

Corrosion or dirt on this ABS trigger ring can render the system useless

Leaking or seized rear wheel cylinders should be replaced with new ones – they are cheap enough.

REAR BRAKE PIPES

Oh dear. This is one job you should really dread. Replacing the rear brake pipes around the differential is a task I would strongly recommend you pay somebody else to do. They really are that bad. The front to rear brake pipe comes up from the master cylinder, threads over the axle and up to a T piece where the pressure is split from left to right rear brakes. The metal pipes then run along to a flexible hose. After a decade or more, the pipes will be rusty and, worse, the 11mm union nuts will be rusty too. A standard 11mm spanner is useless and even a special 11mm brake pipe spanner can struggle. To get it apart, nine times out of ten you will have to sacrifice the rubber flexible hoses. You have to cut them right at the front, wrestle the brake pipe spanner between the axle beam and the fuel tank and whilst you hold the spanner on, use a deep 14mm socket on the metal stub of the cut flexible pipe to get it apart. If the worst comes to the worst, destroy the metal spring clip on the body bracket where the flexible and steel line meet. Taking off the rear part of the exhaust heat shield means removing just four 10mm bolts and makes life easier. So does removing the bolt that holds the differential to the boot floor and letting it hang down. Disconnecting the bottom damper mounts from the trailing arms allows the differential to drop some more and this makes life a lot easier. It is still a complete nightmare of a job though. My recommendation? If you're going to replace the front to rear brake pipe as well (it will be rusty by now), drop the whole rear axle out. The extra work is not much – four nuts for the prop-shaft, drop the exhaust off and using a big trolley jack or two, lower the rear axle down – you will need an assistant for this, and also to get it back in. The advantage is that replacing the brake pipes will be easy.

As for the actual pipes, you have a choice. For doing the job with the axle in place, I would use copper brake pipes that are so much easier to bend and shape than the steel ones BMW use. BMW still supply all the steel pipes, but they are made to length and are not shaped.

One last word on the subject. This is a job for a very patient mechanic with a dry workshop, and one preferably with a ramp or a lift. If your facilities amount to a cheap trolley jack and your workshop is the roadside, forget it.

FRONT BULKHEAD BRAKE PIPES

These run from the master cylinder to each front wheel. One of them goes across the length of the bulkhead and gets rusty. It is also a pain to replace and many have been replaced by copper pipes fitted in an 'approximate' fashion.

FRONT TO REAR BRAKE PIPE

This goes from the master cylinder, down the bulkhead, along the bottom of the car and up over the rear axle. The main point where the pipe rusts and bursts is at the back. BMW will supply a new pipe but they do not come ready formed anymore, but are cut to the right length. The trouble here is getting the pipe over the rear axle beam and with the axle in place it is not easy. The answer is to make a slightly longer one from copper/kunifer pipe and instead run the pipe under the axle.

ABS PROBLEMS?

As built, the E30 ABS systems are pretty good. On early examples the pedal was pretty nasty with long travel but later ones seem fine. On these, the ABS light should come on with the ignition and go out when the engine fires. However, note that wiring the ABS light up to the oil pressure light does that as well! If the ABS light comes back on when you are driving, you have a sensor problem. The sensors could have a broken wire inside but you cannot interrogate the system to find out which one is faulty. It could also be excessive dirt on the ends, or the trigger rings on the hubs could be dirty or corroded.

The ABS block down in the engine bay is pretty reliable but the ECU up above the glove box has a relay that can be blown by jump-starting the car with a big booster pack. So if the light comes on at low speeds it is likely to be a faulty or broken sensor wire. If it comes on at higher speeds, reckon on a corroded hub trigger ring. Removing and cleaning the various bits are the first steps, throwing expensive bits at it comes next.

Be aware that the ABS light should not come on at idle without the car moving. Some cars used a coil that sat upside down and the coil lead could run close to the ABS wiring, something that can cause an electrical interference.

HANDBRAKES AND CABLES
The handbrake on drum-brake cars works on the brake shoes and is adjustable from inside the car – two 10mm nuts on the handbrake lever. If the rear shoes are worn out though no amount of adjustment will help. On disc-brake cars the handbrake layout is a pair of small brake

shoes working inside the rear disc. They last a long time because they only get used as a clamp as opposed to regular shoes that have to slow the car. Replacing them with new ones is pretty simple workshop manual stuff.

Replacing the handbrake cables is quite simple if you know the score. Getting the old ones out is an art. The steel ferrules where the cables go into the body either side of the differential can seem difficult but the way to do it is to use Mole grips and twist them. Use some penetrating oil as well and after a few twists they will come out. Getting the new ones back in is a problem because the inner cables will not want to come past the handbrake lever – so undo the two 13mm bolts and remove the handbrake lever complete. The inner cables will then sail up the body tubes.

ADJUSTING PEDAL HEIGHT
Often, a poor pedal feel can be cured by raising the brake pedal. This is done by adjusting the cross linkage (RHD or) behind the glove box. Slacken the 17mm nut and use an 8mm spanner on the linkage rod - you'll see the pedal go up or down. The clutch pedal can also be raised by slackening the 13mm nut where the pedal joins the master cylinder and turning the 17mm bolt - it has an eccentric pivot.

Components for the handbrake shoes on disc brake cars. Number 7 is the adjuster

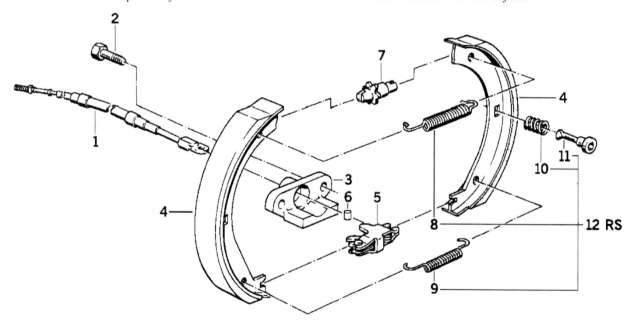

Chapter 7

TRANSMISSION

TRANSMISSION (CLUTCH, GEARBOX, PROPELLOR SHAFT AND DIFFERENTIAL)

CLUTCHES

E30 clutches are as reliable as on any other car, but in time they will wear out and eventually the hydraulics, the master cylinder and the slave cylinders, will spring a leak. The master cylinder is the one bolted to the bulkhead and connected to the clutch pedal. They last pretty well, but when they fail you will get brake fluid running down the pedal and into the carpets below. If you find that you have to top up the fluid reservoir on a regular basis, make the carpet or floor mat you first place to check for a fluid leak. You cannot repair them as no seal kits are available, so it is a new or good used cylinder. If you buy a used one, just pull the rubber dust seal back and make sure it is not going the same way as your old one. With brakes, anyone who fits second-hand or repaired hydraulic parts and then uses the car on a public road is clearly not right in the head. With clutch hydraulics, you would suffer inconvenience as opposed to potentially killing someone.

The slave cylinder is bolted to the gearbox bell housing and eventually they will fail and usually at the most inconvenient time. They are pretty easy to change, but whilst you are down there you should replace the rubber flexible hose as well for the few quid they cost.

Most E30s that have never had the hydraulic parts removed will still have the original fluid. Springy clutch pedal action and crunching into reverse is a sign that the old fluid is full of condensation and is ruined. Every couple of years, when you replace your brake fluid, why not bleed out the clutch fluid too? Most E30s I have seen

have fluid in the reservoir that is as black as sin. Many cars though have a problem here. You undo the bleed nipple, pump the pedal...and nothing comes out. This is because the fluid escape drilling in the slave cylinder body is blocked with rust. Take the slave cylinder off, remove the bleed nipple and run a small drill down the drilling until it's clear. Then you can bleed the clutch. Often the clutch becomes lighter to use with new fluid.

As for replacing the clutch, there are not any real hang-ups as it is all very conventional. The only problem is getting the top starter motor nut and bolt out on the earlier six-cylinder cars; it really is a complete bastard and requires an assistant. Once you have removed the air flow meter and can actually SEE the starter nut (difficult in itself), you will need a very skinny ring spanner to get onto it. Sometimes only an open-ended spanner will do it. From underneath, you will require a very, very long socket extension (about a metre long) with a 'wobbly' end. Getting the nut and bolt back in is a recognised art form. Basically, your assistant has to glue the head of the bolt into the socket using something like mastic and ease the bolt in. Then, with the nut glued into the spanner, you have to get it in there whilst your assistant turns the nut until it catches on the thread and starts to wind on. On the cars with the big starter, basically metal bumper cars, you cannot comprehend just how difficult this is until you do it. Many cars came out of garages and clutch fitting centres with the top bolt in the workshop dustbin and the bottom bolt done up extra tight

Various different types of bolts are used to hold the gearbox to the back of the engine. On older cars plain bolts are used, mainly 13mm and 17mm. Around 1985 BMW started phasing in torx bolts which require special torx sockets, but a set of these is not expensive. On cars like the M10 316, you may find a mixture of both. 17mm bolts around the top but the bottom ones are small torx, which can be removed with a close-fitting conventional 8mm socket because they are not particularly tight. On the bigger torx bolts on later cars, trying the same dodge will just end up is with stripped torx heads so do not try it! In rare cases the steel bolts will corrode into the bellhousing.

Inside the car, the clutch pedal can often be at a different height to the brake pedal. Both the clutch and brake pedals can be adjusted for height. Where the 17mm nut and bolt connect the pedal to the master cylinder push rod the bolt is actually eccentric. Slackening the bolt and turning it will raise or lower the pedal.

One last thing – clutches that squeal at idle. If you have this noise, depress the clutch pedal very slightly. If the noise goes away, you have got a problem that will quickly lead to a destroyed clutch and a big bill. What is happening is that either the slave cylinder, the flexible hose or the master cylinder is at fault. The noise is the clutch release bearing in constant contact with the clutch cover and spinning. When you touch the pedal, the bearing fully engages and the pressure on the bearing takes the noise away. Eventually, the bearing will have enough of being spun all the time, overheat and seize. The next time you use the clutch, the seized bearing will punch through the cover and you will have no clutch and a solid pedal.

If you suspect this problem, jack the car up and place it on axle stands. Fire the engine up and wait for the noise to start. Crawl underneath and slacken the two 13mm nuts that secure the slave cylinder to the gearbox. If the noise stops as you undo the nuts, you have found the problem. Basically, it is caused by a faulty seal somewhere that is not allowing the slave cylinder to fully retract the release bearing. It could even be a faulty hose that has damage inside and is acting as a one-way valve for the fluid. From aftermarket sources the parts are cheap and I would try first replacing the slave cylinder and hose.

GEARBOXES
There are a huge number of different gearboxes fitted to the E30, but just six different basic types. Because only six basic castings were used, Getrag marked and identified the various different types with a number and three letters stamped on the bottom edge of the bell housing on four-cylinder cars, and on the top edge by the cylinder head on six-cylinder cars. On a 1988 316-carburettor type gearbox, for example, you might find a serial number followed by 'BMR' that tells you what it was.

First up is the runt of the litter, the Getrag 242 four-speed unit as fitted to the early 316 and 318i cars. It is not very strong and they were known to break, but as most cars were fitted with the five-speed gearbox it is not a unit to worry about. If you have one, you can cheaply upgrade the car by fitting a five-speed gearbox from any M10 engined E30 but you will need the complete gearbox with the gear linkage and the prop-shaft as well.

Next up is the four-cylinder M10 version of the prolific Getrag 240/5. This was fitted to the five-speed 316 and 318i and it is a very good and strong gearbox. After a huge mileage they might growl or whine, or maybe develop weak second gear synchromesh, but these gearboxes just do not seem to wear out.

The third gearbox is a direct descendant of this unit, and is the Getrag 240/5 as fitted to the M40 and M42 engined cars. It was fitted to the plastic bumper 316i, 318i and was used in the 318iS until September 1990, after which BMW reverted to the E34 518i unit. The M40/M42 unit looks the same as the earlier M10 gearbox, but the spacing for the bell housing to engine bolts is different and they do not interchange.

Next is the third version in the Getrag 240/5 trilogy, the unit as fitted to the 320i. Although the gearbox looks similar to the four-cylinder types, again the bell housing is different enough to prevent it from being interchanged.

320is were also fitted with the rare ZF S5-16 gearbox as used in the earlier E28 520i; another strong old gearbox.

The Getrag 245/10 and 245/11 units were the Sport 'Dogleg' units as used in the 323i. They are both nearly identical and are known to be noisy in old age, caused by worn lay-shaft bearings.

The next unit is the Getrag 260/5 as used in the 323i with the standard five-speed overdrive gearbox. Not much to say about these, but they were replaced in 1985, when the 325i superseded the 323i, by the next version of the 260/5. Wider ratios were robbed from the manual 325e and the gear linkage was revised, replacing the troublesome pressed steel plate gear linkage with the alloy rod type.

Finally, the Getrag 265/5 as used in the 320iS and the M3. There were various different part numbers, but to all intents and purposes they are the same. You can tell a 265/5 because it has a separate bolt-on bell housing.

When a gearbox gets noisy or starts to develop gear selection problems, do not even consider trying to repair it; it is just scrap so do yourself a favour and find a good used one. Now, a word on what gearboxes fit which cars. Four- and six-cylinder gearboxes do not interchange, period. Do you have a car with an M40 engine (1987 on with plastic bumpers) in need of a gearbox? Well, there is a cheap gearbox from a B-registration 318i that looks identical; apart, that is, from the fact that the bell housing bolt pattern is different by a few millimetres here and there and this is enough to make swapping identical looking M10 and M40 gearboxes completely impossible. If in doubt, measure the distance between the top two bell housing bolts on your car and compare this with the one on the gearbox you are about to buy. Even better, remove a gearbox from a car yourself, or see a gearbox still attached to an engine – then you will know.

On six-cylinder cars, the gearboxes from the 325i will fit a 320i, or an older 323i, without a problem. However, you need the complete gearshift assembly, including the gearlever. There is even a metal bracket that bolts to the tunnel of the 325i that holds the linkage in position and you need that too.

Some 323i models came with the five-speed close ratio gearbox where first gear is across to the left and back; this is called a dogleg gearbox. These fit almost any six-cylinder car including later, plastic bumper 325is where there is no timing pick-up in the bell housing. About the time the E34 5 Series came along in mid 1988, BMW abandoned the TDC sensor on the flywheel used on the older chrome bumper, and some very early plastic bumper, 325i models and did it all on the front pulley instead. If you have one of the earlier cars with a black plastic sensor in the bell housing near the clutch slave cylinder you are stuck with this gearbox unless you are really keen, as even replacing a worn gearbox with another one means the same type of gearbox. Some dogleg gearboxes have the lug on the bell housing which you will have to drill, very accurately indeed, as well as drilling and tapping a threaded hole for the retaining bolt. These boxes are 1983 onwards E30 units where the casing was shared with the Motronic 525e. It is possible to

do this, but it is a lot of work and you have to take the gearbox to a specialist machine shop. When swapping a 240 gearbos for a 260, you will need the slightly shorter 323i/325i propshaft.

Is it worth it? Well, the dogleg gearbox has very close ratios and fifth gear is like driving in fourth on your old gearbox. Fuel economy and your nerves will suffer but if you live away from motorways and enjoy driving hard then it is a good thing. Do not forget you will need the complete gear change set-up from the 323i. When swapping gearboxes, you should fit a new rubber coupling for the prop. These are made by SGF and the expensive ones might have the BMW motif on them! When fitting, you will notice some arrows cast into the rubber around the edge. The tip of each arrow must point towards the nut, and not the bolt (shown). If you do not, the coupling will break up in a couple of hundred miles – you have been warned!

Actually changing a gearbox is straightforward, apart from the top starter bolt on six-cylinder cars. On older cars with the big starter motor, removing and replacing this bolt is a horrible nightmare. Later cars, from about 1987, used a smaller starter motor which makes life much easier – but still difficult. When refitting a gearbox, bin the big starter and fit a good second-hand small one.

USED GEARBOX ID CHART

Found a gearbox at a breaker's that you think might be the one? Here is the chart. The gearbox number is stamped into the casing at the front edge of the bell housing. The number is just a serial number; it is the letters on the end in which you are interested.

316 (M10 carburettor) 4 speed	= Getrag 242 LF
316 (M10 carburettor) 5 speed	= MN or BMV (Getrag 240) AY or AW (Getrag 242)
316i/318i (M40) 5 speed	= Getrag 240, BMO, TBCU or BCX
318i (M10) 4 speed	= Getrag 242 LF
318i (M10) 5 speed	= Getrag 240 MD or BMU. Getrag 242 LG
318iS	= Getrag 240 BCO, BCT. Air con cars BCP or TBCU. BCT, BCO, BCP are longer E34 518i units.
320i	= ZF S5-19 THMH, Getrag 240 BMS, MB or BMT
320iS	= Getrag 265 EZ, TCS or HZ
323i	= Getrag 245 GF or GJ (dogleg Sport), 260 NB, TNW, NC or TANC (overdrive)
325e	= Getrag 260 ANO, TNT or NT (April 1986 onwards)
325i	= Getrag 260 NW, TNW, ANB (Standard) or HJ / TNN (Sport)
325iX	= Getrag 260 TNX (overdrive) THB or HJ (Sport)
M3	= Getrag 265 EZ, TCS or HZ. USA Overdrive units TCM and HY

* Note: 240 units do not interchange between M10, M20 or M40

THE GEARLINKAGE – AND HOW TO REPAIR IT

The gear change on the E30 gearbox will eventually wear out. Up until around 1985 the E30s used a gear change that was a shaped steel plate that bolted to the back of the gearbox. It bolted onto two rubber bushed alloy mountings which themselves bolted to the back of the gearbox housing. Not only do the rubber bushes wear out, but also the bolts that hold the plate to the mountings. Also the bolts holding the mountings to the gearbox can come loose and the alloy mountings themselves can break. The bush where the gearlever sits also wears out and by the time it is all worn or loose, getting gears can be a real art form. Finally, the joint that connects the shaft from the gearlever to the gearbox wears out. So, quoting your chassis number to BMW will establish what bits you need and, to be honest, it is such a dirty, horrible job you might as well replace everything – two mountings, new bolts (you can guarantee that one has dropped out in the road if you do not order a new one), a new shift rod to gearbox coupling (order a new spring clip and roll pin as well) plus the spring clip. Buy a new plastic bush where the gearlever sits in the plate too, it is pretty cheap.

On the later cars, BMW used a solid alloy extension that pivots on the back of the gearbox, rather than the earlier type that used the rubber bushed mountings. It is a vastly superior set-up but you cannot fit it to the earlier type gearbox because the rear gearbox casing is different. Again you will need the coupling plus the alloy extension front bush and the white plastic bush where the gearlever sits.

To replace it, you will need to get right under the car so raise the front end and sit it on axle stands. It is a very good idea to disconnect the exhaust down pipe from the exhaust, as is replacing the front prop-shaft coupling. Using a trolley jack and jacking the front of the engine under the sump (using a block of wood to spread the load) raise it three or four inches. This is very helpful as it will drop the back of the gearbox down and give you more room. Open the bonnet though, because if you do not the front engine lifting eye might well dent it from the inside. Take great care not to strain any hoses.

On older types, you can see the bolts that hold the mountings to the gearbox so just undo them. The front coupling is held to the gearbox by a roll pin, and a steel ring that snaps into place secures this. You will need a very small screwdriver to prise the ring out of the way as it can be very fiddly. You may want to take the shift rod off first and can do this by removing the small locating clip. These have a nice habit of springing off, never to be seen again, so buy a couple of new ones before you start.

On the later types, the shift rod fits to the coupling in the same way, but is mounted to the gearbox in a different manner. It uses a steel pin with a clip built in that you have to prise from the gearbox and move sideways. Once it is all out on the floor you can clean everything up and fit the new bits, using grease on all the moving parts.

This is a fiddly and often frustrating job, which is why it is never worth replacing just one part. Most E30s on their original front rubber prop-shaft coupling are ready for a new one so you could do that at the same time. But once it is all back together, the difference in gearshift quality is remarkable.

Post '85 gearlinkage. Components 4 and 13 are the standard parts that need replacing

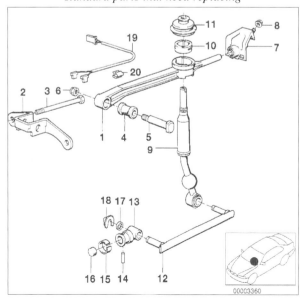

Pre '85 gearlinkage mounting. The front of the steel mounting plate (5) is fitted to the gearbox on rubber mounts which break.

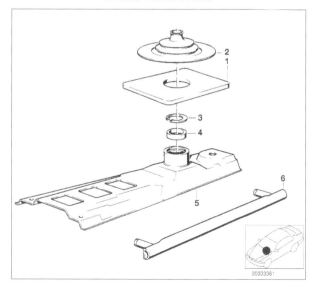

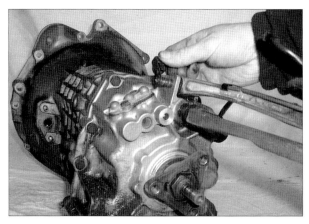

1985 onwards gearlinkage front joint

GEARBOX MAINTENANCE

All you can really do is to drain the old oil and refill it with new every couple of years. Using synthetic gear oils is a very good idea, but before you drain the old oil, make very sure that you can remove the refill plug! If you cannot, you would not be the first!

AUTOMATIC GEARBOXES

Automatic gearboxes? Well, any problems and they are best binned and replaced with a good used one. Signs of a dying automatic gearbox are a reluctance to change up from first gear when used initially (sticking governor), slipping in reverse and engaging second gear with a violent thud. Some can also be reluctant to engage first or reverse when cold unless you give the throttle a quick prod in N or P. All these are signs that the automatic gearbox is not long for this world. Mind you, any weird symptoms on cars with the switchable sport/economy auto box can be down to corrosion in the ECU plug in the side of the gearbox. Older auto boxes use a kick-down cable to tell the gearbox when to change up or down, but the switchable unit relies on the engine ECU and the gearbox ECU in the boot (next to the aerial) telling the electronic solenoids inside the gearbox what to do. If water gets into that wiring plug, the solenoids either work erratically or they do not work at all. On the switchable automatic gearboxes, any weird behaviour in the way the gearbox works can be down to a faulty gearbox ECU. It lives in the boot and gets cold and damp – an odd clicking noise from the unit is a sign that there's a dry joint in there somewhere and a good used unit is needed.

Torque converters will eventually wear out and the first thing to let go is the lock-up clutch. A properly functioning lock-up clutch will engage at about 53mph. Drive the car gently along a flat road and count the gear changes. At around 53 to 55mph the revs should drop as if it has engaged another gear and that is the lock-up clutch engaging. Tired torque converters will also slip at higher

Oil leaks from the reverse light switch can lose a lot of oil

road speeds almost as if the clutch was slipping on a manual transmission car and sometimes they can emit a rattle at around 1300rpm that sounds like a loose exhaust bracket. When this occurs, its days are numbered.

With these gearboxes you should not run the engine in park or neutral for any length of time. With age and a few miles, they can develop a slight cross leak from the oil pump to the forward clutch, applying slight pressure when in neutral. This partially engages the forward clutch, which can overheat and damage the clutch plates inside. Revving the engine in P or N will make things worse and you would not be the first to do a bit of engine tuning and find that you have no forward drive and a ruined gearbox. Therefore, when stuck in traffic, resist the temptation to slip it into P or N as it will do it no good at all. Likewise, when running the engine for engine work (bleeding the cooling system or whatever), raise the back wheels off the ground, handbrake off and in Neutral. This then takes the pressure off. In fact, you might find that the rear wheel turn slightly and this is a sure sign that the oil cross leak is engaging the forward clutch. But because the wheels are turning, it is not harming it – but do avoid revving the engine.

Oil leaks from these gearboxes are not common but the big disaster leak is the front oil seal where the torque converter fits. The oil pump is just behind here and the oil pressure is pretty great. These seals have a habit of just failing. Sometimes the seal will overheat and stick to the converter and will spin its way out of the gearbox but whatever happens, a big leak of automatic gearbox oil from the bottom of the bell housing is bad news. It's a gearbox out job to fix it and none of the additives that claim to stop gearbox oil leaks will halt this one.

Automatic gearboxes also have oil filters. Draining the oil and removing the bottom pan reveals the filter screen and it is a couple of Torx bolts to change it, but do not forget the rubber O-ring. When removing the bottom pan, spray penetrating fluid around the securing bolts as corroded ones can snap off.

When exchanging gearboxes, swap like for like. For example, if you own a 325i do not buy a gearbox from a 525e or 325e just because it is only twenty quid, it will not do. A 1986 320i automatic gearbox will fit a 1984 323i for example, but I would always try to find the gearbox from the correct model.

Automatics also have an oil cooler and it's built into the bottom of the radiator. The steel pipes running to the oil cooler will eventually rust, and keeping them clean and rust-proofed is a very good idea.

Beware the bolts that secure the autobox to the engine, the two long ones can seize in the bellhousing. Using a grinder to cut into the gearbox is often the only way. When fitting a gearbox always fit the autobox and torque converter together - never try to fit the converter to the engine first.

Finally, changing the oil. To do this involves undoing the drain plug in the bottom of the pan and letting the old oil out. This still leaves old oil in the torque converter so what you might want to do is refill it with new oil, run the engine for a few minutes, stop the engine and drain it again. Refill the gearbox again, run the engine, drain it and finally refill. This will get virtually all of then old oil out. It is not essential, but some view maintenance in different ways to others. Refill the gearbox through the dipstick tube, the refill capacity being 3 litres of ATF. The

Automatic transmission with Electro-hydraulic control system.

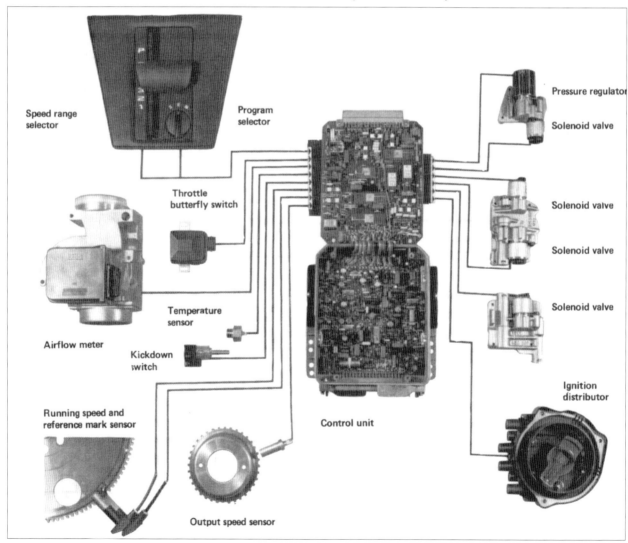

74

The front prop coupling. The arrows must point towards bolt heads, not nuts

The centre propshaft joint. Note paint marks added to ensure correct reassembly

total oil capacity for the four-speed auto is 7.5 litres. That shows how much is held in the torque converter and various parts of the gearbox. To check the level, fire the engine up, have the car standing on perfectly level ground in P or N, withdraw, clean and refit the dipstick. Pull it out again and check that the oil is close to the maximum level. If it is above the maximum, drain about half a litre and check again. If it is only just above the minimum, add half a litre.

PROP-SHAFT

Prop-shafts are the same design for all E30 cars, bearing in mind that the front half of the automatic prop-shaft is shorter. Prop-shafts go on for a long time but there are three main problems:

1) The front rubber coupling eventually cracks and will in time disintegrate and they look like a ball of string with bits hanging out everywhere. When they get really bad, you will feel a vibration on acceleration and often on deceleration too. Automatics seem more prone to vibration on deceleration because there is no engine braking. When they finally let go, the prop-shaft does not fall off because the pilot bearing holds it, but you will get a terrible knocking noise when pulling away. SGF made this coupling with some bearing a cast-in BMW badge, although they are more expensive than those from aftermarket suppliers. Changing a rubber coupling (or doughnut) means dropping the exhaust from the manifold, removing the heat shield (8 x 13mm bolts), removing six 16mm or, more commonly, 17mm nuts and bolts and removing also the two 13mm bolts holding the propshaft centre bearing. When fitting the new coupling, look round the outer edge for small arrows. Do not ignore these. You will see that the arrows point in different directions and each arrow must point towards a flange (see picture). If they don't, the coupling will be stressed incorrectly and could break up within 200 miles.

2) Centre bearings last a long time but not forever. The inner bearing race can get slack and noisy, leading to a weird noise under the base of the rear seat and the rubber supporting the bearing race can crack and break up. When this happens you will get a bad thudding noise when accelerating and general prop-shaft vibration. It is often a good idea to change the centre bearing when you do a prop-shaft coupling and vice versa. To change one, taking the prop-shaft right off is advisable – it involves only another four bolts on the differential flange. Mark the relation of the front and rear prop-shaft halves, to maintain factory prop-shaft balance, and unscrew the large collar nut. Then you can pull the two halves apart. That done, it is easy to remove the bearing retaining circlip and drift the old bearing from the prop-shaft.

3) Universal joints. With the prop-shaft off, move the joints and feel for any stickiness. In particular, joints often develop a "notch" around the straight-ahead and that's not good. Getting some spray grease behind the seals on the yokes will relieve it, but once you have done this, refit the prop-shaft and be prepared to look for another one when the rear universal joints start to get noisy.

When the prop-shaft is due to come off – for a new front coupling for example – you might as well order a new front centring sleeve. This fits in the front of the prop-shaft and is a nice, snug fit on the gearbox output shaft. It is there to locate the prop-shaft perfectly and give the coupling an easier time, but they do wear out. Driving around with a disintegrating coupling will wear the bush out and a new coupling will not last too long if this bush is worn. To replace them, pack the hole in the bush with grease – really fill it up. Then use a 14mm diameter bar, place it in the hole and give it a good whack with a hammer. The hydraulic effect will push the bush out but if it is obstinate, use a hammer and small chisel to break it up. The new one just presses in with a bit of lubrication.

A few more pointers on prop-shafts – it is often a lot easier to put a jack under the gearbox and remove the rear gearbox mounting cross member altogether. Before tightening the centre prop-shaft bearing bolts, push the assembly forward about 2mm to put a slight tension on the bearing before tightening it. When replacing the prop, bear in mind that they differ in length: 318i, 320, 325i, M3. They are not the same length!

FINAL DRIVES

With the E30 come two basic types of differential, the small one and the big one. The small differential is unique to the E30 and is recognised by having six bolts to hold the rear alloy cover to the differential casing. Also the oil drain plug is not directly below the oil filler plug, but the only bolt along the bottom edge of the differential is. Legend has it that big differentials began to be fitted in 1985 when the 325i appeared, but it seems that earlier cars fitted with limited slip differentials used the big casing with eight bolts for the rear cover. On these big units, the oil drain plug is directly below the filler plug. Towards the end of the 323i production run, big differentials were being fitted that were not limited slip. At first, I thought that BMW introduced the big unit with the 150bhp engine in late 1983 but I have now seen enough 150bhp cars made in 1984 to disprove this. However, 323i models made as far back as June 1984 with an LSD use a big differential. My 1985 323i automatic had a big differential but it also had the last type of LE Jetronic with no cold start injector. 323i models began using the big differential in around May/June 1984. All 320i models use the small differential and it might surprise you to learn that the LSD on the 320i is the small type – it is also used on the 318iS and any other four-cylinder (non M3) E30, albeit with different ratios. There's much talk of the letter S on the LSD, but this is in fact a letter S stamped into the ID tag on the differential.

As for the big differential, it is based on the E28 5 Series unit; in fact the casing is the same. The rear alloy cover is different and so are the output shafts, which are bigger.

To use an E28 differential (also used on post 1982 6 Series) in an E30, you need to change the rear cover and also the output shafts. These are removed with two tyre levers and a bit of force to overcome the internal spring clips fitted. E28 LSDs can be bought from a scrap yard for a few quid, whereas E30 ones are quite rare and can be pricey and output shafts from a standard differential will fit an LSD and vice versa. Elsewhere is a table of which differentials came from which car – a 524td limited slip differential is the same unit as an M3 Sport Evo and Evo II. Your only problem is finding one as they were never sold in Britain! The most common E28 LSD's are from the 535i and M535i and these are of no use. They used the very big casing also used on the 635CSi. It will physically fit an E30, but you can't use E30 output shafts. You can recognise these diffs by the number of bolts securing each side cover - 6 bolts on the E30 and small E28 diff (518i-528i), 8 bolts on the big 535i/635CSi unit. The only 6 series LSD you can use is the rare 628CSi unit.

Final drive maintenance is easy because it just involves draining the old oil and refilling it with new. Very few cars that left the dealer network have had the final drive or gearbox oil changed and sometimes the drain plugs and refill pugs can be hard to shift. The golden rule is to tackle the refill plug first, because if the drain plug comes undone, draining the oil, and the refill plug does not, you are in trouble. Limited slip differentials require special oil – use standard gear oil and it will not be an LSD for long.

If you have any problems with the differential the best solution is to throw it away and fit a better one. If it is a rare LSD then by all means have it rebuilt, but the only thing you can do at home is to replace the output shaft oil seals and paint it. Even changing the front pinion oil seal is a problem because of the collapsible spacer – get it wrong and the preload on the bearings will be wrong and the differential will be noisy.

Chapter 8

ENGINE TYPES

THE M10 ENGINE

The M10 engine used in the E30 powered the chrome bumper 318i and the carburettor 316 cars until September 1988. It is a direct descendant of the engine seen in 1962 with the first BMW 1500 and uses an iron block, alloy cylinder head with 'hemi' combustion chambers and a single, chain driven overhead camshaft. Over the years, a few of the 'nice' bits were robbed from the M10. The forged steel crankshaft was replaced by a grey cast-iron crank in around 1980, and the camshaft drive chain was reduced from a twin-row Duplex to a single-row chain at around the same time.

Even so the M10 is a class act. The 1766cc (1.8) version powered both the 316 and the 318i and the carburettor version with a very restrictive carburettor gave 90bhp when a 2-litre Ford engine was doing around 98bhp. The M10's trump card is strength and reliability. Even with

The M10 - 316 engine

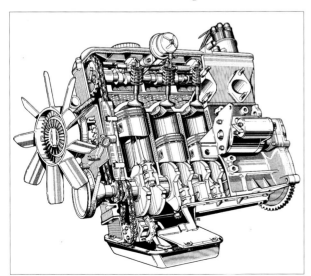

appaling neglect it will rattle on almost forever and it doesn't really have any weak points. Continued neglect of the anti freeze strength will eventually lead to corrosion in the cylinder head water jackets, resulting in a major head gasket failure. The timing chain will be quite stretched at 150,000 miles, and the top chain wheel on the camshaft can wear badly. The block can sometimes crack across a cylinder head bolt hole, but this is normally due to the head bolts being refitted after a cylinder head job and the bolt holes not being cleared of oil. Water pumps are reliable, the camshaft oil spray bar doesn't work loose but neglect of oil changes will lead to the oil holes blocking and starving the camshaft of oil.

Given 6000-mile oil and filter changes, plus reasonable care, the M10 will sail past 200,000 miles. The 316 was also saddled with a dreadful carburettor which was a whole barrel of trouble but the 318i used either Bosch K Jetronic (pre-September 1983 and very rare now) or Bosch LE Jetronic which is pretty reliable.

After 210,000 miles, this 316 crank
was still unworn

THE M20 ENGINE

The M20 six-cylinder engine had a pretty rough start to life. First introduced in the 1977 E21 320/6, it was initially called the M60 and was available as a carburettor 2 litre or a 2.3 litre with Bosch K Jetronic in the 323i. Cylinder head problems were rife and the biggest problem was the head cracking just underneath the camshaft journals. This allowed coolant to pass from the water jacket that ran along the length of the head into the area around the camshaft, mixing water with oil to form the most ungodly mess. BMW worked hard to improve things, making the area between the water jacket and the camshaft thicker but it is a problem that persisted until the very last M20 engine was made in 1993.

For the E30, the M60 was renamed M20 and the M60 tag was later used on the 3- and 4-litre V8 engines. BMW improved the head design on the M20, giving it bigger inlet and exhaust ports, which improved power at the expense of low down torque.

Today, the M20 engine is well known for the cylinder head cracking and it still happens. There is no rhyme or reason for it and heads crack at various mileages and it is not dependant on servicing either. I have seen some shocking 325i models with oil like treacle and 150,000 miles but still on the original head without problems. The

325i seems more prone to this than the 2 litres for some reason but the earlier 320i and 323i cars could be a bit grim as well. Checking the manufacture date on the cylinder head is a good indication of whether the car has had any cylinder head action in the past.

Like the M10, the bottom end of an M20 is very strong and most 150,000-mile 325i models are still fighting fit and ready for more action. Be aware that the 325iX has a different cylinder block to the other cars so an engine transplant is a lot trickier.

S14

This four-cylinder engine was a 16-valve, twin camshaft unit used in the M3 and the 320iS. Based on a modified M10 2-litre block (the two are not interchangeable), the S14 was a pure race engine with steel crank and rods, forged pistons, duplex timing chain and higher quality steel used for the valves and shimmed tappet buckets. Various states of tune were used on the 2.3 version, which is the most common, plus there was the 2.5 litre version used in the 1990 Sport Evolution and a highly tuned 2-litre for the Italian and Portuguese market only 320iS.

The big bone of contention with the S14 is the timing chain. A few years back, some BMW specialists decided it would be a good idea to put about a rumour that M3 timing chains would break if left for over 100,000 miles.

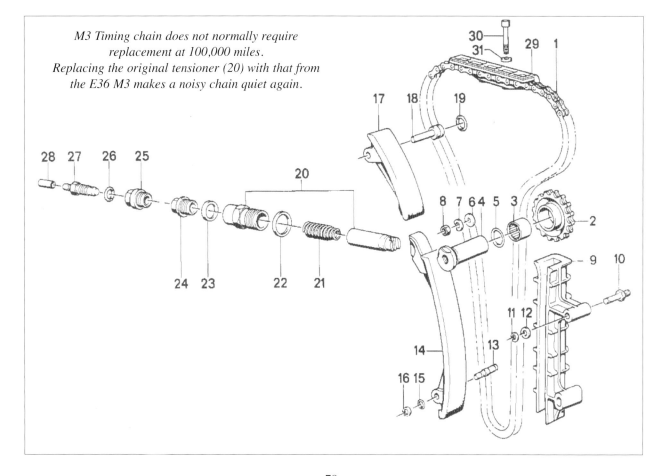

M3 Timing chain does not normally require replacement at 100,000 miles.
Replacing the original tensioner (20) with that from the E36 M3 makes a noisy chain quiet again.

Let us state here and now that this is not true, although it has become folklore. The whole timing chain thing is due to the rather ineffective hydraulic chain tensioner used on these engines. This relies on oil pressure to tension the chain and they can take a couple of seconds to pump up, leading to chain rattle on start up. Some even get so weak that the chain rattles at idle. The cure for this is simple and cheap and involves fitting the screw-in tensioner from the later E36 M3 that uses the same timing chain as the old E30! This new improved tensioner tensions the chain even when the engine is not running and will make a real rattle bag quiet again. Of course, a car where the chain has been rattling away for some years will need a new chain and most likely a new crankshaft chain sprocket as well.

Talk to most M3 mechanics, such as Nigel Moseley and Peter Walsh, and they will tell you that they have never seen a chain break. Someone who wants to take £1500 plus from you will tell a different story. At the end of the day, it is down to you. Of course, any timing chain will be worn at 100,000 miles but if an E36 tensioner makes it silent, forget about it. Replacing the top guide rail (29) is a very good idea too, and cheap.

The S14 is a very, very strong engine built for serious abuse and bottom end problems are rare. Crankshaft, bearing or piston problems are almost unheard of on well maintained engines, but when the engine starts to burn oil, and when the oil lights takes longer to go out in the morning than it used to, it is best to strip and rebuild it before it goes bang. Contrary to popular opinion, the S14 engine is simple to remove and not complex to work on. Think of it as an M10 with an extra camshaft, plus an additional eight valves, and you are not far adrift. Jobs like shimming the valve clearances and setting the camshaft timing need care though.

THE M40 ENGINE

Every car manufacturer builds at least one dud engine. The M40 Series as fitted to the plastic bumper E30 316i and 318i was BMW's lemon. As a brand new engine out of the box it wasn't bad at all. It was a bit livelier than the old M10 and it supposedly weighed less. In theory it required less maintenance, due to having hydraulic tappets, but the theory proved wrong and most M40s sound like a bag of nails. This engine has many problems. Firstly the valve gear is troublesome. The camshaft wears out as well as being horribly noisy. The problem can also manifest itself in a refusal to rev over 4500 to 5000rpm and the worn out camshaft lobes just cannot open the valves wide enough – engines which are otherwise quiet can suffer this problem. Then the camshaft can wear out in the traditional way with the sides of the lobes wearing flat, giving rise to the 'clack clack clack' sound. Then we've got the hydraulic tappets. These fail on a regular basis and, unlike tired hydraulic tappets on

most engines, they can get noisier as the oil warms up. And, again unlike most engines, additives just do not work and can often make them even worse.

The answer is of course to replace the tappets but, without the special tool to remove the rockers, this involves removing the camshaft, which leads to another can of worms. Removing the camshaft means removing the camshaft belt and that is regarded as an absolute DIY no-no unless you have the special tools to set the camshaft timing and set the belt tension, although you can do it without them. On the 320i and 325i engines, a camshaft belt change is possible without special tools and you can adjust the belt tension by letting the spring on the tensioner roller do the work. On the M40 engine, changing the cam belt is probably easier than on an M20 but words of caution. You don't really need the special tools like the prophets of doom will tell you, but you need to be careful. The belt is tensioned by an eccentric roller and unless the old cambelt was virtually falling off it's an idea to mark its position with Tippex before releasing the nut. That way you can adjust it back with the Allen key to exactly where it was before and tighten the nut. As a rule of thumb, the cam belt should have 10mm of slack along its longest run. Another tip is to tension the belt using just your thumb on the Allen key. When you can't press any harder without hurting your fingertip, you're about right! Also, mark everything with Tippex; the crank position (get it to TDC first!), cam position.....everything. Leave nothing to chance because there are no cam timing marks. Summing up? The M40 cambelt is ideally

An M40 engine - air filter is not standard

*A well worn 325i head - when they are this rough,
complete overhaul is the only answer*

replaced with the special tools by a dealer or specialist, but the value of the cars doesn't allow that luxury too often.

Engines with noisy camshafts and tappets are best driven until they give up and then you can stand back and take a view as to whether it is worth spending money or just throwing the car away.

Water pumps, unlike those fitted to the old M10 engine, fail at varying intervals but they do not gradually develop play, they let go suddenly. BMW, in their infinite wisdom, designed the alloy water pump as a reasonably tight fit inside the iron cylinder block. This means that, after a few years, the pump really does not want to come out. Getting to the stage where the water pump can be pulled out takes about 20 minutes and BMW even provided threaded holes in the pump body. The idea was to screw in bolts and ease the pump out by winding these bolts in but all that happens is that the

The M21 Diesel Engine

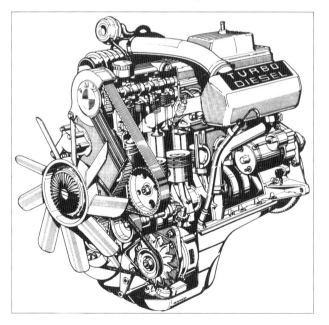

ears of the pump break off. Even carefully applied violence can break the pump body in two, leaving the inner part of the body in the block. Getting it out needs care to avoid dropping bits of alloy into the water jacket – it really is a total pain.

Oil leaks. The M40 gained a reputation early on for leaks. The crankshaft front oil seal, camshaft oil seal and the sump gasket all leak. The last one can be lived with, the first two cannot as the camshaft belt will be soaked in oil and will soon fail.

Camshaft belts. These should be replaced NO LATER than 25,000 miles and many experts say change them at 20,000 miles. Like a Ford CVH, it is very fussy and if the belt breaks, it is goodbye engine.

My verdict? If you have a quiet M40, then get the belt changed by a dealer or a well-equipped specialist and pray. Avoid a noisy M40 engine if you can – a 320i is not much worse on petrol and it is so much better as a car. Later Tourings and Convertibles were M40 only of course, so if you really must own a 316i or 318i, be careful and do not buy one with a noisy top end. With a good M40, change the oil every 5000 miles using synthetic oils – Castrol Magnatec seems particularly suited to the M40. Change the rollers at every other belt change and change the front oil seals every second belt change. That way you stand a good chance of the engine lasting.

As for the M40, it survived the E30 and lived on in the 518i and E36 3 Series up until 1994. Then it was replaced by the vastly improved M43 that was the M40 but with a chain driven camshaft and a revised camshaft and follower layout. Apart from the odd head gasket failure, it is a good engine; but that's not much consolation, is it?

THE M42 ENGINE
This little jewel has been described as a poor man's S14 and all the ingredients are there; steel crankshaft, twin camshafts and 16 valves, plus chain drive for the camshafts. Unlike the M40 on which it was based, the M42 1.8 is a tough old thing that will take quite a lot of neglect but, like any engine, it does have its problems in old age. The best known of these is the dreaded profile gasket that sits at the front between the head and the timing chain cover keeping oil and water separate. When this gasket fails, oil and water will mix and one of the early signs is a bad oil leak from the front of the engine. It is a cylinder head off job to replace the gasket, but once repaired with the latest type of gasket (introduced with the 1.9 litre M44) it will not fail again. Timing chains are also a moot point and, like the M3, a new tensioner will cure most of the problems. By 150,000 miles though, the chain is on borrowed time so at that mileage you can

either get it done, or keep going until it dies. Used engines are available and it is possible to fit a later E36 engine or the even later 1.9 units.

THE M21 ENGINE

This engine was fitted to the 324d and 324td and was based on the M20 petrol engine. However, everything is different, although parts like the flywheel and connecting rods are the same. Being compression ignition, the cylinder head design is very different and so are the pistons. The crankshaft is similar to the petrol unit and was a forged steel item, later used by Alpina for their 2.7 litre engines. As an engine it is very tough, particularly the 324d without a turbocharger. Low stressed and not very powerful, it will eventually succumb to old age and the poor maintenance suffered by old diesels. Camshaft belts need to be replaced every 25,000 miles and this procedure is the same as on the petrol M20, although it has a longer belt to drive the diesel pump. The engine also has piston oil cooling by way of oil jets at the bottom of each cylinder. The cylinder head is a flat design with no combustion chambers and the compression ratio is 22:1. Because diesel engines do not have a proper manifold vacuum, the M21 used a vacuum pump driven off a camshaft lobe.

ENGINE MAINTENANCE AND REPAIRS

REPAIRS POSSIBLE WITH THE ENGINE IN PLACE.

Nobody takes engines out for fun and in particular a six cylinder E30 is an engine you want to leave in the car. To get the engine out, you don't have to remove it separately from the gearbox, as there is just about room to pull the engine and gearbox out in one lump. On the four-cylinder cars there is enough room to remove the engine to gearbox top bolts but on sixes it is pretty hard work. Another way is to remove the front suspension cross member, complete with the lower wishbones and the steering rack, whilst the engine is suspended on an engine crane. The complete engine and gearbox can then be lowered down out of the car and pulled forward but you need to get the car three or four feet off the ground and the car will be immobile until you refit the suspension bits.

Removing the sump

You might need to do this for a variety of reasons – leaking sump gasket, replacing the oil pump or renewing big end bearing shells. On both the four- and six-cylinder cars you will need to raise the engine with an engine hoist so that the sump will clear the oil pick up pipe and strainer. If all you have is a slight weep of oil from the rear of the sump, firstly remove the rear reinforcing cover at the back of the sump that bolts up to the bottom

The best way to remove the 6 cyl. engine.

of the gearbox bell housing. Very often, removing this cover will reveal 10mm sump bolts which have come loose so cleaning the area and tightening the bolts again will often cure this.

Replacing big end bearings

To be honest, when the engine starts making a noise from the bottom end, the time for slipping in a new set of bearing shells will be long gone. With the sump off you can easily remove the big end caps and look at the state of the bearing shells. BMW cranks are very tough but if the crankpins look a bit rough, it is party over. With the oil cleaned off, a good test is to rub a penny across the width of the crank pin. If any of the copper from the coin is left on the crankpin, it needs a regrind. There are stories from individuals with 600 grade strips of emery polishing the crank pins in situ but it is not ideal. You might remove the scratching but the crank pins will probably be slightly oval. It is one way of keeping an ailing engine going, along with some thick oil and additives, but you must never, ever re-use the connecting rod bolts. They are stretch bolts to be used once only. Re-use them and they will break, simple as that.

Replacing pistons

Well, with the cylinder head and sump removed, it is possible to take out the pistons and con rods. But why would you want to do things this way? By the time things have got this bad, you might as well hire an engine crane and just pull the whole engine out – indeed, you might as well just fit another engine and be done with it. But anything is possible – maybe you do not have the room to pull the engine out.

Removing the engine

On four-cylinder cars, including the M3, there is enough room to get at the bell housing bolts connecting the

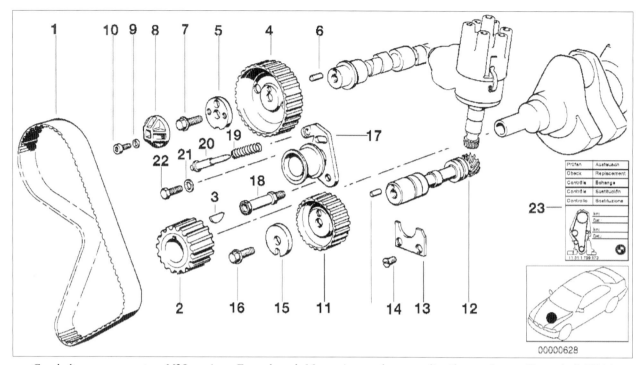

Cambelt arrangement on M20 engine. Even though Motronic cars have no distributor, the auxiliary shaft (12) is unchanged, components 5, 7, 8, 9 and 10 are replaced by a rotor arm on Motronic cars.

engine to the gearbox and you can lift it out of the top. I once bought a 1985 316 for its engine and drove it 20 miles back to remove the engine. The exhaust manifold was still warm to the touch after the engine was out of the car and on the ground! On the six-cylinder cars though, it is not so easy to get the engine out, you don't have to remove the gearbox (manual or auto) first but you remove it as one unit. The easiest way is to drop the whole engine and gearbox out of the bottom of the car. You will need the front of the car about three feet off the ground at the front and the engine's weight supported with a hoist, block and chain or an engine crane. You will need to remove the front wheels and split the ball joints for the front lower suspension wishbones and the steering rack. The engine mounts will need to be undone followed by disconnecting the steering column joint from the rack. Disconnect power steering pipes, if fitted, and then the four bolts holding the back of the wishbones to the chassis. Then it is a case of removing the four bolts that hold the cross member to the front chassis legs and it will all lower down and out of the way. This lot will take you about an hour and a half and once done, the exhaust can be dropped off the manifold without having to separate the sections – the down pipe nuts will be much easier to see and remove as well. From here, you disconnect the prop-shaft from the back of the gearbox, unplug the engine loom and undo the starter wiring and coolant hoses. Support the gearbox on a trolley jack and undo the gearbox cross member nuts. Now you can lower the engine down a few inches- looking for bits you forgot to disconnect – and lower the gearbox as well.

The beauty of doing it this way is that all the nightmare jobs like the starter bolts (you cannot separate the engine from the gearbox with them in place) and getting the gearbox back on are vastly easier. You can build up the complete engine and gearbox as one unit with ease and then lift it back in place. It is still hours of backbreaking toil but somehow it's a nicer way of doing things.

CAMBELT CHANGE, M20 SIX-CYLINDER

All six-cylinder E30 engines were of the M20 type, and they all have a camshaft belt. These should be changed at about 30,000 miles, although some owners do it at 25,000 or even 20,000 miles. It's a job for a skilled mechanic with plenty of experience – or an inexpensive job for a BMW dealer on Four Plus (BMW's GB's servicing scheme for cars older than 4 years), or a very well regarded specialist as there are many areas where mistakes can be made. The manual transmission 320i and 323i cars are easiest as you can quickly remove the radiator to get a lot more room. On the automatic cars, you have gearbox oil cooler pipes to consider and if they look a bit rusty, I would not touch them. Taking the bonnet off an E30 is a ten-minute job that makes life a lot easier, whether or not you have got to keep the radiator in.

Motronic cars are also difficult. There is a TDC sensor cable that goes across the front of the upper camshaft belt cover and it is held in with two plastic clips that just love to break. Order two new ones beforehand as these clips are very important. As for the camshaft belt replacement, it goes like this:

1. Drain the coolant from the engine. You just remove the bottom hose from the radiator.

2. Remove the radiator if you want to – it is advisable if you have not done one of these belts before, but watch those automatic gearbox oil cooler pipes! On older cars it is just one 10mm nut and bolt, on later cars like the 325i, you have a plastic retainer and two 10mm bolts. Undo the hoses and lift the radiator out.

3. Remove the viscous fan coupling which has a left hand thread – i.e. it undoes by turning the big 32mm nut clockwise. A sharp blow on the spanner frees them off.

4. Remove the distributor cap – on Motronic cars it is three 8mm bolts, on others it is two screws on the cap, which actually hook over retaining clips on the distributor body. Remove the rotor arm and black plastic dust shield on Motronic cars - the three Allen bolts are very tricky.

5. Remove the top camshaft belt cover – it is one 10mm bolt which can also secure a hose retaining bracket and one 13mm. Also, slacken the 13mm nut on the alternator bracket and jiggle the cover out, along with the rubber side cover. Let these parts soak in cleaner whilst you are doing the job as they are always filthy and oily.

6. Now remove belts for both the alternator and the power steering pump (if fitted). The bottom 13mm nut and through bolt for the alternator are difficult to get to, but if the top bracket is slackened, the alternator can often be moved by force. See the 19mm toothed nut on the bracket? By slackening the 13mm through bolt, the idea is that you can turn the 19mm toothed nut and the alternator will move. This rarely happens because the teeth on the bracket are usually badly worn. On the power steering pump two 13mm bolts and the toothed 19mm will get it moving. Removing the air flow meter and air cleaner assembly is advisable, and easy.

7. Now you can remove the six 13mm bolts that hold the pulley and damper onto the front of the crank. The pulley is balanced to the crank and on reassembly it can be refitted in any position – unlike the damper that uses a dowel to locate it. Therefore, mark the pulley to the damper. Once the six bolts are out, the pulley and damper can be jiggled off – it can take a little bit of effort with a big screwdriver.

8. Now we have to set the crank and camshaft timing. Thoroughly clean the crank pulley hub, the camshaft

The bottom mark must line up with the notch in the block

The top timing mark, M20

The wonderful 320i/323i distributor. They seize into the block and the advance mechanism can seize too

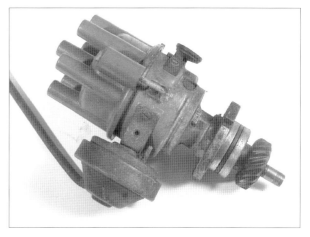

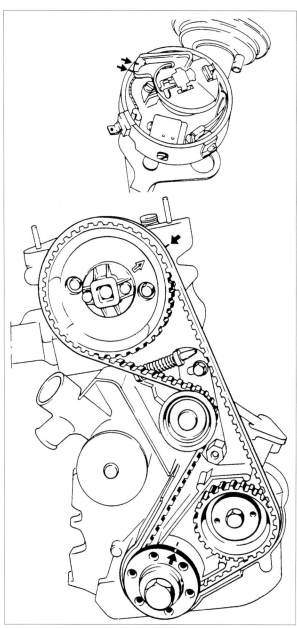

Installing the new cam belt

pulley and the front of the cylinder head. Turn the engine over on the front crank bolt until the line on the crank pulley hub sits in the middle of the V-cut into the alloy casting. On the right-hand side of the cylinder head is an engraved line, it and the line on the camshaft pulley should be aligned. If it is slightly out (i.e. one tooth on the pulley), a previous expert wrongly fitted the camshaft belt. If it is miles out, turn the engine over one revolution, bring the crank back into position and the camshaft marking will line up. On older 320i/323i engines with a pressed steel camshaft pulley you will know when the camshaft is in the right position as the two holes in the pulley will line up with two 10mm bolts that hold the camshaft oil seal retainer – there is still a mark on the pulley and a mark on the head though. On

cars except the 325i and later Motronic 320i, the position of the third, auxiliary pulley that operated the distributor is absolutely vital because the distributor has a habit of seizing into the block. If the auxiliary pulley is moved, the ignition timing will be wrong and if you cannot move the distributor, you are in trouble! Mark both the pulley and the position of the rotor arm on the distributor.

9. Now remove the old belt. It is just one 13mm bolt and a long stud to remove the tensioner and the belt then just comes off.

10. Have a good clean up around this area – use aerosol carburettor or brake cleaner and get this area nice and clean. If it was very oily then you will have to remove the front cover and fit a new crankshaft oil seal – boring as it means removing the auxiliary shaft pulley. If there is evidence of oil leaking from the camshaft oil seal, that is easy as it is just two 10mm bolts and the seal carrier comes off. Replace the oil seal and the O-ring though and use plenty of grease on refitting the seal assembly to the camshaft to avoid damaging it.

11. Now fit the new belt. Fit it to the bottom pulley first and make very sure the belt teeth engage in the pulley teeth. Fit the tensioner, fit it on full spring pressure, as if the belt was un-tensioned, and fit the belt around the camshaft pulley and the auxiliary pulley. Get hold of both sides of the belt just above the crank pulley and try to pull it – very often it will move as the belt moves around and the belt teeth engage.

If the crankshaft, camshaft and auxiliary pulleys are in exactly the right place, slacken the tensioner bolts and the tensioner will spring into position, tensioning the belt. Tighten the tensioner bolts and turn the engine two complete revolutions. If the belt is okay and the timing marks are spot on, the belt is on correctly.

For belt and braces, refit the crank pulley and damper with a couple of bolts and spin the engine over on the starter. Recheck the timing again.

12. If it is all okay, put it back together. An old washing-up bowl full of engine degreaser to soak the oily bits in is important to anybody who likes to do things right as it is so much better reassembling clean parts. Remember to use a medium thread lock on the six front pulley bolts.

Replacing camshaft chain, M10 engines
Over a period the timing chain will stretch and the teeth on the top camshaft sprocket will wear. The result is a chain that really 'jangles' at idle and can sound like a diesel. You have got two choices – either fit a really

strong spring in the tensioner (or the original spring spaced out with half an inch of small washers!), or for a lasting repair fit new bits.

Before you start this job, you need to check the condition of the top camshaft sprocket. It wears badly on high mileage engines and fitting a new chain to an old, worn out sprocket will make the most terrible rattle at idle – far worse than with the old chain. If it is worn out, you will notice that every other tooth is worn down – i.e. good tooth, bad tooth, good tooth, etc. On really grim ones, the chain links actually eat into the base circle of the sprocket. If it is bad you will need a new one. Good used ones are now rare.

1. Remove the bonnet – it is six bolts, the washer fluid pipe and the bonnet stay. It makes life about a hundred times easier.

2. Remove the bottom radiator hose, drain the coolant and remove the radiator.

3. Remove the viscous fan with a 32mm spanner and remember it is a left hand thread.

4. Remove the camshaft cover.

5. Remove the six bolts and lift off the upper timing cover.

6. Remove the fan belt, unbolt the alternator mounting bracket from the block and move the whole alternator out of the way – best to disconnect the battery too.

7. Turn the engine over until the notch on the crankshaft pulley is lined up with the pointer on the lower timing cover and the notch on the camshaft sprocket is aligned with the mark at the top of the head under the end of the oil spray bar. Handbrake on, in fourth gear, and undo the big nut that holds the pulley on. Reset the marks again (it will have moved slightly), mark everything with paint, knock it out of gear and pull the crank pulley off.

8. Unscrew and remove the chain tensioner – oil will come out so catch it.

9. Now you have to drain the engine oil and remove the lower sump cover – a ring of bolts and it will come off with a slight tap from a mallet. Look up and you will see the bolts that secure the sump to the timing cover. Remove them, plus the external timing cover bolts that go into the block, and remove the cover. Be careful not to damage the sump gasket if possible. The water pump comes off with the timing cover.

10. Now you can undo the four bolts that hold the

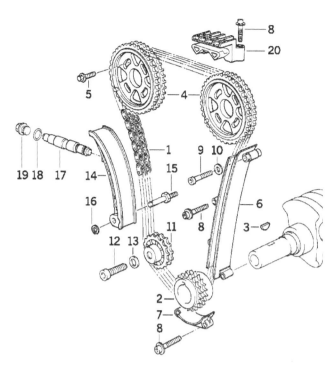

Cam chain, gears and tensioner for the 318iS. Assume almost everything here needs replacing after 150,000 miles, but only a strip down will say for sure.

If the teeth on the cam sprocket are worn (every other tooth) a new chain will still be noisy

camshaft sprocket to the camshaft and remove it, removing the chain from the lower crank sprocket. The lower sprocket tends not to wear badly on the 316/318i, unlike the M3 engine.

11. You have now the choice of fitting a new oil pump drive chain. Most have gone slack so by removing the three 10mm bolts, you can remove the oil pump sprocket, fit a new pump chain and refit it. I recommend using

some serious strength thread lock when refitting the bolts, washing the bolts and the threaded holes in the oil pump with carburettor cleaner. If the new chain is slack, it could well be, you will need some shims from BMW to space the pump downwards, and thus take the slack out of the chain. Oil pumps are pretty long-lived and you could fit a new one – but with an old M10 engined car, where do you stop? You will also need a new O-ring where the oil supply pipe goes into the pump and you may as well fit a new seal where the pipe fits into the block. A tired oil seal on this pipe is often the cause of an oil light that takes ages to go out from a cold start. The part numbers for the shims are 11411250428 for 0.3mm shims and 11411250427 for 0.1mm shims, the number for the timing chain is 11311716986, the camshaft sprocket is 11311265006, oil pump chain 11411716989 and the two seals are 11411250421. You will need a load of gaskets too: a camshaft cover gasket plus timing cover upper gaskets 11141727 978 and 979, timing cover lower gaskets 11141727 980 and 981 and a new sump gasket 11131727974. Although you have not removed the sump, chances are you will break the gasket when the lower timing cover comes off. Cut the front bit off, use the cover for exact dimensions, and use clear silicone sealer to glue it in place of the old damaged bit. The bottom pan gasket is 11131727983 and a new crankshaft pulley oil seal is 11141709632. New tensioner spring is 11310731115. All this lot will come to a fair amount, but you will have a quiet, dry engine.

12. Reassembly is pretty obvious by now and once the chain is back on, along with the lower timing case and the tensioner, recheck the camshaft timing. Use thread lock on the four bolts holding the camshaft sprocket to the cam.

Cam chain replacement – 318iS
I spent a day looking at an old, long dead 318iS engine and managed to figure out how they come apart, but Brendan Purcell of the Irish region BMW Car Club has written all about changing the chain in a far more erudite fashion than I could manage, so he really is the inspiration for this bit. He also replaced the chain and associated bits on his own car, taking pictures along the way, so his bit was written from real-world experience of doing the job. Owners are scared of the 318iS M42 engine but really there is no need because it is not particularly complex. If you are an experienced DIY mechanic and you are both patient and attentive to detail, and cleanliness, then without drama you can do the job in a day.

The bits you will need:
Upper timing case gaskets set 11141721919
Lower timing case gasket set 11141721802
Profile gasket 11141247837
Cam cover gaskets 11121721876, 11121721475 and 3 x 11121721476
Timing chain 11311247160
Crank front oil seal 11141439570
Thermostat housing gasket 11531721172
Tensioner guide rail 11311727342
Guide rail 11311247470
Tensioner 11311743187 and sealing ring 0711 9963355
You will also need a water pump gasket, but it is advisable to fit a new water pump whilst it is apart – a good aftermarket one is only £30 or so.

The job itself
1.) Number one task is to take the bonnet off – for the sake of four 10mm bolts, a clip for the bonnet strut and the washer pipe it makes life so much easier. To remove the bonnet, disconnect the washer fluid hose, unclip the gas strut and close the bonnet but do not push it shut. Remove the four 10mm bolts and off it comes.

2.) Remove the viscous fan with a 32mm socket. It is a left hand thread so standing in front of the car, clout the spanner to the right with a hammer as if you were tightening the bolt up. Remove the fan and the fan shroud. Although Brendan does not mention it, removing the radiator at this point is quick and easy and gives you a bit more room to work and see what is happening.

3.) Mark the plug leads and remove them along with the park plug cover. Two 10mm nuts hold the steel spark plug lead guide in place and the plastic lead tray can be prised out with a screwdriver.

4.) Remove the camshaft cover – it is fifteen 11mm nuts and the two shorter bolts are in the centre. Disconnect the breather tube as well.

Cams must be set like this at TDC.

5.) Rotate the crankshaft so that the two front (number 1) camshaft lobes are angled towards each other.

6.) Now for the fun part – removing the front crankshaft pulley bolt. These are tightened up to a whopping 230 lb/ft (311nm) and are a complete bastard to shift. If you have a seriously big compressor an air gun might shift it, but most are not capable. Either way you will need a serious 22mm six pointed impact socket (the black ones) and a big long bar. If you can get hold of a 3/4-inch drive commercial vehicle breaker bar and socket you might be in luck but as Brendan points out, even with the car in fifth gear and the brakes on you might just slip the clutch. The way to do it is to fit the socket and bar with the end of the bar resting on the left-hand (inlet manifold side) chassis rail with a block of wood in between. Then crank the engine on the starter and that should free it.

7.) Remove the water pump and thermostat housing. Remove the crank and camshaft position sensors – a 5mm Allen bolt and a couple of 10mm nuts.

8.) Locate and remove the small access plug on the engine side of the bell housing, just below the starter motor. Insert an 8mm drill bit into the hole and turn the engine over until the drill bit pops into the hole in the fly-wheel – the engine is now set at TDC. Leave the drill bit in there for now but do not forget it!

9.) Make sure that the camshafts are set – there are squares on the cams and they must be horizontally in line. Clean the area with carburettor or brake cleaner and mark the cams to the head with paint. Also mark the cams to the front chain sprockets.

10.) Remove the front pulley bolt and the pulley. You may need a puller for this, but careful use of a couple of old tyre levers will get it off but do be careful not to break anything. Do not smack it with a steel hammer!

11.) Unbolt and remove the upper and lower timing covers – mostly 10mm but with a couple of 13mm and there are three shorter ones so make a note of where they go.

12.) Release the 19mm chain tensioner, clean the casing thoroughly and fit the new one.

13.) Mark the crank position against the block.

14.) Undo the four 5mm Allen bolts and remove the top and bottom chain guides.

15.) Note the angular position of the camshaft sprocket bolts relative to their slots as the new sprockets need to

Undoing the crankbolt is hard work

This is where the 8mm drill goes.

Use straight edge to ensure cam alignment

*With pulley centre bolt loosened a few turns,
pull the hub off*

Mark crank bottom sprocket to be sure

Cam timing marks (top) and your paint marks

go back on is exactly the same position. Taking out the four 10mm bolts for each sprocket will remove them, so if in doubt just remove one (the chain will come off with it) and refit the new one exactly as it came off. It is an excellent idea to stuff and old towel down the front of the sump to catch those dropped bolts. Remove the crank sprocket with a puller and fit the new one.

16.) Remove the old chain guides and replace with the new ones.

17.) Fit the new chain onto the crank and single camshaft sprocket and finally fit the remaining camshaft sprocket. Before fitting the bolts, clean out the threads in the cams with carburettor or brake cleaner, clean the bolts with the same stuff and apply some mild thread lock to the bolts. Torque them up to 15 lb/ft (20 Nm) but hold the cams still with some suitable grips. Recheck that the crankshaft and two camshafts have not moved. There should be fifteen rivets between them inclusive, arrow-to-arrow. Recheck the squares on the cams with a straight edge if in doubt.

18.) Now to installing the chain tensioner. If you are fitting a new one, you will need to compress it in the vice until it 'clicks'.

19.) You will need to fit the new front crank oil seal now. Hammer the old one out with a hammer and screwdriver, but oil the new one before fitting. Use a suitably large socket or a block of wood to hammer the new one in but remember to hammer it in square. They can be tricky so go easy.

20.) Refit the timing covers. Brendan advises using gasket sealer but I like to use Castrol LM grease. Grease will harden and carbonise as the engine heats up and will form an incredible oil tight seal, plus any inside the engine gets washed away by the engine oil – it is up to you but go sparingly with the gasket sealer – it is ideal for blocking oil strainers and oil ways.

21.) Recheck the camshaft and crank timing AGAIN and refit the crank pulley and its monster bolt. Apply some thread lock and do it up to 230 lb/ft (311 Nm) – or as tight as you can. Use an extension pole on the breaker bar, but put a bit of old carpet on top of the wing – if the breaker bar decides to snap, it will put a dent in the top of the wing.

22.) Pour some clean engine oil over the chain – about half a litre.

23.) Recheck the torque of all eight 10mm bolts holding the sprockets to the cams. And do all eight – it's the one you didn't check that fell out and destroyed the engine.

24.) Refit the camshaft cover with a new gasket (fit it dry) and tighten the nuts/bolts to 9lb/ft.

25.) Refit the water pump and the cam/crank sensors, checking the condition of the O-rings. For both water pump gaskets and the O-rings, grease is a superb sealer.

26.) Refit all the other bits you removed, but REMOVE the 8mm drill bit!! Grease the insides of the hoses lightly where they fit the radiator and water pump, refill the cooling system – basically, reassemble what is left. Slacken the coolant bleed screws on the radiator and the thermostat housing as you refill with three litres of neat anti freeze first, followed by water. Tighten the bleed screws for now.

27.) It is now time to fire up the engine. It will probably rattle like hell for about 30 seconds until the tensioner pumps up but it should then quieten down. When the tensioner kicks in the engine sounds superb. Run the engine until it starts to get hot and then open the bleed screws. When all the air finally escapes and is replaced by running water close the bleed screws and check the heater – it should be set to hot anyway. When hot air is coming from the heater, it has been bled. Run the engine up to full running temperature, shut it off and drain the oil. Replace the oil filter and refill with new oil. Check for oil and coolant leaks; give yourself a slap on the wrist if you do have one and a good pat on the back if all went to plan.

REMOVING THE CYLINDER HEAD

This is well covered in most workshop manuals, but here are a few pointers. Firstly, removing an M20 head is a real drag and the best way is to take it off leaving the inlet manifold in place. That involves locating and removing twelve cleverly hidden 12mm nuts. Getting them back on is fun too. To do some jobs removing the head is essential, a burnt-out valve, broken stud, stripped spark plug thread etc. Some cars use Torx head bolts, others use conventional 17mm bolts but all types need to be replaced with new ones once removed, especially hex types.

The other way is to remove the head with the inlet manifold attached. This is done by disconnecting the injector wiring plugs from the injectors and threading the injector loom back through the centre gap in the manifold. The engine wiring is tie wrapped to a steel trough under the inlet manifold and as long as you make notes of where everything went, it soon comes apart and refitting is not a bad job either.

Removing an M10 318i head is difficult as well because the injection loom is all crammed in there. When skim-

A view of the chain and sprockets
Serious "mayonnaise" like this spells a cracked cylinder head.

Head cracks through the cam journals too

ming an M10 head, the front timing cover that bolts to it MUST be machined with the head. Let us say you machine 20 thou from the head. If you do not skim the front upper timing cover as well, it will be 20 thou deeper and will cause an oil leak once reassembled.

THE CRACKED CYLINDER HEAD PROBLEM

When BMW designed the small six engines in the Seventies, they did not include enough metal above the longitudinal waterway that runs along the length of the head. Because alloy and cast iron expand and contract at different rates during heating and cooling, the head is always under quite a lot of strain. Early M60 type units in the E21s were very bad for head cracking and BMW replaced plenty under warranty.

With the M20 engine that arrived with the E30, BMW added more metal in this area and made the water jackets thicker. They also added 'steam holes' in the head to improve the circulation of hot water on the 2.5 cars, but they still suffer the cracked head problem. As stated previously, there is no set pattern for head cracking problems but when it does happen, it's pricey to put right.

Cracked heads come in two forms. Firstly is the crack from the water jacket upwards. When cold, it is okay but after a few minutes running, the heat generated by combustion heats the head up and the crack expands. Hot water from the cooling system rises up through the crack and starts to mix with the engine oil just under the camshaft – the number one place is between cam journals number six and five, continuing either to journal number four and beyond or ending at the water jacket sealing plug. So, when confronted by water in the oil, do not think for a moment that it is 'just the head gasket' because it is not. With the head stripped and the area between the camshaft journals cleaned, the crack is very, very hard to spot and you may need to get the head crack tested with dye. Some companies weld cylinder heads but it is not ideal. Some of the better welded heads will have been preheated to working temperature and welded with a very extreme welder, which will fully penetrate the crack. The camshaft journals will then have to be re-machined. These higher quality repaired heads can still be expensive though and my money would be on an original uncracked head. When buying a used head, the only way is to find a complete car in the scrap yard with the oil and water still in it. That way you can get a good idea that the head is okay. But basically, if it is clean inside it is probably okay.

The other situation is oil in the water. This means a more severe head crack that is allowing oil back through the crack. This is more serious because oil in the coolant will quickly destroy the hoses. If you have to repair a car with oil in the water, it is absolutely imperative that you replace every coolant hose. Oil quickly eats into the old rubber and they are one hundred per cent guaranteed to explode when up to just above operating temperature – such as in a traffic jam on a hot day.

Another head crack, although not as common, is a crack from the water jacket into one of the ports. On an inlet port, the car will just use water. Oil and water will not mix, it will not overheat, and it will perform as well as ever. But you will be putting water in the header tank every day. This crack is not repairable. The other side of the coin is a crack from the water jacket into an exhaust port. This will cause hot exhaust gas to pressurise the cooling system. The car may not overheat according to the temperature gauge but after a run, you can hear coolant boiling in the block and the hoses will be rock hard. Upon loosening the header tank cap, hot coolant will boil and hiss and try its best to escape. So when you have fitted a new BMW thermostat, made sure the viscous fan is working and the system is properly bled (if the heater pumps out hot air, it is bled) and it still does this, suspect the head. Now, it could be that the gasket is blowing and the only way to find out is to pull the head off and look at the gasket.

M10 engines do not seem to suffer the cracked head syndrome but they can crack between the valves if they have been cooked, i.e. run too hot once too often! These heads are then scrap, but to be honest it does not seem to happen to the M10s fitted to the E30 as much as it did on the old 2002 cars.

I CANNOT AFFORD/JUSTIFY REMOVING THE HEAD – WHAT CAN I DO?

To be brutally honest, not a lot. If you have oil in the water, drain down the cooling system and refill it with an engine cleaner like Gunk or Jizer – use a couple of tins and run the engine for a couple of minutes. Drain the system again, remove one of the heater hoses and run the engine with a garden hose feeding fresh water into the expansion tank. When there is just clean water coming out, refit the hose, drain the system again (use the bottom hose) and add a couple of bottles of liquid leak stopper. Top up the cooling system with anti freeze and fresh water and try your luck – it may work, it may not. But even if it does initially work, it will not be long before it is back to its old tricks again.

REPLACING THE CAMSHAFT

It's been said that you can remove the camshaft without removing the rocker shafts, but let me state here and now that you cannot. I have also seen camshafts replaced without removing the head on M20 engines – it is possible. With the bonnet and radiator off, removing the rocker shafts, rockers and finally the camshaft is no more difficult with the head on the car than it is with the head on a workbench and you avoid the sheer boredom of removing the head. The way to get rocker shafts out is to remove the spring clips on the rockers themselves and use a big screwdriver between the back of the head to move the shafts forward. Then use Mole grips and ease the shafts forward, retrieving the rockers one by one. Eventually you will come to a rocker that is 'rocking' and compressing a valve. Turn the crank over by 45 degrees so that all six pistons are down from the top of the cylinders and then refit the camshaft pulley centre bolt. Use this to turn the camshaft and decompress the spring, removing the rockers as you go. When no compressed valves are left, the shafts should slide out easily. With the rockers out, the camshaft front plate can be lifted out, the oil seal holder removed and the camshaft slid out.

When fitting a new cam, you must always fit new rockers, even if the old ones looked okay. It depends on your conscience if you are just repairing the car to sell on though.

ENGINE SWAPS

Thinking of putting a 2.5 into a 316? Forget it, it is too much work. If you were building a car from a shell then, of course, you could use a 316 shell, but as a conversion job there is too much work involved – engine, gearbox, rear axle, brakes, wiring loom, etc.

Fitting a 318i engine into a 316 is possible but you will need the engine wiring loom. The carburettor and manifold from a 316 does not really fit the 318i engine's bigger ports and there is nowhere to mount the 316's mechanical fuel pump. M10 gearboxes are all the same however. An engine from an E28 518i will fit with the sump and oil pick up pipe from the E30 engine.

On the M40 cars, the 316i and 318i engines can be interchanged without a problem because the gearboxes are the same. Be aware that M10 and M40 gearboxes look the same but they are impossible to fit because the bolt spacing on the bell housing is slightly different. E36 M40 engines will fit after you have fitted the E30 sump and oil pick up pipe, plus the front cover - a lot of work!

320i and 323i LE Jetronic engines will interchange without a problem. Fitting a later 325i Motronic engine is again possible but you will need the complete engine wiring loom.

Be very aware that an E34 engine (1988-90 5 Series) engine is no good because the dipstick fits into the sump (which cannot be used in an E30) and not into the block. An engine from an E28 520i will fit an LE Jetronic 320i with the sump and oil pick up pipe swapped over.

Fitting a plastic bumper 2.5 engine into a Motronic 320i is just plug and play – the engine loom is the same. Use the 320i flywheel and clutch and the 320i gearbox as it is very strong and you need to give it serious grief for it to go bang.

On the M20 engines, the mounting points on the block were revised when the E34 came out. Earlier and later blocks will interchange though but, if in doubt, buy the complete engine with the alloy engine mounts still bolted on.

Servicing and repairs, 324d and 324td

Setting up the injector pump

This is the method for setting up the basic static pump setting:

1.) Set the engine up so that number 1 cylinder is ALMOST at top dead centre (TDC). When TDC occurs, both valves on number 1 are fully closed but the valves on number 6 are overlapping, i.e. one just about closed, other just opening. You want it a few degrees before TDC.

2.) Now remove the plug in the centre of the injection pump and screw in the special BMW adaptor 135330 into the threaded hole for the plug you've just removed and fit a dial gauge with 2-3mm pre loading. The BMW adaptor is pretty important, so you will have to beg, borrow or hire it from your dealer!

3.) Turn the crankshaft over until the dial gauge is at its lowest point, and set the gauge to zero.

4.) Turn the crankshaft (always in direction of engine running rotation which is CLOCKWISE) until TDC occurs. Put the car in gear with the handbrake on so that the crankshaft cannot turn, or in P (park) on automatics. Mark the front pulley if need be.

6.) The dial gauge should now be reading 0.74 + 0.02mm for an engine with a recent camshaft belt change (new, or up to 9000 mile old belt) or 0.76 + 0.02mm for cars with a camshaft belt with 9000 miles or more of service. Correct any wrong values by turning the injection pump until the correct value of 0.74 is achieved.

7.) Adjust this value by loosening the pump mounts and moving the pump. If the value is too big, pull the pump AWAY from the engine block. If the value is too small, move the pump TOWARDS the engine block. Tighten the mounting bolts only in this order. Nut of front flange inside of engine, nut on front flange outside of engine, and lastly the rear nuts. Turn the engine over a couple of complete revolutions and recheck.

Adjusting the idle speed
1 - The locknut
2 - Idle Screw

Setting up the idle speed, hot and cold.

This can be done with or without a special screw-in tachometer, although doing it with one is vital if the car had a clock and not a rev counter!

1.) Start by warming the engine up – go for a five- or ten-mile drive to get the engine up to full temperature.

2.) With all the electrical equipment turned off, heater fan, heated rear window, radio etc, loosen the locknut on the idle speed adjusting screw and adjust the idle speed to 750rpm, 800rpm maximum.

3.) Turn the toothed nut on the cable until the gap between the throttle lever and the toothed nut is between 0.5 and 1mm – use a feeler gauge to get it spot on.

4.) On cars with automatic gearboxes, check and correct the adjustment of the throttle cable after doing this. Unless the adjustment was badly wrong, I doubt you will have to do anything here.

Changing the camshaft belt

This is a pretty similar procedure to doing the belt on the M20 petrol, so if you have done an M20 belt before you will not find a diesel belt change too horrifying.

1.) Initial procedure is the same – radiator out, bonnet off, timing belt cover removed and the front crank pulley removed (six 13mm bolts).

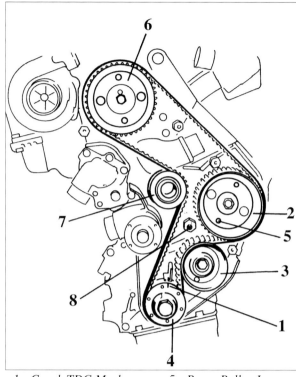

1 - Crank TDC Mark	5 - Pump Pulley Lugs
2 - Diesel Pump Pulley	6 - Camshaft Pulley
3 - Auxilary Pulley	7 - Tensioner
4 - Crank Hub	8 - Tension Adjuster

Adjusting Valve Clearance
1 - Camshaft
2 - Valve Clearance
3 - Adjusting Eccentric

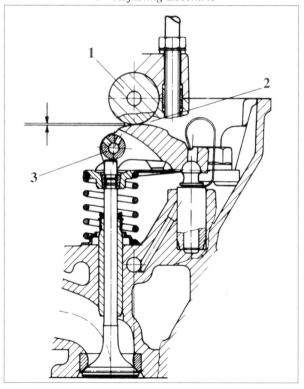

2.) This is where the diesel gets different. Align the notch on the front crank hub as you would on the petrol – you will see a mark scribed on the hub and this must be in line with the 'V' cut into the alloy front housing. Put the car in gear (manual) so the engine will not turn, or P for automatics. Just make sure it doesn't turn.

3.) With the camshaft cover off, make sure the engine is at TDC with both valves closed on number 1 cylinder, valves number 6 will be 'rocking', i.e. one closing and one opening.

BMW say you need to use a special tool (11 2 300) to hold the camshaft, but use vice grips on the camshaft to hold it still. Use a rag to avoid marking the camshaft and use a paint mark or two to ensure perfect alignment. A piece of metal plate with a square cut in will do. This is to locate onto square lug on camshaft.

4.) Paint mark the injection pump for perfect alignment, undo the tensioner and remove the old belt.

5.) Clean everything up, and begin by starting the new belt off on the crank sprocket and work the belt around the auxiliary shaft pulley, the diesel pump pulley, camshaft pulley and finally around the tensioner pulley as shown. The tensioner will need to be fully 'back' to allow the belt on and it is quite tight. Release the tensioner; turn the engine over a couple of times. Final tension of the tensioner is 50Nm for a new belt or 35 for an old one. But who the hell refits an old camshaft belt?

Engine rebuilds
If you have got something pretty rare and a good used engine is not available – or you want to build a 2.7 – then rebuilding an engine is an option. The big, big thing about engine building is utter cleanliness. One speck of dirt will quickly ruin a new shell bearing so operating theatre cleanliness is desirable. If you have just pulled an old engine out of your car, or you have just collected an old 525e engine for your 2.7 build, the first thing to do is to get is steam cleaned or pressure washed. Take off the

A ruined rocker. The pad on the left should be a smooth curve

camshaft cover, spray some degreaser in there and steam clean inside the head too – it just makes stripping the old unit less oily. Also invest a few quid in some latex gloves as engine dirt really ingrains itself into your skin and nails and can take weeks to get it out again.

If you can find one at an auto jumble, the original Haynes manuals are very useful for engine rebuilds – look for the big 317 page orange Owner's Workshop Manual for the 320i and 323i/325i as opposed to the later skinny Service and Repair Manual. For the M10 engined cars, I have found the E21 316 – 320 manual that is still in print in original form to be very handy as well.

As you strip the engine, keep things in order. Mark piston tops lightly with a sharp screwdriver to number them and centre punch dots or numbers into the connecting rod caps. Be very careful not to mix up the main bearing caps either, although they are numbered.

As you remove bits, place them in a container filled with engine degreaser. Wearing washing up rubber gloves, you can clean everything using a stiff brush and if you choose to use some old petrol, for goodness sake do it outside and not in the garage because the fumes and the fire risk are too dangerous. Nuts and bolts left in a container of cleaner for a day or so will scrub up well.

Engine blocks need to be cleaned before, and after, machining work but if you have a block acid cleaned, do not leave it in there too long because the acid will damage the white metal auxiliary shaft bearings and you cannot buy new ones. The oil-way plugs at each end of the block will need to be removed so that the central oil gallery can be completely cleaned to perfection – refitting the old main bearing shells upside down so that the oil galleries to the crank are blocked is a good way of cleaning out this oil gallery because the cleaning fluid can only go straight through. Basically, clean everything once, twice, and again for good measure.

What bits can be re-used? Well, if the engine ran okay and did not use oil, the pistons will probably be okay for re-use. You can carefully remove the top ring from each piston and put it in the bore to check for ring wear. Most old BMW blocks need a re-bore and if you can still see the cross-hatched honing marks, a quick bore clean with a drill operated honing tool will be enough. Most engine shops will have the proper tools for doing a professional job but it is only really needed when you have had the block re-bored.

In most cases, a set of new piston rings is not a bad idea but if you have never changed rings before, let a professional do it because they are easily broken and if you fit one or two upside down, you will end up with the piston giving compression as it goes down the bore.

Skimming heads and blocks – take off only as much as you really need. If a block or head face will clean up with just 2 or 3 thou, leave it at that. If you take anything more off either surface, play it safe on reassembly and use the thicker head gasket. New oil pump, crank bearings, connecting rod bolts and of course all oil seals and gaskets are mandatory. If you are on a budget and the oil pump seems in good condition then you can re-use it.

Lastly, but most importantly, do not use any form of gasket sealer – the mark of a bodged job. BMW did not use any of this rubbish when building the engine so neither should you. A light smear of clear silicon sealer on a sump gasket is okay but no more. Instead, give the gaskets a light coating of Castrol LM grease. This carbonises as the engine warms up for the first time and creates an incredibly oil tight seal. Not only that, but what gets washed off inside by the engine oil will just dissolve. Gasket sealer will not, but it will find an oil way to block. As for painting the engine, resist the temptation to use thick enamel paint for the block as it acts as a heat barrier and it looks horrible as well. With the block acid cleaned, use a conventional aerosol primer followed by Satin black. The block will not get hot enough to burn off the paint. Cylinder heads and alloy parts can be painted using etch primer followed by a regular silver paint from an aerosol.

Sudden misfires and weird noises – M20 engine
These are symptoms of a broken rocker. It only really happens on an old engine with a worn camshaft, or on one that was over revved, but it is a problem. If an inlet rocker breaks, it will just run on five cylinders but fuel will build up in that inlet port. If an exhaust rocker breaks, you will get a horrible coughing back though the air flow meter. That cylinder is sucking fuel and air in, but because the exhaust valve cannot open, the burnt mixture is being forced back out of the inlet valve and out of the air flow meter.

It is a real nuisance, but if you are really lucky it will be cylinder number one, which can be changed without the head coming off. You will need to remove the camshaft cover to find out which one it is. Either way, the camshaft belt needs to come off so now is the time to fit a new one. Remove the radiator, fan, front top camshaft belt cover, including the distributor cap on Motronic cars, and finally the camshaft wheel – you are best off undoing the securing bolt when the car is in gear and the camshaft belt is still on. This may well strain the camshaft belt so you must fit a new one. Now lift out the plate at the front that locks the two rocker shafts in place and remove all

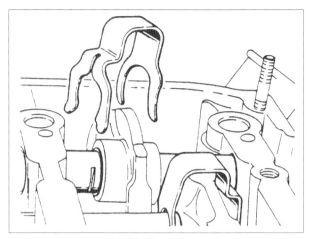
Rocker shafts and rockers

rocker retaining clips on that shaft. If it is rocker number one at the very front of the engine, use a hammer and a soft drift to punch the rocker shaft back. Obviously you will have turned the engine over before the camshaft belt came off to ensure the camshaft lobe on the rocker you are replacing is pointing down otherwise you will not get the new rocker back on. When the shaft is back far enough, slide the old broken rocker off and the new one on. Now just reassemble the engine, but do replace the camshaft belt unless you personally fitted a new one no more that 5000 miles ago. Camshaft belts do not like being tensioned, run for a few thousand miles, released from tension and then tensioned again. If number two rocker has broken, the shaft will not go back far enough. If it is the very back one, you can pull the shaft out of the front using Mole grips but you must use a bit of old aluminium to protect the shaft. If it is a centre rocker, you still do not have to take the head off. If you are changing number one inlet rocker, number one exhaust has to come off first. The inlet rocker is behind the exhaust rocker and there just is not room to punch the exhaust rocker shaft enough to remove the broken rocker.

ENGINE MOUNTINGS
Engine mounts are probably the most neglected part of a car. As long as the engine doesn't actually fall out in the road we just assume that they are okay. BMW mounts do seem to last a very long time but after fifteen years and 100,000 plus miles it could well be time for a pair of new ones. Replacing them is pretty straightforward and the bits from BMW are cheap enough too. Replacing the gearbox mounts at the same time is a very good idea. Once you have replaced them, you will feel the difference when pulling away and driveline shunt will be reduced considerably.

REMOVING EXHAUST MANIFOLDS
Taking these off can be a complete swine, as they do not often give up without a struggle. Basically, do not

remove it unless you absolutely must. BMW thoughtfully cast a hole halfway along so that you can get a socket onto the fourth lower nut (six-cylinder cars) but they are still quite hard work. For some obscure reason best known to them, BMW used 12mm nuts for the inlet and exhaust manifolds. These nuts are rusty and just love to round off so you will need a 12mm six pointed impact socket because the nuts will just laugh at anything less. If you do not have such a socket (3/8-inch drive as well), go and buy one before you start. Also douse the exposed threads with releasing fluid.

The down-pipe connections are normally either 14mm or 17mm, although 15mm have been known to be used. You will need another heavy-duty six-point socket and a half-inch drive breaker bar to crack these.

The ultimate nightmare is a stripped thread in the cylinder head for a manifold stud because very often the studs come loose. Just one over-zealous mechanic can ruin the thread. When this happens, the only option is to remove the head and have the thread repaired. I have seen some great bodges here – the best one was a piece of steel tube hammered into the head and the exhaust manifold refitted with plenty of exhaust paste so as to sleeve the joint. It looked awful, but to be fair it did the job!

TOP END OIL LEAKS

All engines will eventually leak oil. BMWs leak oil from the camshaft cover and the M20 has a gasket here, plus four rubber bungs to plug the slots where the rocker shafts slide in and out. BMW oil pressure switches seem to leak oil for a pastime and because it is right on the end of the main oil pressure gallery it is amazing how much oil they can leak. The real problems are oil leaks on the M20 front camshaft, crankshaft and auxiliary shaft oil seals because it is a labour intensive, camshaft belt off job. One puzzling leak on the M30 Motronic engines (such as Alpinas) is oil coming from the distributor cap. This is because there is an oil seal for the camshaft behind the rotor arm.

Restoration Notes

Chapter 9

COOLING AND HEATING

COOLING AND HEATING SYSTEMS

E30 cooling systems are as reliable as with any other car. The problems are mainly old age and neglect. If you changed the anti freeze every year, like BMW told you, most of the problems would never have happened, although the cracked head bogey is something that cannot be avoided. If it happens it happens, end of story.

THERMOSTATS

The job of the thermostat is to make the coolant in an engine warm up as fast as possible. It cuts off the flow of

This is the coolant level sensor - it's very important and could save your engine.

water from the engine to the radiator until the water in the engine is good and hot, and when it is hot enough, around 88 degrees, it opens up and allows the hot water into the radiator to cool off. As the engine cools, such as a fast run on a motorway on a cold day, the thermostat will partially close as the water temperature drops below 88 degrees and the water will heat up again. It is there to keep the engine coolant at a specific temperature. Thermostats for cold climates will open very late, those for cars in hot climates will open early.

Like any car part though, it will fail one day and when yours does, buy a genuine BMW thermostat, swallow the expense and accept no substitute. Too many aftermarket thermostats are cheap rubbish. About 10 years ago I had a 1984 316 that ran cold because the aftermarket thermostat had jammed open. I went to my local motor factors and bought a new one and fitted it. The car got less than a mile up the road before boiling because this one was faulty and would not open.

E30s use two types of thermostat. M20 and M40 engined cars, plus those with the M30, 333i, Alpina B6 and B6S for example, have a thermostat in the top of the cylinder head on the front by the radiator. You will notice that there are a lot of radiator hoses here. Let us take an M20 engine for example (320i, 325i etc). The one on the inlet side of the engine goes from the thermostat housing to the bottom of the radiator. This is the bottom hose, where hot water from the engine goes through the thermostat into the bottom of the radiator to be cooled off. The next, middle hose, goes from the other side of the thermostat housing to the water pump. This is the bypass hose. When the thermostat is shut (engine cold), water is just pumped around the engine and the radiator is bypassed completely. The next, right-hand hose (we're looking from the front of the car here) is the top hose and it goes from the thermostat housing to the top of the radiator. Cooled water from the bottom of the radiator rises to the top, being cooled by the air stream or fan as it goes, and when it is at the top of the radiator, it goes back into the engine via the top hose.

Let us look at a scenario with a failed thermostat.

1.) Thermostat is stuck closed. Water is pumped out of the block by the water pump through the bypass hose into the cylinder head where it is heated more and more. The engine boils and blows a hose – or blows the head gasket.

2.) Thermostat is stuck open. Water is pumped through the radiator from the minute the engine starts. With cold air going through the radiator, the water takes forever to warm up.

Now, if you've got a car with an overheating problem, the way around it is to take the thermostat out – right? Wrong! Maybe your E30 is an old nail that just is not worth spending money on, a car with a short MOT and just months or weeks to live. If the thermostat and viscous fan are in order, it could be a cracked head or a corroded waterway in the head just clinging to the head gasket for dear life. In this case, do not just REMOVE THE THERMOSTAT! If you do, water will arrive at the thermostat housing via the bypass hose and go straight down into the radiator without cooling the engine. Sure, the temperature gauge might read normal because the water around the sender in the thermostat housing is cool, but the coolant down in the block and the back of the head is well and truly boiling. If you have problems and need to delay the coolant from heating up, try this bodge – it is only a bodge mind, and has no place on a decent car. Remove the thermostat, and then remove the top radiator

This is the hole that needs sleeving to run without a thermostat

hose from the thermostat housing. You will see a big hole, and you will also see a couple of coolant temperature senders sticking out. What you need now is a 70mm length of tubing about 29mm thick – the right diameter to fit snugly in the thermostat housing. You will need to drill a suitable hole in the tube to clear the protruding sensors – about 40mm from the top. When you've done, unscrew the sensor, insert the tube and refit the sensor that will hold it in place. I would also advise drilling about three or four small holes in the tube on the thermostat side to allow trapped air to escape. What will this trick do? It will basically mean the cooling system is permanently running as if the thermostat is open. It will seriously restrict water movement in the bypass hose but because of the three or four small holes in the tube, bleeding the air out is easy enough. Doing this will have the effect of having a stuck open thermostat with coolant doing the whole circuit of the engine. The problem that caused the overheating will surface some time or other, but this trick can keep an ailing car going for a while. Now you can make that 10-mile trip to work without the car boiling its head off.

Now for the M10 engine cars and the M3. These cars used a remote thermostat, a three-way alloy unit at the bottom of the hose. These do not often fail, but when they do, it is dustbin time and a new unit. The M3 thermostat also has the electric fan switch and is a different unit to the M10 but is the same in principle – top hose, bottom hose and a by-pass. We will not go into the kind of bodge we discussed with the M20 engines, but on the M10 you can remove the thermostat, pull out all the internals until you have just an alloy shell and refit it. Now the engine will really overheat, so insert a cotton reel into the hose that goes across the front of the engine above the water pump – the by-pass hose. Do that, and an engine in trouble will run cooler, unless it really has got a major problem with the head gasket. But if you are on holiday, or just miles from home, these tricks can get you home but are not proper solutions. As for the M40 and M42 (318iS) engines, no such fix is possible because it is a modern design engine with no by-pass system. Just removing the thermostat altogether is the 'get you home' fix on these.

THE RADIATOR TO EXPANSION BOTTLE PIPE
On cars with an expansion bottle (or header tank), there is a small pipe from the top of the radiator to the bottle. If this blocks, or the rubber hose collapses inside, it will create a massive air lock and overheating problems; producing the same symptoms as a blown head gasket. It will also make bleeding the cooling system completely impossible.

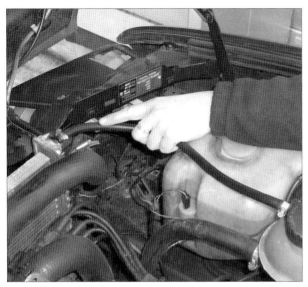

If this pipe blocks, the system will pressurise and the engine will overheat and spit it's water out

Radiator bleed screw for M40/M42 cars. Overtighten it and it will break!

BLEEDING THE COOLING SYSTEM (M20)

This can be either hard, or it can be easy. The hard way is to chuck all the coolant in one go and try to bleed it on the bleed screw – good luck, you will need it.

Assuming you have a dry engine with no coolant, the easy way is to remove the top hose and disconnect the bottom hose from the thermostat housing. You will need 5 litres of anti-freeze and do not buy a cheap variety as the alloy used for BMW heads does not like it. I use a litre container or bottle for this bit. Fill it with anti freeze, and slowly pour it into the header tank (expansion bottle). Now get another litre and pour it into the bottom hose – that is the one that goes from the bottom of the radiator to the thermostat housing. Leave about a minute between each litre, and then pour another litre into the header tank. Leave it a minute and pour the next one into the bottom hose. After a break of a minute, put another litre into the expansion bottle (slowly, remember) followed by the last litre into the bottom hose.

Now start with fresh water (distilled is best), leaving it a minute between each litre. Why? To give the coolant time to find its own way. You should have the ignition on and the heater set to hot for this so that the circuit is fully open. By now you could be seeing coolant in the hose and in the thermostat housing. As soon as there is coolant starting to spill out of the thermostat housing, refit the top hose, but do not fix it to the radiator just yet. Keep adding water, nice and slowly, into the bottom hose and the header tank until water is at the top of the bottom hose. Now refit it to the radiator. Keep adding water until it is coming out of the radiator. Refit the top hose. You should have taken over ten minutes to get this far, and now you can fire the engine up. It is full once

you have added about nine litres of coolant. Make sure all the hose clips are tight, and go for a drive up the road, using up to 4500rpm. Because you added the coolant slowly and in two places there should be no air locks. As soon as the heater is pumping out warm air, the system is bled. To finish off, you can open the 8mm bleed screw if you want but if the heater is hot, it's bled. If the heater will not pump out warm air (wait until the needle on the gauge is at a quarter), stop the engine and open the bleed screw. As soon as it stops hissing hot air and a steady stream of coolant is coming out, it will be bled. Carefully unscrew the header tank cap, let any pressure escape and top up the header tank with either water or anti freeze. Job done!

The 8mm bleed screw on the thermostat housing is well known for being a complete swine because it corrodes. Before you get involved with any work on the cooling system just see if it will shift. Only ever use a close fitting 8mm socket, although a 5/16-inch (English) is 7.9mm and a very snug fit. If it rounds off, try Mole grips but if no luck, go to BMW and buy a new housing with bleed screw.

BLEEDING THE COOLING SYSTEM (M40 AND M42)

These are a lot easier because the radiator has a bleed screw as well. Follow the steps above as for the M20, but open the radiator bleed screw as well.

REPLACING WATER PUMPS

On the M10 and M30 engines, changing the water pump is a rare occurrence. They just never seem to fail. When they do, fitting a new one is so easy it is just not worth me elaborating.

On the M20 six cylinder engine, change the water pump every camshaft belt change because to remove the pump, you ought to change the camshaft belt too. Why is this? The camshaft belt tensioner pulley has a tensioning spring that sits between the pulley mounting plate and the water pump body. So, to remove the pump, you have to release the spring and trying to get the pump back on against the spring pressure can be very difficult. Even if you do manage it, the chances of the water pump gasket being damaged are quite high. So when the camshaft belt is off, and you have no record of a new pump recently fitted, please buy one and save yourself future grief. Likewise, you may as well fit a new camshaft belt when doing a water pump.

If you have just had a camshaft belt done, change the water pump like this. Remove the viscous fan, radiator shroud, top camshaft belt cover (deep joy on a Motronic car) and remove the top two water pump bolts. Slacken the bottom bolt until the pump can be rotated anti-clockwise and the spring pressure from the camshaft belt tensioner relived. The tensioner roller will not release because it has two bolts holding it in place, so do not worry about the belt losing tension. When refitting the pump, lightly grease the gasket on both sides and stick it to the pump. Refit the pump with the lower bolt with about three or four turns, and refit the tensioner spring whilst turning the pump clockwise into position and refitting the top two bolts. Not easy, but...

Now the M40/M42 pump, which can be either a very simple one-hour job or a three-hour battle between you and the car. The problem is this. On the M10 and M20 engines, the water pump is a surface fit against the block. You remove the bolts, give the pump a tap with a hammer, it falls off – easy. On the M40/M42 though, it is an alloy cylindrical pump that fits inside the block. Thankfully, it is very easy to reach. Remove the two clips and the radiator shroud lifts out. Remove the viscous coupling with a 32mm spanner as described in the viscous coupling section following and there is the pump in all its glory. Just four bolts and it should come out. BMW even tapped two threads in the pump body so that you could wind two of the bolts in and push the pump out. In reality, a big pair of grips and plenty of penetrating fluid are needed. A hammer and a big screwdriver are needed to get it moving and the idea is to get the old pump turning in the block. The worst that can happen is that the cylindrical part of the pump body breaks off in the block. At that point, you can remove the radiator (easy – about three minutes) and the front centre grille (two clips) to give yourself a good view. If the pump body has broken off inside the block, the impeller will still be stuck inside which makes removing the main part of the pump a bit of a pain. But, with some careful leverage and applied vio-

lence, the impeller can be forced out but it is better to remove the TDC sensor wire from the camshaft belt cover to avoid damaging it. Once the pump impeller is out, use a hammer and sharp chisel (or big flat blade screwdriver) to break up the alloy pump body but do catch all the old bits. Once you have made one cut in the pump body, it will release its grip inside the block and come out. Fish out all the bits of impeller and alloy from inside the block. M42 water pumps are easier because they fit into the front timing covers and tend not to corrode in so badly.

Refitting, thankfully, is not a reverse of removal...

VISCOUS FAN COUPLINGS

Every E30 made, apart from the European market M3, has a viscous fan. Rather than a solid fixed fan droning away and sapping power, the viscous fan has a viscous coupling which, when heated enough by air around the radiator, will lock up and power the fan. Then the air around the radiator has cooled enough, the fan will disengage.

This is a great theory and it works well until the day the fan coupling decides it has had enough of life in the fast lane. A good viscous fan will engage from a cold start and then shut off after a few seconds. It will engage when the needle on the temperature gauge gets to a point in a jam or slow moving traffic between the half and three-quarter marks and is a kind of howling, high pitched drone – you will notice it. When you increase the rpm to around 2000, the noise should gradually fade away. As a rule a car that gets hot in traffic, but cools down once you are out on the open road or runs at normal temperature on the motorway, needs a new viscous coupling.

With these viscous couplings, it is often best to buy a genuine BMW item. I do not know why, but both others and myself have had problems with the cheaper ones, even those that are said to be the 'genuine' parts. Mind you, Behr made a lot of the original units for BMW, as well as radiators and the heater matrix, and Behr couplings are available from companies in Britain such as Euro Car Parts and GSF. Believe it of not, incorrect storage can damage the units to the extent where they can fail straight out of the box. So do not ignore the 'this way up' markings on the packet.

Fitting a new coupling is not hard. It is a 32mm size and you can use either a 32mm open ended spanner or a special viscous coupling spanner, which is very slim. These couplings screw onto the front of the water pump and use a left hand thread. That means to unscrew them from the pump, you need to go in the opposite direction; i.e. turn the nut clockwise when viewing from the front of the car.

Stand on the inlet manifold side of the engine bay, fit the spanner and give it a good sharp clout with a hammer towards you. This will loosen the nut and then you can spin the fan off. Refitting can be a pain and if you find that you really cannot get the thread to engage, try this. Pull the coil lead from the coil to disable the ignition, hold the fan nut against the water pump threads and get an assistant to crank the engine. BE VERY CAREFUL HERE! No loose clothing, no ties and wear some heavy-duty gloves – old gardening gloves are perfect. The engine will not fire and run but there are alternator fan blades and drive belts in there. But doing this makes the water pump spin over and it quickly catches the thread in the viscous coupling. To tighten it, fit the spanner and give it a good smack anti-clockwise. Do not use any thread lock on the threads because one day you may have to remove it again. Some cars, like the 325i, are a bit harder because you need to remove the viscous coupling and fan along with the radiator plastic shroud but it is not that bad a job.

The M3 ELECTRIC FAN

All E30 M3s except the federal (USA/Canada) versions had an electric fan. This was a one-speed fan on cars up until around 1988 and a two-speed fan from there on, so cars like the regular 215bhp M3, the Evo II and Sport Evo have a two-speed fan. This is a reliable system but the weak link is the wiring plug that fits onto the thermostat switch on the thermostat. There are two or three wires going into this plug and they are a power supply and an earth. Power comes along one wire, goes into the switch that will connect to earth and bring the fan on when the coolant gets hot enough. The actual switches do not fail that often but the contacts in the plastic plug corrode and don't work. The first you know of the problem is when the car boils up in traffic. Testing to see if the fan itself works is easy by bridging connections on the end of the plug but if it is really badly corroded, you need to cut the plug off and solder on new wires and a new connector. The BMW part numbers for the bits you need are 61 13 0 007 446 for each wire (90 degree angle connector) or 61 13 0 007 442 for the wires into the straight connector. The plastic connector itself is 61 131 378 410. The wires slide in and click into place and the new wires are soldered onto the old loom. I have noticed that the new wires are of thinner gauge than the original loom but it doesn't seem to cause a problem.

RADIATOR REPLACEMENT

Changing the radiator on a manual transmission car is very easy. If you do not want to remove the viscous fan assembly, unclip the fan shroud and pull the radiator up and out without it.

On automatic transmission cars, things can get pretty nasty because of the automatic gearbox oil cooler pipes.

Unlike the M30 engined 5 and 7 series cars, whose pipes screw into the connections on the side of the radiator, the E30s pipes screw in from below, although some US market cars and later cars, have the pipe connections on the side. This can make them a complete nightmare to remove and, to add insult to injury, the pipes can really rust. Rather than trying to do them from within the engine bay, as you would on an E28 525e, you can access the pipes from below once the undertray (if fitted) is removed. The 22mm union nuts will come undone without too much drama, but when the union nuts are rusted to the pipes it can be real problem. The way to get around this is to clean them up with a wire brush. If you have access to either a industrial strength heat gun or oxy-acetylene, heat the union nuts up until they glow red. Once that is done they should move. If you do not have this equipment, you will have to rely on penetrating fluid and holding the pipe still with mole grips clamping along the length of the pipe whilst you undo the unions. Once the unions start to move, spray on more releasing fluid and wind them back and forth until they are free enough to be unscrewed. If the pipes look really rusty and the unions are stuck fast, get a pair of new pipes because the old ones are absolutely guaranteed to break and leave you with an immobile car.

RADIATOR MAINTENANCE

Whenever the radiator has to come out it should be reverse flushed, which means using a hose on the bottom pipe and flushing the water back against the normal direction of travel. These cooling system flushes that are poured into the expansion bottle seem to do something. Old radiators can be cleaned by using a lime scale remover normally used in old kettles and washing machines but they can be a bit too vicious and will find any holes. Small holes in the radiator fins can be sealed up with a soldering iron and low melting point solder but you are just putting off the evil day when a new radiator is needed. The worst solution is to use a stop leak additive. This will normally block the heater valve and cause an air lock. In Britain, BMW issued a recall on faulty radiator caps and most cars will have had a new one. Overheating at speed without coolant loss means a blocked radiator.

COOLANT LOSS

You may have a problem where the car is using water but there is no sign of where it is going. Head gasket failure would mean overheating, a cracked head would mean water in the oil, whilst oil in the water could be either a cracked head or a head gasket blown across from an oil way into a water jacket. A leaking heater matrix would mean damp carpets and severe condensation inside the windows and any external water leaks would be pretty obvious. You would also smell antifreeze.

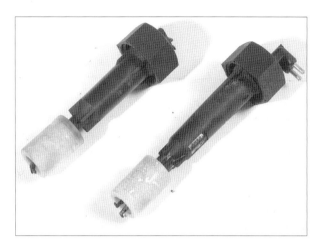

Make sure the level sensor works.
There are two types - fitting the wrong one will
give the wrong reading and indicate coolant loss

Here's the electronic heater valve.
To the left of the picture is part of the brake
linkage on RHD cars

One place where water can leak is the throttle body. On the older M20s, the throttle body is water heated. It is not unknown for the throttle body to corrode and a pinhole appear. The water is then sucked into the engine and burnt along with the fuel and air mixture.

One very visible place for coolant to leak on the Motronic six-cylinder cars are the hoses. The hoses that go across the front of the engine. These use a steel link pipe that is bolted to the engine above the front crank pulley that will eventually rust and spring a leak. New ones are available from BMW.

REPLACING HOSES

With the newest E30 now being ten years old, most of them will need a hose or two. By all means keep an eye on them but when the hoses feel saggy, it is time to replace them. Hoses are reinforced with thin wire but this will not last forever and when it decides to let go, that old hose will just pop. Just one overheated moment in traffic is all it takes. When fitting new or old hoses, use standard grease like Castrol LM to seal them. Do not use a silicon sealer as the bits that drop off will only block something important.

THE HEATER MATRIX

These do not often leak but when they do it is difficult to replace them. Basically, you have to remove the glove box and the centre console, as well as a lot of the brake linkage, to give yourself room. On LHD cars, like the M3, it is a nightmare job. On any E30 removing the four nuts that hold the heater box to the bulkhead can help. To access these you need to remove the steel panel at the top of the bulkhead from under the bonnet. This will allow the heater to drop down and make things a bit more flexible.

THE ELECTRONICALLY CONTROLLED HEATER

All E30s use an electronic heater control valve. It takes

an electrical signal from the rotary 'hot or cold' dial on the dashboard and opens and shuts accordingly. Not much kills these valves, but those lovely radiator sealers you can buy do a fine job of blocking them.

So, it is midwinter and your heater does not work. Excluding for a moment any cooling system issues (is the system properly bled?), you need to find out if there is hot water getting to the valve. With the engine running and up to temperature, feel the hoses on the bulkhead going into the heater valve. If they are hot, or at least one is hot but you still have no heater, the valve is at fault. The first trick is to open the glove box (or on LHD cars, remove the lower dash shroud) and remove the plastic side trim. When you have located the heater valve pull the single wire from the top of the unit. This will open the unit up. You see the E30 heater valve is in an open condition at rest without 12 volts. It needs 12 volts to close the plunger so, when you pull that power wire off the unit should open. If you get a torrent of hot air from the heater after that, the valve is okay but the rotary switch on the dash has gone west. And joy of joys, fitting a new one is just such fun.

Changing a heater valve

1. Firstly, remove the centre console – to do this will first need to remove the rear console that fits between the seats and taking out the rear ashtray will reveal how the rear console is secured. Removing the gearlever gaiter will reveal the plastic securing nut for the front console whilst at the front there are two 8mm bolts going up into the dash. Do not forget the wiring connection for the cigarette lighter.

2. Now drop the glove box down and disconnect the two supporting straps – these attach to the glove box by a plastic through-pin that you simply push out.

3. Now remove the plastic trunking and the plastic side trim that covers the heater valve. It is pretty obvious how it comes off but be careful as it is easily broken.

4. From under the bonnet, locate the two heater pipes and remove the lower one. Expect a slight loss of coolant so have an old cork or bit of rag ready to stuff up the hose. Make sure the coolant is not too hot when doing this.

5. Back inside the car, remove the two 8mm bolts that secure the heater valve to the heater – have an old towel and a container ready to catch any coolant that will escape. There is also another single crosshead screw that holds the valve to the heater body and it is a complete and utter swine to remove – especially on RHD cars because the brake pedal cross linkage is in the way. Be patient!

6. The valve should now come out and it can be tested. Blow into the long tube and it should be easy to blow though. If it's difficult or impossible, the valve is finished. If it's clear, test the valve by putting 12 volts through it – do this using a battery and a couple of wires. With 12 volts, the valve should shut with a click and be impossible to blow through. If the valve passes these tests, it looks like it is okay and the problem lies elsewhere. If the car is just a banger, or you have taken it apart in the winter and you do not have a replacement valve, you can do the following bodge. You see the flange where the valve bolted to the heater unit with the two 8mm bolts? Run a 10mm drill up that hole until you break though into the inlet passage. This will bypass the valve and allow hot water straight though into the heater. This is all you can do if the valve did not open even with the wire removed.

Removing the heater heat control switch

Firstly, the radio needs to come out, followed by all the switches above the radio – heated rear window, hazard warning lights etc. With that little lot removed, look up into the void and you will see a couple of small crossheaded screws securing the whole heater control and radio support panel to the main dash. Remove the centre console as described in the heater valve epic and you will see another pair of screws going up through the dash into captive clips in the heater control board. On some cars the two front centre console screws go all the way through into the heater control board, meaning you do not have to take the console out.

Pull the complete unit forward out of the dash, but before you start pulling the heater control cables off, make sure that you have enough room to get in from behind with a screwdriver and remove the three tiny screws that hold the switch into the panel. Pull the knob off the front of the switch and the switch unit will pop out. Disconnect the power supply cable as well. As well as being an electronic switch, this unit also operates a cable that goes down to the main heater unit and opens a flap. Make sure this cable has not broken – it is very rare but not unheard of. As for the electrical switch, clean it with methylated spirit to get any crud off the contacts. To test the, use an ohmmeter on the two contacts. In the cold position there should be no continuity, full open circuit in the hot position and half the value obtained in the halfway position.

Air conditioning

This was a common feature on US market cars but quite rare on European ones. Repairing air conditioning systems is not a DIY task because of the gasses involved, but there are a couple of checks you can carry out. Firstly, the compressor should engage with the engine running and the button pressed. With the engine running, get an assistant to press the a/c button and see if it engages. If it does and the air conditioning still does not work, it has probably got a leak somewhere and the gas has escaped. If it does not, the compressor could be seized. With the engine switched off, try and turn the outer part of the pulley (the disc in front of the belt). If it doesn't turn, it is seized but if it does turn there is either no power getting to the compressor or there is some other fault. Either way there is not a lot you can do about it, although running a direct 12 volt feed to the compressor to test the system will not hurt. It may just be a blown fuse or relay so check this first. These older systems used 'Freon' or R12 gas that has been superseded by R132, which is supposedly environmentally friendly. BMW do a kit with new seals and other bits to convert the system, and there is also an additive that will convert R12 to something like R132. Needless to say, the BMW conversion kit is the best option and whilst the system is in bits being repaired you might as well go this route.

This is the rear of the heater control switch.

Restoration Notes

Chapter 10

FUEL SYSTEM

The E30 range uses a variety of different fuel systems with three fuel injection systems, and a couple of carburettors too. Some of these are now getting rare and Bosch Motronic as used on all 1988 onwards cars is the most common.

The 316 carburettor

All M10-engined 316 cars used a carburettor. The early cars in 1982 and early 1983 used the Pierburg 2B which was sort of okay but later cars used the dreaded Pierburg 2BE, the ultimate nightmare carburettor. BMW were forced by emissions regulations to use this carburettor when what they should have done is equip it with an injection system. A horribly complex device, it used various sensors, vacuum control units and was electronically controlled with a Bosch ECU. It really was a terrible thing and when it starts to malfunction, the only sensible course of action is to take it off, throw it away and fit a Weber replacement. Many of the repair parts are no longer available for the Pierburg and there is very little service information around. You would not be the first owner to spend £100 on parts, along with many hours of tearing your hair out, only to give up. If you can find one, you can go the second-hand route and try a different carburettor but there are not many good ones about. Even the 316s ending up in breaker's yards now seem to have had Weber carburettors fitted and, of course, these offer a good saving over new ones. As for buying new carburettor bits to try and make yours work, do not bother. The parts are very expensive and you have absolutely no guarantee that the damned thing will work. ECUs do not often fail but it is not unknown. Before assuming the carburettor is at fault, check all the ignition system, make sure the fuel pump is delivering enough fuel and check all the vacuum pipes and electrical connections – you never know, you might be lucky. A carburettor and inlet manifold assembly from an old 2002 or E21 316 can be fitted but again, the age of these parts is against you. If ever there was a reasoned argument to buy a 318i, this is it!

BOSCH K JETRONIC

This system was used on the European and Australian 318i until August/September 1983 and no UK or US market cars were fitted with this system. It is a mechanical system with electronic elements. The main unit is the fuel distributor (or metering head) – it has five fuel lines coming out, four injectors and the cold start valve. It is fed pressurised fuel by the electric pump. The metering head is bolted to an air flap. As the engine cranks over and starts to draw air in, the flap opens and as it rises, the lever on which it pivots pushes a steel pin in the centre of the metering head which opens the valve and allows pressurised fuel to the injectors – think of how a toilet cistern works and you are spot on!

Problems are mainly poor maintenance and old age related. Remove the big rubber bellows between the throttle body and the metering head unit and check it for splits – obviously in a system that relies on air being sucked in a split would cause a pressure drop and not lift the flap enough. Also check that the round air flap is sitting perfectly central and that it lifts easily – use a pair of small grips on the central bolt. The plate must not only sit centrally but at the correct height. If it sticks at all, wash out the unit with carburettor or brake cleaner and a toothbrush – in fact, do this anyway. If it sticks, loosen the central bolt and carefully realign the plate until it is a perfect fit. It must be able to lift without touching the sides of the bowl. If it touches, it will stick and cause a big misfire.

The warm-up regulator is the unit with two fuel lines and a single electronic connector plug and when it fails it causes all kinds of problems. Test it by pulling the plug off, connecting an ohmmeter and checking for an open circuit. Now switch over to voltmeter and check the plug – with a running engine you should have 11.5 volts minimum, preferably 12.

There is also a temperature time switch and this controls the time the cold start injector is open. Pull the plug off and use a test lamp on the plug at battery + and W terminal on the switch itself. The lamp should be glowing at coolant temperatures below 35 degrees centigrade or 95 degrees Fahrenheit, but should go out above this.

Used parts are hard to find for those now, but this system was used on cars like the Golf GTi and Escort XR3i until around 1988.

BOSCH LE JETRONIC

Bosch LE Jetronic was the staple fuel injection system for the E30 until Motronic arrived in 1986 - even then it lingered on until late 1987 when the 320i and 318i finally went over to the Motronic system. Chrome bumper 318i, 320i and 323i cars use it. Bosch LE is really quite a simple system. An electric fuel pump delivers fuel to a fuel rail to which the injectors are attached and the fuel rail has a fuel pressure regulator which keeps the fuel pressure up depending on what load the engine is under - it has a vacuum pipe with manifold vacuum as well. A return pipe delivers spare fuel back to the tank.

The injectors are triggered by the engine ECU (Electronic Control Unit) which takes signals from two devices. The first is the throttle position switch (TPS) on the underside of the throttle body. This is a device which measures the opening of the throttle butterfly: closed for idling, slightly open for part throttle and full throttle. The ECU also takes readings from the air flow meter (AFM). This provides more accurate information on exactly how much air is going into the engine. The throttle position switch is there to give instant information when the throttle is snapped open and before the AFM can respond.

Like all fuel injection systems, LE Jetronic has cold start and cold running enrichment. On cars up until 1985 this was done with a cold start injector. A sensor on the thermostat housing measures the coolant temperature and tells the ECU to open the cold start injector, closing it when the engine is running. The injectors are also held open for slightly longer on each cycle until it's warm enough to run without the added enrichment. Cars after 1985 had it all done on the injector opening times.

As an added 'refinement', these cars also had an added air supply when cold. On the 320i and 323i this was done with a water heated slide valve which, when the coolant was cold was open, allowing extra air into the idle circuit.

When the coolant heated up, it would close off. 318i M10 cars used an electronically heated valve which was better.

The E in LE means economy, and this was an economy biased system. On coasting (down hill on zero throttle for example) the fuel is cut off, cutting back in when the throttle is opened. It's so smooth you'll never notice. You'll notice on these cars a strange vacuum operated throttle damper and this is to hold the throttle open slightly on the overrun to prevent the engine from stalling when the fuel is cut.

Problems? The TPS fills with oil seeping past the throttle shaft, rendering the unit non functional - taking it off and cleaning it out is the answer. The rest is down to DIY fiddling because really, there's nothing to go wrong and it's a really reliable system. The fuel pump relay is known to play up - intermitting non-starting is the main giveaway.

BOSCH MOTRONIC

This is now the most commonly found system on E30's. Fitted to the 325e first in 1984 it found its way onto the first 325i in 1985, the M3 in 1986 and catalyst 320i's from the 1987 model year. Basically, it's LE Jetronic but with the ECU taking care of the ignition timing as well. On the chrome bumper 325i and 325e, this was done with two sensors on the flywheel. One told the ECU when the engine was at TDC (top dead centre) for firing, the other was a speed sensor for telling the ECU how fast the engine was spinning round. Many driveability problems are caused by a failed speed sensor; the engine will idle fine but over 2000 rpm it loses the will to live because the ECU isn't advancing the timing. Plastic bumper cars had a different system where just one sensor on the front pulley gave the ECU info on both parameters. That's why on Motronic cars there is no distributor as such. The ECU picks up the signals and does the rest. The only way the timing can be altered is by reprogramming the ECU. You may have read how older Motronic BMW's are not suitable for unleaded; this is purely because adjusting the timing to suit lower octane fuel was not a five minute job.

This is the later type "in-tank" fuel pump

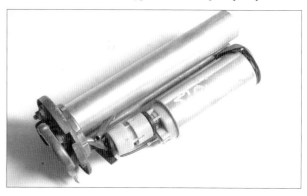

FUEL PUMPS

The 316 uses a conventional mechanical fuel pump bolted to the cylinder head – if you used a second-hand 318i head you will soon find out that there is nowhere to fit the pump!

Fuel injection E30s mostly used a standard Bosch electric pump that is mounted on the rear inner sill by the rear subframe mounting, on the opposite side to the fuel filler. The pump is a tough old thing, but when you run it dry it will never be right again and will probably fail after a few days of noisy operation. These pumps spin over at very high speed and need the fuel to lubricate them. Between the pump and the tank is the reservoir and after the pump is a pressure damper which damps out the pulses from the fuel pump. From here we have the steel fuel lines which just love to rust and, unlike the brake lines which run over the rear axle, these fuel pipes are easy to change although to shift the crosshead screws that secure the clamping plates can require some brute force and ignorance.

The next pump is the in-tank type that was phased in with the plastic bumper cars. 99% of these cars will have the in-tank pump but some very early, September 1987, cars are known to have still used the external pump – I have owned one (a 318i) but they are rare and I have only seen the one. These pumps fit in the tank and are accessed by removing the rear seat base and taking off the black, round cover plate – it is on the same side as the fuel filler neck. Once the plate is removed you will see the fuel hoses and the electrical connections. The pump is removed by twisting it and lifting it out, but you will have to remove those little 8mm nuts first. These hold the fuel pump and the fuel gauge sender together and it is impossible to remove both at once. Like the external pump, the in-tank pump does not like being run dry.

These later pumps are around second-hand but are E30 only – however, the older external pump is a generic unit used on cars as diverse as the M635CSi and the E28s. Four- and six-cylinder pumps are the same too. Some M3s used an external fuel pump and also a lifter pump in the tank (called a 'w-suction device' on BMW ETK). The lifter pump can fail causing fuel starvation – either fit a new one or replace with a standard sender unit and a 325i type pump.

FUEL PUMP RELAYS

I would not say that the E30 fuel pump relay is notorious because the same part was fitted to thousands of other German cars and also GM cars – anything that used Bosch fuel injection or engine management. Signs that a pump relay is on the way out include a refusal to start. This can come in many forms. Maybe you have driven

On the right is the fuel pump relay for the LE Jetronic cars

DME and fuel pump relays, Motronic

20 miles, gone away and come back to the car after 25 minutes. Leave it another 20 minutes and it will start. Maybe it will lose power, and then come back to life again once you've coasted to a start – it will slowly die as opposed to cutting out altogether.

On Motronic cars, the fuel pump relay is the very same orange relay as is used for the horn. So, if your Motronic car stops, cuts out, refuses to start or whatever, pull the relay from the fuse box (Marked K2 on the fuse box lid) and fit this in place of the fuel pump relay.

Total, sharp cutting out can be the DME relay, which is the white one. It really is worth buying a new one of each (they are not that expensive) and keeping them in the glove box – or a couple of used ones from the scrap yard. 525e cars use the same relays, as do the E34 and E32's.

On the older LE Jetronic cars, the 'fuel pump' relay does more than just control the fuel pump. It also gives power to the injectors. If an older chrome bumper 320i, 318i or 323i will not start, check for a spark at the plugs, and that there is fuel getting to the injectors rail. If there is a spark

The screwdriver is pointing to the fuel filter

ECUs for the early Motronic cars (left) and the later types (right) the third (bottom left) unit is for the ABS

Coil unit for 318iS. Running with one faulty could damage the ECU

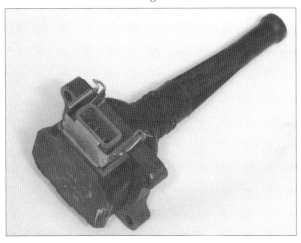

but no fuel, the relay could be faulty. If you do not have a spare relay to hand, make up a Y shaped jumper wire with three male connectors. Remove the relay and fit the jumper wire to terminals 30 (12 volts), 87b (pump) and 87 (injectors). It should now come to life! K Jetronic 318is use a different relay system; remove the diode relay and the pump relay, connecting contact 87 from the pump relay base in the fuse box to the battery plus terminal and the pump will run. If not, grovel under the car, and use wires with crocodile clips from the fuel pump to a battery.

FUEL FILTERS
These are either hidden down below the brake servo on older cars, or on the M3, under the back where the fuel pump sits on external fuel pump cars.

ECUs
As a rule, the ECUs on cars with Bosch LE Jetronic (M10 318i, chrome bumper 320i and 323i) do not fail. The only thing that would damage one is a bad water leak past the screen, or a car with water leak elsewhere that resulted in bad condensation. Used ECUs for these cars are everywhere and about £10 will buy one, as they are just not items that sell. A full list of ECUs is given below.

When the 325e arrived, it used the early type of Motronic engine management that took the engine TDC position from sensors on the flywheel. These ECUs could fail, but not very often. The same goes for the early chrome bumper 325is, which used a similar type of ECU, and there were a spate of failures.

When the plastic bumper cars arrived in September 1987, BMW switched to a new type of Motronic system that took crank position and timing from the front pulley. The ECUs became bigger and Motronic was also fitted to the 320i for the first time. These ECUs are very reliable, but the early 325i cars with the 173 numbered ECU could give starting and idling problems. It was replaced in June 1988 with a revised ECU, the 380 unit. A good friend of mine had an automatic 325i built in June 1988 with the early ECU and it could idle too fast and need a good churn on the starter to get it started. Fitting a second-hand 380 both reduced the idle speed to 750rpm (good on automatics) and cured the starting problem. Early E34 cars like the 520i and 525e also suffered the early ECUs and BMW sold a retro fit kit of bits to fool the ECU and give more fuel on cold starts. A second-hand later ECU is a better idea.

On the 318iS, the ECU has to fire four coils and if a coil fails, it can often damage the ECU. M3s use a conventional Motronic ECU.

Here is a list of most E30 ECUs:

Carburettor ECUs

0260 200 005:   316 with Pierburg 2BE carburettor

LE Jetronic ECUs

0280 000 318:   Early 318i 1983 – 84

0280 000 330:   Later 318i 1984 – 87

0280 001 301:   Early 320i and 323i 1982 – 84

0280 001 309:   Later 320i

0280 001 308:   Later 323i

0280 000 310:   Late 323i

Motronic ECUs

0261 200 174:   316i 1988 onwards

0261 200 157:   318i 1987 – 88

0261 200 175:   318iS 1989 onwards

0261 200 164:   325i Auto 9/87 onwards

0261 200 381:   320i 1987 onwards

0261 200172:   320i 1987

0261 200 073:   Early metal bumper 325i 1985 – 87

0261 200 173:   Plastic bumper 325i 9/87 onwards

0261 200 380:   325i from 9/88 onwards

0261 200 071:   Early 195/200bhp M3 cars and Evo I

0261 200 090:   Evo II

0261 200 091:   M3 with 215bhp

0261 200 092:   Sport Evo

0261 200 042:   325e until 9/85

0261 200 087:   320iS

0261 200 074:   325e 9/85 onwards (low compression)

The two sensors: The upper one is for the temperature gauge, the lower one is for the ECU and is a swine to replace.
Break off the plastic bit and use a socket.

Note: Some 318i also fitted with (0261 200) 986, 386 and 387 ECUs. Some 320i with 172 ECU. Some catalyst equipped 320i with 405 ECU.

Trouble shooting fuel injection faults

This is an area where many amateur mechanics fall and it is amazing the number of cars you see with a whole host of expensive new bits fitted under the bonnet as the owner/mechanic threw parts at the car in an attempt to cure the fault.

Engine will not start:
Firstly, you need to check for the two essentials – a spark at the plugs and fuel at the injectors. Pull the plug lead off number one plug, stick an old plug in the end of the head, rest it on the camshaft cover and crank the engine. If it has a spark, move on to the fuel system. If there is no spark, pull the coil lead from the end of the distributor cap and put the plug in the end of the lead. If there is still no spark, you need to be looking at the coil and the ignition 12-volt wiring so check for voltage at the low-tension terminals. If there is a spark from the coil but not from the plug leads, suspect a damaged rotor arm or distributor cap.

Okay, so assuming you have a good healthy spark at the plugs, either the fuel pump is not working or the injectors are not being triggered. On older cars with the external electric fuel pump, you should hear the pump buzz briefly as the ignition is turned on. Either way, pull the fuel supply hose from the front of the fuel rail and put the end in an old bottle. With the ignition on and the engine cranking, there should be fuel gushing out. If not, first check the fuel pump fuse – it is number 11 and it is a 7.5 amp fuse. If it is not obviously blown, clean it up, tighten up the connection by bending the fuse mounting tabs inwards slightly and try it again.

Still no joy? Then you should be thinking in terms of the fuel pump relay. On cars with LE Jetronic such as the old M10 318i, chrome bumper 320i and the 323i, the one relay controls the pump and also the injector firing. Locate the relay on the inner wing by the inlet manifold and pull it from its socket. You will need to make up a jumper wire to connect three terminals together. The terminals you need to bridge are 87 (injectors), 87b (fuel pump) and 30 (12 volt power supply). With this done, you have bypassed the relay and you might want to run another wire from terminal 31 (earth) to the battery earth although it should work without this. With a spark at the plugs and the fuel pump and injectors working, it should now run. If the fuel pump has failed, well, you will just have to fit another one.

On Motronic cars, it is all a bit more complex. For a start you have timing sensors either on the flywheel (chrome bumper) or on the front pulley (plastic bumper and M40), plus not one, but two, relays for the pump and injectors. The relays are in the same place as on the LE Jetronic cars (on a bracket on the inlet manifold side front strut turret) and the fuel pump relay has four pins; there are five pins on the injector relay. The same rules about spark and fuel apply to these cars but if the fuel pump relay has stopped (i.e. no fuel getting to the fuel rail), you can go into the fuse box and rob the horn relay, which is the same type. As for the five-pin relay, this controls the injectors and takes signals from the ECU, as well as taking 12 volts and providing an earth. If you read through all of this before your car stopped, you will have a spare relay...

Intermittent cutting out, and/or engines that will not start for twenty minutes after stopping, are suffering from this problem. Cars that drive fine but suddenly cut out at traffic lights and will not restart indicate this fault. The engine will crank and try to fire but cannot quite manage it. Then after a few minutes it will restart and run fine. The irony of this is, a few hours after typing this, I went out in my own car and this happened!

The engine feels very flat – or will not respond to the accelerator
If the engine idles okay but just dies when you press the throttle (or takes forever to pick up), suspect the air flow meter (AFM). The way to go with these is to remove the air cleaner box and just have the air flow meter dangling on its inlet pipe. With the engine idling, try to rev the engine and watch what the air flow meter flap is doing. Watch out for loud backfires, but if the flap is not moving, try opening it with a screwdriver as you open the throttle. If it suddenly picks up, that is your problem. Every 10,000 miles, it's a good idea to take the AFM off and give the inside a good clean with carburettor cleaner and an old toothbrush. Polishing the bore with some paint cutting

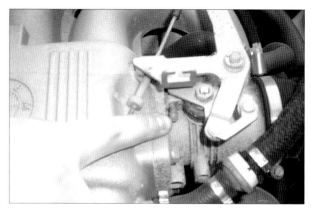
The idle stop screw - never, ever use this to raise the idle speed!

paste can help a 'sticky' unit, but to be honest it's best to just replace it. The options are a brand new unit from either Bosch or BMW, a genuine Bosch reconditioned unit or a used one. Do not bother with a cheap reconditioned AFM, as nine times out of ten they are a load of rubbish. All they have done is tightened the spring inside and given it a quick coat of silver paint. They do not last very long before all the old problems are back.

It uses loads of fuel
This could be a very dirty, old air filter, wrongly adjusted air flow meter or possibly the coolant temperature sensor. On the M40 engine this is buried down the behind the inlet manifold and is a sod to find, but on the other models it is screwed into the front of the head on the thermostat housing. If you suspect that it is faulty, pull the connector off with the engine stone cold and use an ohmmeter. There should be no continuity when cold, but with the engine at running temperature (or the coolant above 86 degrees Fahrenheit) there should be continuity. A failed switch will not only cause high fuel consumption but also, in a really bad case, the engine will not even start. When hot it will just flood the engine – cranking it over with the throttle wide open, but the fuel pump fuse removed, until the engine clears and burns the fuel in the cylinders is the only way to clear it. Changing the temperature sensor (that is the blue one) on the six-cylinder cars can be a really awkward. There is not enough room to get in a deep socket or a conventional ring spanner. Instead you will need a steeply cranked ring spanner and you will have to damage the blue plastic bit. The other way is just to chisel the blue plastic bit off the top and use a standard 19mm socket. Removing the brown sender for the temperature gauge is essential for this little task, but is dead easy.

A faulty oxygen sensor on catalyst equipped cars can also cause rich running as it continually adjusts the CO_2 reading (mixture) by analysing what comes out of the engine. They should be replaced every 30,000 miles as a service item, but keeping the contacts clean helps. Testing an oxygen sensor requires proper equipment so, if in doubt, fit a new one. Avoid the cheap ones, as they do not last very long, so fit a proper Bosch sensor or one from BMW.

A rich idle mixture and poor MPG can also be caused by...

THE THROTTLE POSITION SWITCH (TPS)

Modern engine management systems are horribly complex, but the systems used on the fuel injection E30s are not that bad. A very reliable system, most problems are caused by amateur tinkering. The throttle position switch is a case in point, although old age can be partly to blame. With the engine switched off, go under the bonnet and just open the throttle slightly. You should hear a slight click, not unlike the mouse on your PC. This click is the throttle position switch telling the ECU that the engine is no longer idling but is now above idle and would like some more fuel please. The ECU then tells the injectors to squirt in more fuel; you will notice that the throttle only has to open a tiny amount to make the switch 'click' its command to the ECU. So, when amateur mechanics want to raise the idle speed, what do they do? Easy, they just turn the throttle stop screw on the throttle body a couple of turns and hey presto, another 100rpm. What they have also done is to activate the TPS. So what's happening now is that the engine is idling, but the ECU thinks it's doing 3000rpm on light throttle and the injectors are squirting in loads of fuel. The result is terrible fuel economy and, often, a bad idle. Now, six-cylinder cars have the TPS mounted on the underside of the throttle body. It is no problem being there, but to take it off and service it you have got to remove the throttle body, which is about half an hour of fiddly work. The main problem with the TPS being upside down is that as the engine gets older, it starts to 'breathe'. This means the burnt combustion gasses getting down past the piston rings into the crankcase. Normally this would cause enough crankcase pressure to blow the dipstick out of its tube but BMW wisely looked ahead and built a positive ventilation system and an engine that eats its own crankcase gasses. The oily vapour comes up into the rubber tube between the air flow meter and the throttle body and is sucked into the engine and burnt. This is fine, but it leaves an oily film on the inside of the throttle body. This can cause the throttle disc (or butterfly) to stick slightly open and cause the TPS fault, but it also causes oil to build up at the base of the throttle body that even speeding air travelling through cannot shift. It therefore seeps down the throttle disc shaft, into the TPS. Eventually, the TPS will be completely full of old engine oil, impairing its performance or causing the unit to fail completely.

What to do? Easy. On any six-cylinder E30 that has never had the TPS removed, take it off, split the unit open and wash it out. Ignore manuals that state that special gauges are needed to set the unit up again – they are not! You might even feel flush and pay fifty quid for a new one. To remove the TPS take off the rubber pipe from the throttle body to the air flow meter, disconnect the throttle cable, take accurate notes of where all the various pipes go (DON'T rely on memory!!), remove the four 10mm nuts – a tricky job – and pull the throttle body away. Turn it upside down and wash the whole unit with carburettor cleaner, or a stiff brush and some petrol. Mark the TPS position on the throttle body, remove the two crosshead screws and pull the TPS off the throttle shaft.

The TPS is in two halves, and what you need to do now is to use a small, sharp screwdriver and separate the two halves. It can feel as if you're going to break it but it will come apart and do not worry, nothing will drop out, apart from lots of old oil. Once you have split the unit open, you need to let it soak in petrol or carburettor cleaner for an hour. Really wash the unit clean with aerosol carburettor cleaner and be liberal with the stuff. You will see in the unit a tiny white Burgess micro switch – this is what you really need to get clean. This is the bit that 'clicks' and tells the ECU what to do. Use the aerosol cleaner to get all the crud out and use compressed air to dry it off. You may even have to take three goes at getting it one hundred per cent clean but take your time and do it. When the white switch audibly clicks when depressed with a small screwdriver, you know it is okay.

Once clean and dry, snap the two halves back together and refit the TPS to the throttle body, which also needs to be completely cleared of all oil. Adjust the position of the unit so that the switch clicks the very moment you open the throttle. Make minute adjustments on the throttle stop screw to get it just right – by minute, I mean half a turn maximum.

Now refit the throttle body, all those little hoses and the big rubber pipe. When it is all back together check again that the switch clicks the moment you open the throttle. Now fire the engine up – it might take a couple of goes. If the idle is very slow, raise it on the idle speed screw (LE Jetronic cars, 320i and 323i). On Motronic cars you have an electronic idle control valve, which on most cars is not adjustable. For poor idle, take the valve off and give it a good clean out with carburettor cleaner. If it refuses to play ball, you need a new one.

With the throttle switch clicking nicely and the engine turned off, you will also need to get out your voltmeter/ohmmeter. There are three terminals. Eighteen is the centre terminal, terminal two is the one to the left and

Electronic idle control valve, 325e

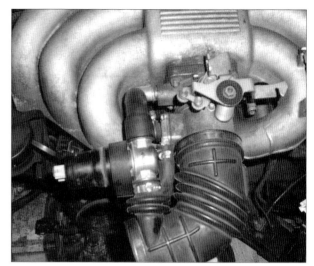

Electronic idle control valve, 320i and 325i (Motronic)

number three is to the right. Unplug the connector plug. Now connect your ohmmeter between the centre terminal (18) and the outer terminal (2). With the throttle closed, you should have a reading of zero ohms. There should however be continuity when the throttle is open by about 15 thousands of an inch – use a feeler blade between the throttle lever and the throttle stop screw. Basically, zero ohms with the throttle shut, continuity when the unit 'clicks' open. Now connect the ohmmeter between the centre terminal (18) and the other outer terminal (3). Open the throttle fully and you should have a reading of zero ohms, and continuity when the throttle lever is about 10 degrees away from being fully open. Make sure also that there are volts getting to the unit. Using the voltmeter, switch on the ignition there should be 5 volts (VDC) minimum between the centre terminal and either of the two other terminals.

A final note on this. If you do buy a new or used TPS, be aware that the units for cars with the switchable automatic gearbox are different. Also, units from M30 engined cars look the same but they actually work back to front so they will not do either!

THE DREADED WATER HEATED IDLE VALVE

320i and 323i cars with Bosch LE Jetronic injection, i.e. metal bumper cars, used a water heated idle control valve. This is mounted on the inlet side of the cylinder block in front of the starter motor, an alloy 'H' shaped device. Two pipes are for water, and are linked into the cooling system, and the other two are for air, linked to the idle system. So when the water is cold, the valve is open and lets air into to the idle circuit, helping it to idle slightly higher – only 100rpm or so. Like a thermostat, the valve slowly closes as the water temperature increases and when the engine is up to operating temperature, the valve is fully closed. It is a great idea, but after ten

years or less, the alloy valve is all corroded inside and does not work any more. When the engine is cold and idling, clamp the pipe that runs from the idle speed screw housing to the H valve. The idle speed should slow down noticeably, and it might even stall completely. When the engine is good and warm, try this again. It should make absolutely no difference to the idle speed whatsoever. If it does, the valve is stuck open. If clamping the pipe makes no difference to the idle speed when the engine is still cold, i.e. just started from stone cold, the valve is stuck shut. Because of the age of these cars, forget any notion of nipping down to the local scrap yard and getting a good used one because there are no good ones left. Even if you do find one that works, it will not work for very long. So, the answer is a new one from BMW and keeping the antifreeze and coolant fresh so that it doesn't corrode. Whilst you are down there, you really might as well replace all the water pipes.

There is another solution which costs much less. Find a later, plastic bumper 320i with Motronic and scavenge the rubber bellows from the throttle body to the air flow meter as well as the electronic idle control valve and it's wiring plug. With this lot, you can replace the old water-heated valve. You will have to join the two water pipes either side of the old water-heated H valve together, or even better, fit a new, one-piece pipe. You could even leave the H valve there, but a bad one might cause a blockage or an air lock so best remove it. Wire the idle control valve into a 12-volt ignition-operated source (not the coil!) and it should all work. A second-hand electronic idle control valve will need some attention with carburettor cleaner to make sure it works fine.

You will, however, still have the old air speed screw. Either wind the screw right in against its stop, or remove it and insert a bit of plastic between the housing and inlet manifold.

On balance, fitting a new water heated H valve is the easiest way because it's just nuts and bolts – but they are quite pricey. If you can get the electronic valve for a few quid and fancy a morning's work, then go for it. It has to be said that the water heated H valve when new was pretty reliable, whereas an old electronic valve can be a bore.

Crank position trigger (325e and metal bumper 325i)
These older Motronic systems use two sensors in the bell housing. One counted the flywheel teeth, much like an ABS trigger ring, to measure the speed of the engine, and the other relied on a marker peg on the flywheel to give it a reference of when the engine was at TDC. The trouble is, these marker pegs can fall out and when that happens, the engine stops dead. Without a TDC reference, the ECU does not know which is TDC and cannot fire. I have seen a self-tapping screw wound in as well as bits of metal welded on. A good repair is to drill a hole on the flywheel (tedious) in EXACTLY the right position and use a 10mm nut and bolt with some thread lock.

This problem is another good reason to own a later car where one sensor on the front crank pulley did everything! The speed sensor gives the ECU info on speed and this can cause mixture problems.

Wiring socket, Motronic 320i and 325i
Look under the inlet manifold just above the engine mounting bracket and you will see an electronic plug. This is where the engine loom joins and many a misfire or unexplained running problem has been caused by moisture getting in here. It is not unknown to unscrew the plug and find water running out. Obviously spraying something like WD40 or Plus Gas in there followed by an electrical contact cleaner will sort out problems here, but if badly corroded, you will need to solder in a new socket.

Air flow meter
This clever device is bolted to the air cleaner box on all fuel injection E30s. Inside is an alloy flap that opens and closes. As the engine cranks over, it sucks air in through the air flow meter. The air being sucked in opens the flap and the flap is hinged on a potentiometer. This tells the ECU how much air is being drawn in and thus how much fuel to inject. The faster the engine runs, the more air is drawn in and the more the flap moves. Accelerate suddenly and the air flow meter will respond – well, it should. In time, they wear out because the spring on the flap weakens. Cheap reconditioned air flow meters (or AFMs) just have the spring tightened which is not much good. Generally, a good second-hand AFM is better than a reconditioned unit, although the genuine Bosch recon AFMs are very good and are basically new units but at a cheaper cost.

Here is a list of the various AFMs. All numbers are found on the black plastic top cover and begin with 0280.

200 201:	316i 1987 onwards (plastic bumpers)
202 050:	318i 1983 to 1987 (metal bumpers)
202 203:	318i 1987 onwards (plastic bumpers)
202 031:	320i and 323i 1982 to 1985
202 090:	Later metal bumper 320i and 323i
202 083:	320i 1987 – 88
202 040:	325e
203 028:	2.3 litre M3

Note: 2.5 Sport Evo cars used the 027 unit from the E32/E34 530i, 535i, 730i and 735i

FUEL TANKS
Leaking fuel tanks are becoming the bane of the E30 owner's life and it is a problem that seems to affect the later cars more than the older ones. Maybe the steel used was a bit thinner to save weight but when you fill the car with fuel and you get a major petrol leak or at least a strong smell of fuel, it is time for a new one. Look also at the state of the fuel filler neck that runs from the body down to the tank because this is made from mild steel and will not last forever. Do not think for a moment that the fuel filter will catch everything because it will not. Replacing rusty tanks is a nuisance because there is quite a bit of dismantling involved. For a start, the exhaust has to come off as well as the prop-shaft. If the car has never had a new prop-shaft front coupling now would be an excellent time to fit one because it is such a boring job. The tank might look like a two-piece unit, as used on the old E21, but in fact all E30 tanks are made in one piece. There are various different types but they all seem to interchange, although fitting a different tank will render the fuel gauge slightly inaccurate. With the exhaust and prop-shaft off, there is still plenty of scope for various dramas. The bolts holding the tank can snap off and getting the breather hoses on and off without breaking them can be a bit of a challenge. You should pay close attention to the fuel filler neck because they too can rust. In short, a fuel tank change can either be a day's work or a three-day drama. It is best to just have the car right up on axle stands, take the fuel tank out and go to your dealer or parts specialist with a list of bits. If you go for a used tank, bear in mind that getting one out of a scrap car will be as much fun as taking the one out of yours and it might be just as rusty. So buying

a used tank from a BMW specialist who has already removed the tank so that you can examine it is a good idea. Try as well to get all the breather pipes. The breather canister is buried up in the rear arch area behind a screw-on plastic trim cover and it is next to the fuel filler entry. Some tanks were specifically for cars with a single pipe exhaust.

E30 fuel tanks come in various different sizes, and these are 58-litres for the early cars up until September 1983, the 55-litre tank after this that was used in later cars plus the 63-litre. Here is a breakdown on which tanks were fitted to what cars.

58 Litre: Pre-September 1983 316, 318i (K Jetronic), 320i and 323i.

55 Litre: All post-September 1983 saloons, 316, 316i, 318i, 318iS, 320i, 323i, 325i and 2.3 litre M3, all diesels, pre-September 1987 Convertibles. The M3 often came with an additional 15-litre tank in the boot.

63 Litre: German market 318i Edition, plastic bumper 320i and 325i, 320iS, M3 Sport Evo 2.5, all Touring models, all post-September 1987 Convertibles.

The inevitable question of the special Sport Evo fuel tank arises, and it is not special at all – it is a standard 63-litre fuel tank as fitted to a humble 320i – the same part number. It is claimed that the 2.3 litre M3 had a special 70-litre tank – not true. What it did have was a standard 55-litre tank and a 15 litre supplementary fuel tank in the boot!

Fuel tanks are interchangeable, and the sender units in the tank are not volume sensitive – put another way, if you wanted to fit a 63-litre tank into a 318iS (or any car with a 55-litre tank and the tank mounted fuel pump), you will need the tank and the fuel gauge. The sender units are the same.

FUEL HOSES
Most E30s will now be ready for a set of new fuel hoses. The transition from stone cold to very hot under bonnet temperatures takes their toll. External cracking is a sure sign that the hose is about to let go. The M40 engines seem very prone to this because the hoses run under the inlet manifold – a smell of fuel is a giveaway. Fitting new ones is fiddly but worthwhile.

Chapter 11

ELECTRICAL SYSTEM

Ratings in amperes, items of equipment supplied, relays

1 = 7.5 A Left high beam headlight (relay K3)

2 = 7.5 A Right high beam headlight (relay K3)

3 = 15 A Auxiliary fan, 91° C (relay K1)

4 = 15 A Flashing turn indicators

5 = 30 A Wipe-wash, headlight cleaning and intensive cleaning fluid systems (relay K10)

6 = 7.5 A Brake lights (15 A if additional brake lights are fitted), automatic cruise control

7 = 15 A Horn (relay K2)

8 = 30 A Heated rear window

9 = 15 A Engine electrical system (carburettor engine), speed-range indicator for automatic transmission

10 = 7.5 A Instruments, on-board computer, reversing lights

11 = 15 A Fuel pump, fuel supply pump

12 = 7.5 A Radio, Check Control and instruments

13 = 7.5 A Left low beam headlight (relay K4)

14 = 7.5 A Right low beam headlight (relay K4)

15 = 7.5 A Rear fog light (relay K4, switching off when high headlight beams are selected: relay K9)

16 = 15 A Seat heating (relay K5)

17 = 30 A Sliding roof (relay K5), electric window lifts

18 = 30 A Auxiliary fan, 99° C (relay K6)

19 = 7.5 A Mirror control, mirror heating (relay K7)

20 = 30 A Heater blower, air conditioning (relay K7)

21 = 7.5 A Interior, glove box and luggage compartment lights, hand lamp, clock, radio memory, on-board computer

22 = 7.5 A Left side, rear and parking lights

23 = 7.5 A Right side, rear and parking lights, licence plate lights, instrument lighting

24 = 15 A Hazard warning flashers

25 = 30 A Not in use

26 = 30 A Not in use

27 = 30 A Central locking system, door lock heating, thiefproofing system, on-board computer, horn

28 = 30 A Cigarette lighter, motor-driven radio aerial, independent fuel-burning heater

29 = 7.5 A Left fog light (relay K8)

30 = 7.5 A Right fog light (relay K8)

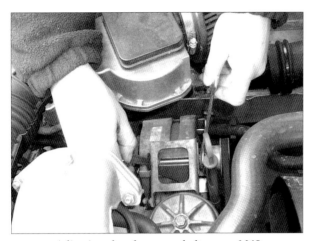

Adjusting the alternator belt on an M40 engined car is shown

This photos shows why the M20 starter is such a nightmare to replace

In the centre of this picture is the earthing point (10mm bolt). If it comes loose you will have weird electrical problems - find them behind the glove box

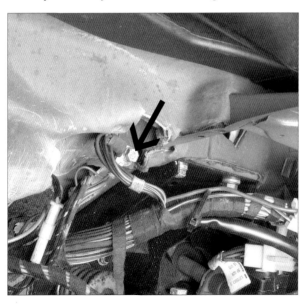

Fuses

All cars use the press-in fuse. They can corrode with age and cause a myriad of electrical problems. A good idea is to buy a new set, clean up the fuse connectors in the fuse box (disconnect the battery first though!) and fit them. Spraying a contact preservative is also a good idea.

Fuses that blow are caused by a short circuit somewhere. A problematic central locking system can blow its fuse and fuse 10 can be blown randomly with no immediate cause. However, it's known now that the wire that passes though the gearlever rubber boot going to the reverse light switch can rub through and short out, blowing the fuse.

Alternator bushes

All BMWs have an alternator that is mounted with rubber bushes to damp out vibrations and improve engine refinement. This is a great idea but, after a decade or two, the bushes wear out and the alternator begins to sit at a strange angle. Rather than putting up with it, it is very easy to fit new bushes. You just take off the alternator, remove the circlips holding in the centre guide pins and remove them followed by the old bushes. Refitting new ones is equally easy and the whole job should not take more than an hour. A toothed nut that runs on a toothed bracket takes up the alternator adjustment. Over the years they rust and the teeth wear out but new ones are surprisingly cheap.

The Starter

E30 starter motors rarely fail – in fact, I have never actually heard of one failing. If all it does is spin without turning the engine over, try turning the engine over by hand half a turn. If, when you try again, the starter engages and the engine starts, the problem will most likely be a worn ring gear. This is a problem because the engine will ninety-nine times out of a hundred stop at exactly the same place – that is why ring gears wear out because the starter will always start on that point.

Replacing a starter is quite simple on the M10 and M40/42, but is a complete nightmare on the older M20 with the big starter. The problem is getting to the top starter bolt because everything is in the way, you cannot really see it and, to make matters worse, you cannot get a socket on the nut. Have a go by all means, but when you feel the red mist coming down, shut the bonnet and walk away. My advice? Take it to a garage, look big and pay up – believe me, paying is a lot easier than doing.

Sorting instrument problems

Every E30 will, at some stage in its life, suffer from flaky instruments. Like the E28 5 Series that pioneered this system in 1981, the E30 used a computerised system for determining when the car needed servicing. It would

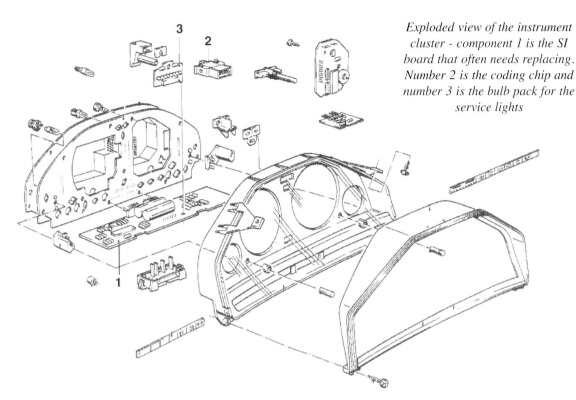

Exploded view of the instrument cluster - component 1 is the SI board that often needs replacing. Number 2 is the coding chip and number 3 is the bulb pack for the service lights

take readings from various sources and based on information of how the car was driven (i.e. number of cold starts, how long the journeys were, how fast it was driven) and adjust the service intervals accordingly. Therefore, a car that had many cold starts and a number of short trips would need an oil service much sooner than one which was driven 200 miles a day on the motorway. On the early cars built up until August 1985, the dash had nine service lights. The first five are green, the sixth is yellow and the remaining three are red. When the car has returned from a service, there should be all five green lights lit up with the ignition on and no yellow or red lights. As soon as the car starts and runs, three green lights go out. This happens every time the car is started. As time goes by, the number of green lights reduces until none come on. This is followed by the orange light that tells the owner that it needs a service. The three red lights will then come on to tell the owner that it is overdue. There are also signs for 'Oil Service' (an oil and filter change plus a look over) or 'Inspection' which means a proper service. After August 1985, this system was changed slightly by reducing the number of red service warning lights from three to just one. BMW also added a small clock symbol which when illuminated, alerted the owner that the car needed an annual check, which means new brake fluid and anti freeze.

Overall, this is a very clever system that, if adhered to as BMW intended, means the car will live a lot longer – witness the condition of one-owner cars with full BMW service history. The problems come when the NiCad batteries that power the system fail. These are actually rechargeable and are charged by the main electrical system. When they fail, you will probably find that the Service Indicator (SI) lights do not work anymore. The car is old; it does not go to the main dealer anymore so big deal, who cares? It might go the other way and have all the lights illuminated and they just cannot be put out, even with one of the many non-genuine reset tools available. The problem is when the batteries start to leak, which is absolutely guaranteed. The acid leaks all over the SI board (The main circuit board that controls the system) and this in itself would not be a major drama if the SI board didn't also control the rev counter and the fuel/temperature gauges as well. So when the SI board gets really bad, the temperature gauge will be all over the place. I once bought a very clean 1988 316 from an auction cheaply with an overheating problem – that overheating problem was cured with a new SI board!

So when you have instrument problems, it is best to dig the cluster out, split the unit and have a good look. If all you have is a fluctuating temperature gauge (assuming the SI lights all work as they should) then it might just be a loose earth nut. Remove the instrument cluster as described later and just tighten the small brass nut on the back. Also, drop the glove box down, remove the plastic rear cover if fitted and locate the earth point on the bulkhead. If it is rusty, remove the earth wires and give it all a good clean. These two small points are the cause of many electrical problems related to the instruments. Before you go charging in, check that the fuses are okay

Two views of an E30 SI Board

– it is fuse 10, a 7.5 amp fuse that operates this lot. If your rev counter and temperature gauge are dead, it could well be something that simple.

Removing the instrument cluster

First off, do yourself a favour and remove the steering wheel. It is held by just one 22mm nut and it generally makes life a lot easier. The way to do this is to remove either the centre BMW badge (cars with the original 4 spoke wheel or the M Technic 1 wheel) or the horn push (cars with SE three spoke leather wheel or the M Technic 2 wheel). Centralise the steering wheel straight ahead, pull the key out of the ignition lock to lock the steering and undo the nut. Refit the key and turn to position one to release the steering lock, re-centralise the steering wheel to the straight ahead position, unscrew the nut and pull the steering wheel off.

Now you have the lower dash under tray to remove. This is held on with four plastic twist clips – using a flat blade screwdriver, twist them though 90 degrees and they will come out. The bottom edge of the undertray locates in a plastic clip at the base of the steering column.

Now for a tricky bit. There is a plastic trim panel between the steering column shroud and the instrument cluster. At first there seems to be no obvious way of get-

ting this off but they are held by a pair of fine-threaded alloy knurled nuts. Look under the dash and you will see them – unscrew them with your fingers and press on the studs to pop the panel out. Now you can see the lower retaining screws for the instrument panel. Unscrew all of these, taking note of where the long and short screws go, and then remove the two at the top which secure the inner black plastic shroud to the dash. Keep a note of where all the different screws go. Once you've done that, you can pull that shroud out to reveal the final two screws that secure the mounting legs at the top of the cluster unit to the dash itself. With those two out, the cluster will now jiggle out of the dash. There are still a couple of connectors to remove and you do this by pulling the black centre clips outwards with a small flat-blade screwdriver and the plug will then come out. Access to these plugs can be a bit tight but be patient and it will come out fine.

Stripping the instrument cluster

With the cluster out, turn it upside down and remove the nine identical gold-coloured crosshead screws – you will see the ninth screw hidden in the middle above the centre connector plug. With these removed, you can then carefully prise the two dash cluster halves apart. You will find the main SI board in the front part. Remove the single crosshead screw and lift out the plastic retainer. You can now carefully remove the SI board, although it can be a tight fit and requires great care. This is the moment of truth. Even if the batteries are dead, you can buy and solder in new ones but nine times out of ten there is corrosion on the board and then they are just scrap. If the car has any value to you at all, the best course of action is either a reconditioned unit or a brand new one from BMW. In the old days, battery replacement was a sure fire fix but these cars are now much older and generally the SI boards are beyond repair.

Now we get to a tricky problem. New boards are just about unavailable right now for the early 'three red light' type of dash. Reconditioned units are very hard to find and unless you are a real stickler for originality, you need to be looking for the later type cluster. These will fit straight into an early car without problems and yes, the VDO and Motormeter dashes will swap over. Eh? VDO? Motormeter? Look at your dash between the speedometer and the rev counter, but above the SI lights, and you will see either of these two names. They were the original manufacturers of the clusters and there is no difference in quality or longevity between the two, although fitting a VDO SI board into a Motormeter dash is fine. A specialist like Phil Crouch in the UK will often have a good range of new used and reconditioned SI boards for old and later type clusters. A new BMW board will have a shiny laquered finish and an orange arrow sticker.

If the SI board is not obviously corroded, you can have a

go at replacing the batteries but the tagged NiCads that BMW used are now extremely hard to find. What I am trying to say here is forget about just replacing the batteries, as it will probably be a load of grief for nothing. Ordinary NiCad batteries will last about three days because it gets surprisingly hot inside a cluster and ordinary batteries will not tolerate the heat. Don't forget to swap over the bulb board to the new SI board.

Reassembly is a reversal of removal, although getting those two alloy knurled nuts back on can be a pain if you have sausage fingers. Resetting the service lights is easy if you have the special tool – lots of companies make them now and you can buy one for about £15. Follow the instructions given, but I will outline how to use the average unit. Start with the oil service light first. Plug it in, switch the ignition on and hold the button down. A light should come on. When the unit clicks and the second light comes on, wait until it clicks again and the light goes off. If a proper reset tool does not do it, your attempts to fit new batteries didn't work!

Coding plugs

When BMW went to the coding plug system in 1986, the idea was that they would no longer have to use different rev counters for four- and six-cylinder cars. Instead, a white coding plug specific to the car's engine would provide the adjustment needed. This is also very handy when buying a second-hand instrument cluster because if you own a 325i and the only E30 in the breaker's yard is a 316i, it is really no problem. You just remove your existing coding plug and fit it into the replacement cluster. Earlier cars had no plugs and so these older four and six cylinder clusters cannot be interchanged. However, an old 323i or 320i cluster can be fitted to a later 325i but the chances of finding one with a good SI board are now minimal.

This is the chart that tells you what coding plug you have. It is at the base of the unit under the rev counter (tachometer), visible from the front when the cluster is removed. They are virtually all white with the part number clearly visible.

316:	1 377 361
316i:	(M10 and M40) plus all 318i: 1 385 364
318iS:	1 394 321 (Catalyst)
318iS:	1 394 110 (non catalyst)
320i:	1 372 264 (early cars up to 1/86) plus early 324d and last 323i
320i:	1 377 364 (later 320i/324d)

Early socket for service lights

The later service light socket

320i:	1 381 635 (320i 12/86 onwards)
323i:	1 372 264
325e:	1 377 646 (cars up to 12/86)
325e:	1 381 682 (cars 12/86 onwards)
325i and iX:	1 377 670 (metal bumper)
325i and iX:	1 381 683 (plastic bumper cars 9/87 onwards)
M3:	1 380 873
324td:	1 385 339
320iS:	No coding plug officially fitted, although some do use the M3 cluster and plug.

Wiper motor problems

E30 wiper motors are generally reliable and long lasting. However, there are two main problems and one of them is spindle wear. This is easy to check, although wipers that clonk are a dead giveaway. Prise out the plastic scuttle vent above the wiper motor and move the wiper arms manually. If the spindle has lots of side-to-side play it is finished and either a good used motor or a new one is needed. The other possibility is the wiper relay unit – this is the long black one in the main fuse box. When these go wrong they can cause various wiper ailments.

With the wiper motor out, unclip the rear cover, clean out the old grease and use Vaseline

Wiper motor relay in the fuse box.

The other problem is a very reluctant wiper sweep when on intermittent. Most owners assume the motor is dead, although it can often be a dodgy wiper motor relay. If another relay does not fix the problem, this is the straightforward repair you can do for free. This also covers wipers that do not park properly. But first you have to remove the wiper motor.

1. On all cars, open the bonnet, remove the scuttle vent cover above the wiper motor and also remove the rear rubber seal that goes across the scuttle. Remove the three 7mm bolts that secure the bulkhead cover panel and unclip the wiring from this panel. You will also find some plastic nuts in all probability, but it is pretty self-explanatory.

2. With the bulkhead cover panel out of the way, you can now remove the wiper motor. On LHD cars, like the M3, it is difficult. On RHD cars it is not so bad. Mark the position of the cranked arm on the spindle with paint, remove the centre 10mm nut and jolt the cranked arm from the spindle – it comes off with a bit of a wiggle. Alternatively you can prise the main wiper linkage arm from the cranked arm ball socket, although it is hard work.

3. Now unplug the electrical connector and remove the three 13mm bolts that secure the complete wiper motor and bracket assembly to the body. Lift the motor out through the hole in the bulkhead. If your car has a strut brace, such as the Hartge type, you might want to remove that first.

4. With the motor out, remove the three 10mm bolts that secure the motor to the mounting bracket – mark the position of the motor to the bracket first though. You can also use a small screwdriver to prise the electrical socket connector from the mounting bracket.

5. Now remove the plastic/rubber dust cover. The black plastic cover where all the wires go is secured to the main motor body by four 'legs'. These are easily prised off with a small screwdriver and the cover lifts away.

6. Now you will see loads of orange coloured grease. You will also see the gold coloured 'C' ring, a round metal circular contact with a segment missing. This missing segment is there to tell the contact that the wipers have completed a full sweep. When grease and dirt get everywhere, the contact can be broken anywhere around this disc, which causes the jerky wiper movements. What you have to do now is to use methylated spirits, white spirit, carburettor cleaner etc, to really clean all the grease off. Clean up the disc and the contact in the plastic cover with some very fine emery, bend the contact tab in the plastic cover outwards by about 3mm (this increases the contact pressure on the disc) and LIGHTLY smear Vaseline on the disc – just a very light coating is needed. Now reassemble the motor but before you refit it to the car, plug it into the wiring socket dangling from the car, switch on the ignition and try the motor. If all is well, rebuild the motor into the car. If it is not, well, you need another motor.

Central locking faults and door lock problems
Many E30s came from the factory with central locking and for 1990, all models had it as standard. Mostly, it is a good, reliable system but it can, and does, go wrong. Central locking failure can be divided into sections, which are:

Total failure: The central locking system is dead. Turning the key in any lock does not trigger the system even though the doors can still be manually locked one-by-one with the key. This is most probably corrosion in the door pins where the central locking loom plugs into the main loom or a dead central locking control unit. We will see how to repair a dead unit later.

Partial failure: Where one door or two doors (four-door and Touring models) do not lock even though locking the car with the key will lock the other doors. This will be a problem with the central locking motor on that door, or the wiring to the motor. The wiring loom for each door's components (central locking motor, electric window motor, electric door mirrors etc) is a loom that plugs into the doorpost electrical socket. These can be corroded over time by water ingress and ruined.

Trying to lock: This is where locking the door with the key locks and then unlocks the door – it is trying to lock but something is knocking the system back. This can be caused by a stiff door lock assembly, needing lubrication, or a door latch pin (they screw into the door posts) that is out of adjustment. This is just a long-winded process of elimination. You need to remove each door trim one by one and disconnect the central locking motor on that door. When you have identified the problem door, the rest of the system will function correctly. Do not forget the tailgate or boot lock and do not overlook the fuel filler cap lock either.

Corroded door pins

As part of maintenance, it is a good idea to unplug these sockets and spray in some penetrating fluid or, even better, proper electrical contact cleaner followed by a dab of Vaseline which will protect it in the future. You may find that when the system is dead, the pins are so badly corroded that they just fall apart. The answer here is to find another E30 in a breaker's yard with good pins and remove the entire socket, along with a good length of the loom. Then you can cut and solder in the replacement section (do not use crimp connectors). If the socket coming out of the door is bad, then just fit a complete second-hand door loom. Not the easiest job in the world I'm afraid.

Faulty door lock barrels

The biggest killer to door lock barrels is moisture and old age. Given time they just corrode, like door locks on any other car, but they can be saved. Spraying penetrating oil into the lock itself, where the key goes, is a start but to do a proper job you will need to remove the door trim and soak the inside of the mechanism. Using a screwdriver, operate the door latch (as if you were closing the door) and using the key, give the lock some exercise. Try using the deadlock as well, but you might find that it just clicks over and nothing happens. In the worst case you will find that, after partially seizing, a previous owner got a bit heavy handed with the key and the lock barrel end is broken. In this case, you will need a complete new door lock and key from BMW. You can buy a repair kit from BMW so that you can use your existing key but it is really fiddly work. Also, operate the door lock micro switches with a small screwdriver. If a previously dead system comes to life, it indicates that the lock is not operating the micro-switch.

The screwdriver is pointing at the fused link - this is what blows. It is repairable with solder.

Central locking motors do fail - testing for power supply and substitution is the answer

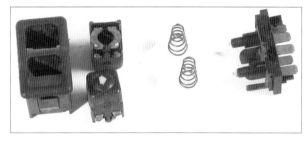

The electric window switches can be taken apart and cleaned up.

If you can live with having two keys, a complete new lock and key is the best answer. The trouble with using a repair kit is that sometimes they just do not want to work with an old key. If you do try a repair kit, it comes as a bag of bits that you fit together. What you need to do is fit all the brass plates into the lock barrel with the springs, slide your old key all the way in and then file down the exposed parts of the plates until the barrel fits together. When you withdraw the key, it should all spring into place and lock. But it is horrible fiddly work with no firm guarantee of a result. If a new lock is too expensive for you, there are still lots of good used ones but remember that left- and right-hand locks do not interchange. If you are looking through a British scrap yard for a driver's door lock for your M3, you will need a passenger door lock, which in most cases will be relatively unworn.

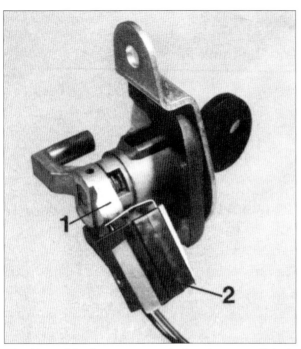

Locking of the front passenger's door is accomplished with microswitch (2), which is operated by a cam (1) on the door lock and triggers the electric system.

Failed central locking control unit

These can fail with water ingress, or with a bit of overloading they can fail by blowing a thermal overload. If water has got in and you can see obvious signs of corrosion on the soldered terminals, the unit is scrap. But on taking the cover off, you might find that the thermal overload has blown and this is easily corrected.

First though, you have to remove the unit. On the driver's side of the car (RHD cars) or passenger side (LHD cars), you need to first remove the plastic panel that covers the front speaker. On RHD cars you will need to remove the dash under-tray, on LHD cars it is useful to disconnect the two glove box retaining straps and let it hang down. On any car you will first need to pull the rubber door seal away. The plastic panel is held on with a couple of crosshead screws but on older cars there is carpeting, as opposed to the plastic panel. You will need to pull the door seal off and remove the speaker first.

So, once the plastic panel is off, the speaker is exposed. Remove the screws and remove the speaker. Below the speaker you will see a pair of crosshead screws. Remove these, put your hand down into the hole where the speaker sits and lift the control unit out. It is a black plastic box with a gold coloured anodised steel bracket. If it is at all wet or damp in there, you may have found your problem.

Now, before you unplug the unit, try operating the central locking and listen for the unit clicking. Sit in the seat, window open, locking the car with one hand with the control unit in your other hand. Feel anything happening? If not, that unit is dead.

To remove the unit from the plug, just use a small flat-blade screwdriver to disengage the tang. Now unscrew the triangular mounting plate from the unit and using a small screwdriver, prise the cover off the unit. The remaining plastic end cover just slides off. Now you can see the circuit board for the control unit. The thermal overload is shown and if that has blown, it is a simple matter solder it back together using a low melting-point solder to. More often than not, the unit will now work again. If the strip blows again, you have got to repair it again and disconnect one door motor at a time to identify which of the door locking motors is causing such high resistance. The actual motors themselves very rarely fail. It's almost always sticky locks and locking mechanisms that cause the problem.

Oh, and one last thing. Do not forget that the central locking system is fused, 30-amp fuse number 27.

Replacing electric window motors

If you've narrowed a fault down to an electric window motor, here's how to change one. They look like they're going to be a total pig to remove and the first time you do one they aren't as easy as they should be. The first thing to do is to lower the window more than half way by inserting an allen key in the motor spindle. The first thing to do is take the window itself out. At the bottom of the door glass towards the back the glass has a bonded on bracket which bolts to the slider with two 10mm bolts. With those undone the glass will lift up and slide off the front runner, up and out of the door. Then it's a case of undoing every 10mm nut and bolt you can find on the inner door frame but take a hint and mark all the mounting points on the door with contrasting paint because the whole motor and lifting mechanism has to come out as one - and it can be a bit confusing refitting it all and not knowing which bit went where. With the door glass out, you can jiggle the motor and lifting mechanism out. Replace the motor by removing the screws holding it to the lifting mechanism.

Replacing a noisy heater fan

These are hidden behind the steel panel on the back of the bulkhead. Using WD40 is a waste of time because it evaporates, and it will also stink the interior out the first time you use the fan. Instead, remove the fan unit and grease the bearings – even a bit of engine oil will do the job.

Batteries

Always use the correct battery. Very often, genuine BMW batteries are cheaper than others. Convertibles need the proper BMW "vibration damping" battery.

Chapter 12

INTERIOR RESTORATION

Few things let a car down more than a really grotty interior. There are still enough damaged E30s around in the breakers to ensure that you can get used trimming bits, but new items are available. Rare bits are good driver's seats (I have always fitted good passenger seats instead), good door trims and rear shelf trims that have not had holes for speakers hacked into them.

The problem with the door trims is that, with time, the vinyl eventually begins to become unstuck from the edges. Various attempts to get the door trims off break the clips from the hardboard base and if the plastic membrane sealing the doorframe has ruptured, damp can warp the door trims and at that point they are just useless. A pair of mint black vinyl door trims for a two-door E30 are valuable and hard to find these days. Early E30 cars had a kind of check pattern cloth inserts, and these are hard work to find in good condition.

Full spec E30 interior - The M3 differs only
in the instruments

Replace that cracked dash
The other problem is the cracked dashboard. E30 dashboards eventually sprout cracks in the top face around the middle and there is just no way of successfully repairing them. Even if you did manage to do an invisible repair (unlikely), the crack will only reappear. Therefore, replacing the dash is the best option. The last time I checked, new dashboards were still just about available from a limited stock, but they are expensive. In that case, a good used dash is the best option and, believe it or not, they are not hard to fit – just long winded.

So, you've found an E30 in the breaker's yard with a nice un-cracked dash – how do you get it out? The first step is to remove the steering wheel, which, if the breaker kept the key, is easy. If he did not, you have to cut the steering lock pawl with a hacksaw. Run the hacksaw between the steering wheel and the plastic column shrouds, cutting for about two or three minutes. With the centre 22mm steering wheel nut removed, the wheel will eventually yank off but it is quite hard work cutting through the pawl.

Now the instruments have to come out and this is described in the repairs section. Now remove the centre console. The rear bit comes out first and the securing nuts are located underneath the rear ashtray. The front half is held in by a plastic nut hiding underneath the gear-lever gaiter and by two screws at the front going up into the dash. The glove box can stay on, although the two straps need to be disconnected. With the radio and all the push button centre switches removed (they just pull out) you can access the screws that hold the centre heater control panel – they screw up into the dash and are accessed through the now-vacant push-button holes. Remove the ECU complete with its bracket and look for the 10mm bolt that secures the dashboard at each end. With these removed, the dashboard should be getting pretty flexible. You should also remove the door rubber seals both sides, as well as the windscreen pillar plastic trims. Two more centre retaining bolts, plus the air vent trunking, and the dashboard really wants to come out. The dash wiring loom is tie-wrapped to the back of the dash so, as the dash comes out, you need to deal with these. Replacing an old dashboard is a good day's work, including taking out the old one, and with it removed you can give all those hard-to-get-to areas a good clean.

Replacing door trims

Replacing these is a nice easy job. Firstly, remove the electric mirror switch by prising it out with a small flat-blade screwdriver – you will need something between the screwdriver and the door pull to avoid marking it. The plug on the end just pulls off easily. Inside the hole where the switch, or the blanking plate on the other side, went you will see a single cross-headed screw and this needs to come out. Look at the underside of the main door pull and you will see two holes going up into the door. The remaining two screws are up those holes. With that done, remove the plastic trim ring around the interior door handle by pushing it forward and out – you may need that small flat-blade screwdriver again. On cars with wind-up windows, remove the centre cover for the winder handle and use a Torx driver to remove the centre screw and the handle. Finally pop off the triangular bit of plastic at the front of the window. To remove the trim you need a flat bladed screwdriver to pop out each of the retaining clips one by one. Once one of the clips has popped out of the door, you can often use you fingers to pull carefully on the door trim to pop the rest of them. When they are all out, use a screwdriver to lift the door trim complete with the top chrome strip out of the door – do not try to leave the chrome bit behind!

Should any of the plastic clips break, remove them by pulling and twisting with a pair of pliers and refit the new ones by pushing and twisting – it is obvious how they fit when you see them.

Replacing rear trims – two-door cars

This is another of those jobs that is easy if you go the long way round. The first thing to do is to remove the rear seats. The base is clipped into a pair of tongs in the body and a single (or pair) of 10mm bolts cunningly hidden in the carpet. The rear seat back is bolted into the body at the bottom on each side by a 10mm bolt. Remove these two bolts and the seat can be lifted up and out (you will need some brute force for this).

Now the rear trim panels can be unclipped and some cars have a self-tapping screw behind the ashtray (when fit-

ted). The trim panels then lift up and out. Refitting is pretty simple, but it is all but impossible with the rear seats still fitted. Some cars did not have a piece of plastic sheeting taped over the big hole in the rear inner wing panel exposed when the trim panel is removed and this can lead to the hardboard trim backing panel getting a bit damp and distorted. Making up and fitting one is a good idea, as is spraying some Waxoyl or similar anti rust fluid in the inner sill and wheel arch area.

Trim cleaners

This book wasn't sponsored by BMW, but I have found that the best trim cleaner for door trims, and especially dashboards, is the stuff marketed by BMW. The BMW Williams Formula 1 branded stuff might seem a good sales ploy but it really works and does not leave that disgusting sticky sheen over everything. Black trim is easy enough to clean but I have found that very dirty beige or grey door trims are best thrown away and better ones found. You can clean them up using one of those dish scouring pads and a gritty hand cleaner but it is hard work and not always successful. BMW's own leather-cleaning foam is pretty good too.

Repairing damaged seats

Well, I can give you an excellent word or two of advice here – forget it. BMW do offer new seat covers for various trims and it is surprising how many trim items are still available. The problems will come when you try to fit a new BMW seat cover. This is strictly a job for a professional trimmer, or the extremely brave and patient. It involves taking the entire seat apart – the backrest cover comes off to reveal the seat back release cables (two-door cars only) plus the large crosshead screws that hold the seat back to the base. Then you have to remove the seat tilting mechanism and, finally, unbend the seat cover tangs and remove the entire seat foam. Sound easy? Believe me, it is not. Then you have to separate the seat cover from the foam and the foam has steel rods moulded in. These rods are used to attach the seat covers using metal C clips – trying to remove and refit these is a complete nightmare and many trimmers will just use plastic tie wraps which are the DIY solution – not that there is anything wrong with that.

Four-door seat re-trims are easier, but they are both very, very hard work and the two door seats are an appaling job that I really recommend that you avoid.

The other, more sensible option is to fit a good used seat. The trouble with fitting a new seat cover is the same as fitting a freshly re-sprayed front wing – it will look very new and a bit out of place. E30 driver's seats are like those from any other car – after a few years and a six-figure mileage they will start to look a bit threadbare. This

A passenger seat from a LHD car makes a perfect driver's seat for RHD

makes good driver's seats rare items indeed. But there is a very cheap and easy solution that I have used many times and that is to fit a passenger seat. There are two ways of doing this. The hard way is to transfer all the base sliding and tilting mechanism over, or swap the base foam and cover plus the backrest onto your existing driver's seat base. It is not impossible but it is fairly tough work. The advantage is that the driver's seat will be in good original condition and it will not look out of place. They are also cheap because there is little demand for them. The easy way is to simply remove the seat belt stalk and swap it over to the other side – about ten minutes work. You then just bolt the seat in.

But what about the seat adjusters? Well, contrary to what you might well think, they do not get jammed down there between the seat and the tunnel but are actually very easy to access. In fact, those who have gone down this route have found that this arrangement is better. I mean, how often do you have to adjust your seat? Not very often.

You soon get used to using your left hand for seat adjusting because you use this hand for gear changing, radio, heater etc. and because the passenger seat comes with a backrest release knob on both sides on the two-door cars, you just have to swap over the two plastic levers. Okay, so it is not one hundred per cent original, but does it really matter?

Leather trim

Leather trim is a bit of a holy grail in E30 circles, but good ones are now rare. Most of the 'mint' leather interiors offered for sale are anything but and, to be honest, if you are doing a restoration the best course of action is to find a pair of ruined cloth Recaro front seats and take them, along with your back seat, to a reputable trimmer. With brand new hide fresh off the cow, the interior will feel like new. By the time you have paid through the nose for a second-hand leather interior and paid a trimmer to clean and re-Connolise the leather, you might as well have had a re-trim. BMW leather was always of the slightly shiny variety – look at a hidden portion of the leather (underneath the seat for example) and you will see what it looked like when new. Although it is pricey, Buffalo hide looks superb and was an incredibly expensive option new.

Detailing

It is the details that make a perfect interior. Cleaning, rubbing down and repainting the pedals is one overlooked job, along with new rubbers and things like a new gear lever knob and gaiter. These do not cost a fortune. Be aware that the original style plastic gear knobs fitted to pre-1988 metal bumper cars are now in very short supply. A new windscreen is one of those luxuries that you may, or may not, want to afford but they make a surprising difference.

By now, most instrument panel glasses are looking a bit tired. They are actually plastic but even so they can be restored using a paint-cutting product like T Cut – the same goes for dull and scratched rear light units.

Original trim colours

Unlike older BMWs, such as the 2002, a phone call to your local dealer with the chassis number (or registration number in the U.K) will tell you what colour trim your car has along with the colour code number.

As a rule, red and black cars have grey or beige trim, blue cars have blue or beige trim, green cars have green or beige trim and silver cars would have grey or blue.

Restoration Notes

Chapter 13

RESTORING OTHER PARTS

RESTORING 'HARD PARTS'

By hard parts, I mean bits like the suspension cross members, steering racks, differentials etc – big and small lumps of the car that came from the factory in a black painted finish. The best way of getting parts like this clean is by sandblasting, but be careful with mechanical components, like the differential, because you really do not want to get sand inside them. Once blasted they should be primed, but resist the temptation to do what most restorers do and get parts stove enamelled. Stove enamelling really is not that good. It is a thick, yet often brittle, coating that once cracked, allows moisture underneath. The best finish is obtained by etch priming and them using a satin black paint, either from a gun or from an aerosol can. Put it this way – BMW did not stove enamel their bits so why should you? A few good coats of paint are all that's needed. If you just want it to look nice and presentable, rather than exactly as factory finish, then use a brush-on paint like Hammerite, which is good, tough stuff.

Parts that were not painted – like many differentials – came in a bare cast iron and these can be really rusty. All you can do with these is to get all the loose rust off before using a plastic filler to tidy up the casing. Then use a thick primer and a satin black paint. Parts like the differential rear casing and the gearbox were always left in bare alloy so once thoroughly cleaned (steam cleaning with chemicals), paint them using an aerosol of aluminium paint. Having restored a Mini Cooper S in the late eighties, I can tell you that it gives you a real buzz to look under the car and see everything refinished in this way. It literally looks like new, but please resist the temptation to finish bits in glossy or polished finishes because BMW never built them that way. These were mass production cars, not hand built masterpieces.

THE CONVERTIBLE HOODS

The Baur hoods are still available and, unlike the BMW Convertible, there is not much to go wrong. The BMW hood on the full Convertible is a great thing when working but when it is not, it is a pain. The hoods used are the manual hood, the electro-hydraulic hood and the hydraulic power hood. Both of the latter are a real nuisance when they go wrong and repair in not a DIY job. There are two good bits of advice though with these. Even though they are power hoods, when activating them to open, give it a helping hand because it takes away a lot of the initial strain and pressure that they do not like much in old age. The second thing is to periodically lubricate the linkages and joints. So many hood failures are caused by broken joints and snapped rods due to seizures.

Many DIY owners have got hold of the BMW setting-up procedure for these hoods and got nowhere. This is one of those jobs you only get a feel for after doing them every day, so leave it to a professional. This can be either a BMW body shop that knows all about them or a well regarded hood specialist – ask about and take advice on this. Be warned that any repair – or a new hood covering – will not be cheap. When buying a new hood, do not buy the cheap one with obvious stitches because these rot over time and the seams will come apart. As ever, the proper BMW ones are the best bet, but are also the most expensive.

RESTORING WHEELS

Alloy wheels are best left to a professional. On the old 14-inch bottle-top type wheel fitted to the original E30 you can rub them down and paint them with Polaris Silver followed by lacquer but you will need proper paint and a spray gun for this. Cross-spoke BBS wheels are difficult to restore at home and so are the Alpina wheels. Lepsons in the UK have a proven track record for restoring tired alloys and the cost is not that great; like any high quality restoration, the money is soon forgotten when you see your wheels returned like new.

Steel wheels are easy to restore. The best way is to get then grit blasted back to bare metal and start again. You can use a decent etch primer from an aerosol can followed by Polaris silver. Avoid the temptation to lacquer them because it is not original. Instead, apply plenty of silver, leaving 30 minutes between light coats, and when dry polish them with T-Cut and wax polish them. Be aware that E30s with the plastic BMW wheel trims had black finished wheels, which makes life easier for you. A brand new set of wheel bolts from BMW is inexpensive and a nice finishing touch and so are new BMW decals for the centres.

De-chroming

This is a tricky subject that can go very wrong. At the end of the day, no primer known to man will stick to shiny chrome. This is why the bumpers on factory de-chrome cars were painted from primed steel. But it is not impossible. Once you have removed the bumpers and taken off the black rubbing strip, the trick is to use a DA (Orbital) sander with some really vicious 40-grit discs on the chrome. This will really dig into it and the idea is to do the whole of the bumper with this until the surface is really rough. Then the bumpers will need to be painted in etch primer followed by primer filler from a gun – aerosol paints are not man enough for this. Once primed, you then have to apply a guide coat and rub it

down. A guide coat is a light covering in matt black. You then rub the bumper down until all the matt black has gone and the surface will then be perfect and ready for colour. You use the same technique for filler repairs. The idea of the guide coat is that the black paint settles in all the pits, scratches and depressions in the surface of the primer. As you start rubbing the primer down with a block (no need to use a block on the bumpers) the dips and scratches will show up black against the coat of primer.

As for the side mouldings, these are harder because they are made from an anodised alloy. Rub them down with 400-grit wet and dry, followed by aerosol etch primer and then a grey primer. Once hard, rub the primer down with 1000-grit and paint with satin black. Matt black looks totally wrong. Although not de-chroming, it is worth mentioning painting black bumpers on plastic bumper cars. I always think the colour-coded bumpers look a million times better. This is not strictly an aerosol can job, but it depends how skilled you are. The main problem is getting the paint to stick to the plastic. You need to degrease it with something like brake cleaner before rubbing down with 400-grit and applying a special plastic primer. The cars with body-colour bumpers always had the clip-in centre bits finished black, so resist the temptation to body colour these too! They just unclip with a small flat blade screwdriver. Once plastic primed, they can be wet flatted with 800-grit wet and dry and then painted. To be honest, the best way to do this job is to buy a pair of cheap bumpers from a breaker's yard and take them to a body shop. Take the door mirrors with you because they, too, look better body colour.

Chapter 14

MODIFYING THE E30

It is now twenty-two years since the E30 3 Series went into production, and ten years since the last Tourings and Convertibles were built. Yet, despite their age, the E30s still capture the imagination like no 3 series cars built since. Put simply, the E30 was the last of the hooligan "sideways special" BMWs and they had a sporty character the later E36 did not quite have. Whether you want to pep up your 316, or build a 200bhp 325i, here is how.

ENGINES

Starting with the old M10, we have got the 316 and the 318i. Now, the only 318i's to use the M10 (i.e. 2002 type) engine are the chrome bumper cars made up until the end of 1987, whilst the 316 carried on using the M10 until the end of 1988 when the M40 engined 316i appeared. The M10 is a great little engine but because the 318i uses Bosch LE Jetronic with an analogue and not a digital ECU, you cannot re-chip them to give more power. However, a decent exhaust, a free-flow air filter in the original BMW air box and possibly an up-rated fuel pressure regulator will give you anything up to 10bhp. A camshaft change also works well, but you will need that up-rated fuel pressure to make it work. An old bodge used to be putting the standard pressure regulator between two sockets in a vice and giving it a 2 or 3mm squeeze but it's not a very elegant solution – it puts the spring inside the unit under more tension. As for the 316, the best way to get a bit more power is to sell it and buy something else! Seriously though, you can give a 316 some extra life for very little money. What you need is the Solex 32/32 DIDTA twin choke carburettor from an E21 320 four-cylinder or the 2002 carburettor – not an easy thing to find now in good condition but they are out there. Combine this with the 320 inlet manifold and a free-flow air filter in the 320 air cleaner box and you will be up from 90bhp to about 98 to 100bhp and a lot of extra sparkle.

If you were really keen, and could find a decent engine, the 2-litre from the 2002 (or early E21 320) will fit. You will need to change the sump over to the E30 type but, that apart, it will drop in easily enough. Because the M3's S14 engine was based on a modified M10 block, it is possible to fit the crankshaft, connecting rods and pistons into a 2-litre M10 block to create a 2.3-litre M10. I am not sure just how pointless it would be, given that a 171bhp 325i is available for so little, but if you had access to some cheap M3 engine bits it would be an interesting project.

Something many 2002 owners wanted to do was to fit twin 40DCOE Weber carburettors. What most did was to rob a pair of old carburettors from a rusty Alfa and expect them to perform; whilst in reality they had a car that wouldn't start, drank loads of fuel and just became a horrible heap. If you want to fit twin 40s, about the best kit around is the Mikuni twin 40mm side-draught kit, which I believe is still available from 2002 specialists like Jaymic in Norfolk, England. Using a 2002Ti inlet manifold you could strap a pair of these onto a lightly tuned 2-litre engine (use an E21 320 unit) with a 285-degree camshaft and have a decent 140bhp engine, by which time you could have just bought a 325i or a 318iS.

Now for the M40, the engine most BMW specialists would like to use as an anchor for their yacht when they retire. This engine has Bosch Motronic, which can be re-chipped, and this combined with an exhaust and an air filter can give you 10bhp. Apart from that, it is an engine best left alone. Camshafts are available and if yours, like most M40s, has top end problems it might be an idea to fit something a bit more radical. As for the M42 engine used in the 318iS, it is a great engine and you can get another 10 or possibly 15bhp with a re-chip and an exhaust system but that is the lot. One emerging problem with this engine is timing chain failure, so replacing yours now is a good idea if it's noisy as after about 150,000 miles they are getting tired. A nice conversion is to fit a complete 1.9 litre engine from a later model E36, using the engine management and loom from the E30.

With prices of E30s being so low right now – and still dropping – the cheapest performance upgrade is to sell your four-cylinder and buy a six, with the 325i the hot favourite.

As for the 320i and 323i, think about it long and hard. Of course these engines can be tuned, with a gas-flowed head, decent 270-degree camshaft and a 325i exhaust system, but you have to weigh up the pros and cons. The pros are that they are now cheap to buy. The cons are that you can buy a 325i with 171bhp as standard for less money so you have to ask yourself – why bother? Okay, if you own a truly immaculate example with low mileage and you really want to keep it, then go ahead. Gas flowing the head is a waste of time because the ports are already more than big enough. In fact, the 2-litre's lack of low down torque was due to the ports being if anything too big, which resulted in slow gas speeds at lower rpm. Instead, leave the head standard and fit a 270-degree camshaft, which will really bring it alive. The 320i head has got big ports, but having a better camshaft to open those valves deeper and for longer will make good use of them. Fitting a 325i throttle body is hard work, but combined with a rechip will give 15bhp.

The pre-1988 320i is not a bad car at all with a standard 125/130bhp but it is very limited on the tuning front and most are just worn-out old heaps. From 1987 BMW began to equip the European 2-litre, in both the E30 and the E28 520i, with a catalyst and, whilst these cars did not come to Britain, from 1987 the 320i had catalyst engines complete with Motronic, but without the catalyst itself. Chrome bumper cars had LE Jetronic, apart from the late European catalyst cars. If you are confused by this, Motronic is an engine management system that takes care of the timing and fuelling, LE Jetronic does the fuelling only and these cars have a conventional distributor and not the Motronic distributor cap on the front of the cylinder head. The distributor on the old LE Jetronic 320i has vacuum advance and retard (advance only on automatics) and it becomes a problem in old age.

Without a doubt, the Motronic 320i is the one to have. As standard it is a bit faster and more driveable than the earlier car and all plastic bumper cars have this engine. If yours has a noisy camshaft, as many do, fitting a suitable Schrick/Piper/Kent camshaft, such as a 272, will work wonders, as will a Fritz Bitz tubular manifold. With these bits, and a re-chip, that 129bhp will quickly become around 145bhp. It's not impossible to fit a larger throttle

body to the 320i/323i manifold, but tricky work grinding out the inlet manifold to suit.

What about the 323i, former darling of the yuppie set? Most of these are so old and worn now that it hardly seems worthwhile, but if you have one the rules of the older LE Jetronic 320i apply. Sure, you could fit a better camshaft and an adjustable fuel pressure regulator but no 323i had Motronic. Unless you own a really nice low-mileage example, your budget is better spent on buying a 325i.

The 325i – now we are talking! As standard, these cars had Motronic and 171bhp and that was just the beginning. Early chrome bumper cars were marginally faster, the later plastic bumper cars having the Motronic set up for a catalyst. Question number one concerns the inevitable 2.7 conversion. Why bother? With a simple re-chip, a good 325i will be up to 180bhp and that is before you get involved with camshafts and exhaust manifolds. The standard early 325i exhaust manifold is a horrible, restrictive thing – with a Fritz's Bitz manifold (probably the best one out there right now), a good exhaust along with a 272 (or 284/272) Schrick camshaft and a re-chip you are up to around 190bhp. Also, the 2.5 has a shorter stroke than the 323i and it likes to rev – stories of 2.7s with broken crankshafts from over revving are not unknown. Also consider a Piper 274 camshaft, which is slightly cheaper than a Schrick, whilst the 285 is pretty fierce. Opening up the head and manifold ports to match the gasket helps, but not a great deal, as does using the older type plugs from the chrome bumper 325i.

Continuing on the 2.5 theme, both E30 Zone and Richard at Fritz have made up an enlarged throttle body and are looking into fitting an air mass meter in place of the restrictive air flow meter. These air mass meters come from the E36 325i and use a heated wire to measure airflow and not a big alloy flap – expect around 8bhp from this.

A Hartge Exhaust Manifold for LHD cars

ETA (2.7) ENGINES AND 2.7 CONVERSIONS

BMW designed the Eta engine in the early 1980s for the USA market in an attempt to avoid gas guzzler penalties. Basically, if the combined fuel economy figures of your entire range of cars exceeded a certain limit, you would suffer big fines. So, cars like the 323i and 745i Turbo were kept out and cars like the 528e were launched.

Basis of the first 528e engine was the M60 2.3 litre engine as found in the European 323i E21. Crank stroke was increased from 77mm to 81mm, bore size from 80mm to 84mm. Low friction pistons and rings were used, and the existing 323i (and 320) '200' cylinder head was retained, but with a new camshaft that had both very conservative valve timing and only four bearings. The surplus three bearing housings in the head had their oil holes blanked off. A special inlet manifold with twenty per cent longer tracts was used, along with an 11:1 compression ratio and Bosch Motronic engine management.

The result was an engine that gave around 125bhp (same as a 320i) and loads of torque around 2000-3000rpm, but would not rev over 4800rpm, not that there was much point. This engine found its way into a European model called the 525e (e stands for ETA, the Greek symbol for efficiency) in 1983 and the following year, also into a 325e for Europe and America – but not Britain. By the time the 525e turned up, the M60 engine range had been renamed M20, but it was much the same engine. Fuel economy was good, 30mpg plus, even on a heavy, un-aerodynamic E28.

The ETA engine is a good one, but its odd shaped camshaft lobes that were needed to give such 'backwards' camshaft timing are prone to wear more than any other BMW engine. Some last 100,000 miles, others 150,000 and when they go, you have to fit another Eta camshaft as the normal M20 camshaft will not do. It will work, but only for a few minutes because the three bearing housings not used in the Eta camshaft are not supplied with oil and the thing will seize. You can drill the extra holes, but...

When it comes to the ancillaries on your hot E30 engine build both the standard radiator and fuel pump are man enough to cope, but forget about using anything other than Bosch Motronic. On the old E21 there was a vague excuse to use prehistoric injection systems, on the E30 there are none. In the old days of K and L Jetronic, you would be forever messing about with distributor advance curves in a futile attempt to get the timing right and fuelling alterations meant messing about with the fuel pressure – all very crude. Motronic is fully mapped. This means that the timing at any given engine speed can be advanced or retarded precisely to suit, along with the fuelling. It is now twenty-five years old, but Motronic is

still a very sophisticated set up. 325i injectors seem to be okay but bigger ones from an E34 530i flow a bit more, although setting them up is tricky. Bigger air flow meters are also hard to fit and the gains are not always worth the hassle. For cooling, a good condition standard 325i radiator works fine. Exhausts are a moot point and I would either use a standard BMW-made 325i system, or a Fritz stainless exhaust which works very well, as does the Sebring system. Some of the cheaper drainpipe stainless steel systems are just rubbish, loud, poor quality and not very well designed. Magnex seems to be a favourite at the moment and are highly regarded and Sebring systems are nice too.

BUILDING A GOOD 2.7

Building a good 2.7 engine does not cost a fortune if you do it yourself. In fact, it can be ludicrously cheap but it depends on how far you want to go.

First, you need a 2.7 engine to start with. Any 525e or 325e will do, but the Euro versions are better because they have a high compression to start with. Let's run through the possibilities depending on your car.

Converting a 320i or 323i

If you own a 320i or 323i and just want to give it a bit of extra grunt, just substitute the old short engine (block/crank/rods and pistons) with a 2.7 Eta. Do not change the pistons, but it is advisable to use a later (post 9/85) engine with the lower 10:1 compression. The 320i and 323i both use the '731' cylinder head casting which has exactly the same chamber volume as the 2.7 Eta head. Therefore if you start with an early 11:1 compression engine, you will still have an 11:1 compression engine that now revs to 6000rpm and will probably be detonating on 95 octane fuels – it would go like hell on 98 octane fuel! These earlier Eta engines are getting rare now though.

A 525e like this is a cheap source for a 2.7 litre engine. This car cost just £40 and its engine is now in a 325i

*This is the head casting number -
this one is a 325i or "Super Eta"*

Replacing the 2-litre short engine with a 2.7 will give you about 150bhp. Still not as much as a standard 2.5 but you still have the 320i inlet manifold, the smaller throttle body, air flow meter and exhaust. But it will have plenty of useable torque. The standard injectors are just about okay for this state of tune and so is the standard ECU although setting the car up on the dynamometer might reveal the need for more fuelling higher up in the rev range. The next stage would be to add a 325i inlet manifold (you'll need to open up the head inlet ports), 325i injectors, air flow meter and a 325i ECU. This will give you another 5 to 10bhp. Conversion cost? A standard Eta bottom end in good condition is about £100, plus a head gasket and odds and sods like camshaft belt and tensioner, oil, filter and bits like that. This is a cheap conversion that gives very good results.

Building a 2.7 for a 325i

Because you're using a 325i head, things can seem a bit more complex but other people have made it much easier for you by doing all the research. The 325i uses semi-dished and domed pistons and longer con-rods, plus a shorter stroke crank, in the Eta block. By semi-dished and domed, I mean the piston has a dish one side and a raised section on the other.

You have various choices here. You can simply fit a 325i "885" cylinder head to a standard, untouched Eta bottom end and it will work, but the valve to piston clearance can be a bit tight, even with standard cams. Fit the 325i head to an early 11:1 compression Eta engine and you will have a compression ratio of 10.4:1, which can be reduced to 10.2:1 using the thicker BMW head gasket. Fit the 325i head to the later 10:1 compression Eta engine and you will have a compression ratio of 9.4:1 with the standard head gasket – this is more practical with today's poor fuels, but it will lose about 5bhp to the higher compression motor.

When fitting the 325i head to a 2.7 with standard Eta pistons, you really should check the valve to piston clearance. Put some blu-tac on the piston crown, fit the head with a cleaned up old head gasket (no need to tighten the bolts), fit the camshaft belt correctly timed and turn the engine over a couple of times. Take it all apart again and see what the clearance is. This is normally fine on standard cams but if you are fitting anything really high lift, you may need to get your machine shop to cut the valve pockets a bit deeper. If you get to this stage, the cost benefits of using the Eta pistons becomes negated and you may as well invest in a set of new, later 325i pistons and some second-hand 320i/323i/Eta con rods – of course, if you started with an Eta engine you already have six of these rods!

ETA blocks

Although the 325i and the Eta block both look similar, and use 84mm bores, there are some differences. Early Eta blocks used, for some strange reason, a big core plug (freeze plug) on the back of the block behind the flywheel. 325e cars also use this plug as do some 325i's according to the BMW parts catalogue. BMW seem a bit confused over this and the parts catalogue gives conflicting information, but it seems that only the really early Eta engines used this plug. Certainly, engines made in 1985 and 1986 do not have it and BMW would not make two separate block castings.

The block with the extra core plug is reckoned by some to be weaker and also the main bearing caps are not as strong. However, these earlier blocks have been used in cars like the Alpina C1 2.5 (the Eta block and 323i crank combo) without dramas. But if you can find the later block then by all means use it.

Using the 325i pistons?

Using the proper 325i pistons is a very good idea because

325i dish/dome piston

they were designed to run with the 325i matching combustion chamber shapes and give better fuel burning and more power – indeed, the 325i combustion chamber and piston crown shapes were half the secret of the 325i. The valve cut-outs are also present and correct. These pistons have a deep dish on one side and a raised crown on the other side to force the burn over towards the spark plug. But you cannot just stick these pistons in a 2.7 bottom end and expect them to work, especially the early ones. Look at the 525e pistons and you will notice that there are weird cut-outs at the bottom of the skirt. These were machined in so that the crank webs would clear and the early 325i pistons do not have them. So if you build a 2.7 using early pre-1988 pistons the crankshaft will not complete a full revolution without catching on the bottom piston skirts – machining 11mm from the skirt will cure this. Later pistons had a much shorter skirt (11mm shorter) and the crank will normally clear, dependant on the piston manufacturer, but with the older types you need to machine in the crank web clearance slots – all very boring. The ideal combination is to shave 2mm from the deck of an Eta or 325i block (they are the same), use the Eta crank and con rods with European 325i pistons – if you can use the early pre-1988 pistons with 9.7:1 compression. 325i con rods are 135mm long as opposed to the Eta rods, which are the same 130mm long items as used in the 320i and 323i. If you use 325i rods and pistons with an Eta crank, the pistons will poke 3mm over the top of the block so that will not work.

If you shave the top of the block, you will need an adjustable vernier camshaft pulley to correct the camshaft timing.

Early 325i pistons will need to be shortened to clear the 2.7 crankshaft as shown

THE SUPER ETA

By 1988, the E28 525e and European E30 325e were dead, and it was not worth producing the old '200' Eta head anymore for the American market cars. So, BMW adapted. They used the pistons from the European Catalyst 525e and fitted the standard, unmodified head from the 325i. A special inlet manifold was made, combining the long inlet tracts of the original Eta with the bigger port sizes of the 325i head. A new camshaft combining the seven bearings of the standard M20 camshaft and the Eta valve timing was made, and a 325i exhaust manifold was used, along with Eta engine management. The compression ratio was 8.5:1 and it gave 127bhp, 6bhp more than the old unit, but the same torque. The Super Etas arrived for 1988 and are in the facelift cars. Fitting a 325i camshaft and valve springs plus a 325i ECU and inlet manifold, throttle body and air flow meter will unlock the horsepower – reckon on a jump from 127bhp to about 180bhp.

The very last batch of European 325e's also used the 325i head and the same rules of tuning apply.

So, the bottom end is now built. Even though Eta engines led a stress-free life, you should strip it, hone the bores (or re-bore with new pistons if need be), polish the crankshaft journals and fit new bearing shells. You must **always** fit new connecting rod bolts as they are only to be used once. Invest in a new oil pump if the old one is worn and fit the E30 alloy sump, as opposed to the steel E28 one which does not fit past the E30 suspension cross member. If the bores are okay and you heard the car ran well without rattle or oil burning, just have bores honed, the pistons chemically cleaned and re-use them. If the engine was a really sweet one it would be tempting to just fit it as is, but if you are building something with 180+bhp it is just a smart move to strip and check everything.

Notice the 5mm difference in length between the longer 325i conrod (top) and those used in every other M20 engine.

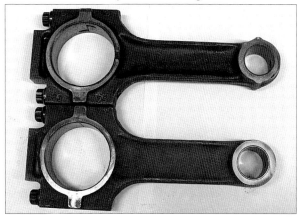

2.7 BUILD CHART

Standard Eta short engine (10:1 c/r)	= using 320i/323i 731 head	= 10:1 c/r
Standard Eta short engine (10:1 c/r)	= using 325i 885 head	= 9.4:1 c/r
Standard Eta short engine (11:1 c/r)	= using 325i 885 head	= 10.4:1 c/r
Eta engine with late 325i pistons and Eta con-rods	= deck 2mm from block	
Eta block/crank/rods + 325i pistons (any) + 320i/323i head	= bent valves!	

WARNING! Do not skim any BMW head more than 20 thousandths/inch.

Now you have to think about the cylinder head and other add-ons. As BMW made it, the 325i head flows very well and you do not really need to touch it. However, if you have a spare £500, then have the head gas-flowed with three-angle valve seats. You might pick up 5bhp from this, but at the very least you need to fit a new set of valves and springs. The valves in your 325i head have worked hard for a decade or more so buy new standard ones – exhausts at the very least. Alpina and Hartge used inlet valves that were around 2mm bigger – using these might give you 5 or 6bhp but they are expensive to buy and fit. Standard 325i double springs are more than good enough, but get confirmation of that from the supplier of your camshaft.

Ah, camshafts. If you are serious about this, forget about using the standard 325i camshaft because it's not good enough. Like most BMW engines, the designers chose a really tame profile to keep the power output down. Choose from Kent, Piper or Schrick, but go for a profile of around 272 degrees, which is similar to the 268-degree camshaft Alpina used in the C2 2.7. Piper does both a 270-degree camshaft and also a 285, which gives a lumpy idle and no real power until 2200rpm. Schrick do an excellent camshaft with a 284 intake duration and 272 exhaust that works well. The Schrick 288 is really a bit too wild for a road car and will drive you mad after a week. In the real world, a 270 or 272-degree camshaft will give you about 12bhp and the car will remain really driveable with loads of torque. Take the time also to check that the camshaft timing is spot on and if you cannot do this yourself get someone to do it for you. Most camshaft people sell the adjustable 'vernier' pulleys that enable the camshaft timing to be set one hundred per cent

This picture shows the difference in inlet port sizes between the three M20 heads. Left to right: 525e Eta, 320i/323i and the 325i. As you can see, 325i ports aren't hugely bigger but have a different shape at the top, easily achieved with a rotary file. The 320i/323i head is actually very efficient.

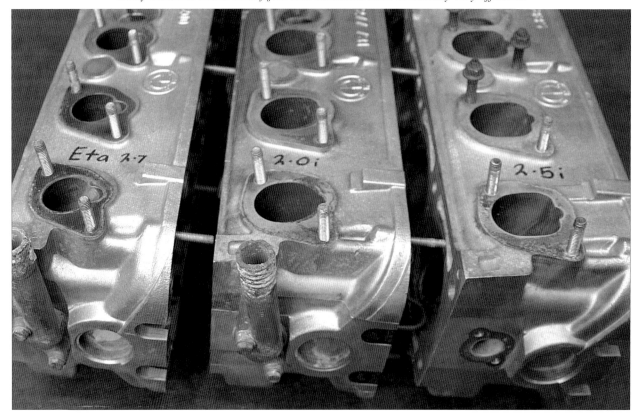

perfect. If you shaved the block 2 mm, the timing will be very slightly out (retarded). With higher lift cams, check with the camshaft manufacturer that you do not need to do any piston machining.

Forget about 2.7 engines that rev to 7000 plus – if you want those sorts of thrills, buy an M3. The 2.7, like all M20 petrol engines, uses a grey cast iron crank that will not tolerate too much 7000rpm action – they are known to shatter. You could use a modified 324 diesel crank because it's made from forged steel, but it is a pain to get hold of them in the UK, and also in the USA where these cars were never sold, although the shockingly bad 1984 and 1985 Lincoln was available with a diesel and thousands (71,000 to be exact) were sold and most are probably in American junkyards. The rockers will also break at that kind of rpm and to be honest, it is just pointless. For the sheer time and effort – not to mention money – to build (or have built for you) a 230+bhp 2.7, you could have just gone out and bought a good used 3-litre or 3.2 M3 engine with rather more power and reliability. In reality 210bhp is a nice useable power number, topping

out at 6000rpm, retaining loads of low-end torque and still giving 325i fuel consumption.

What would be an ideal build? A 2.7 block, decked by 2 mm, 2.7 crank and rods, early pistons with the skirts machined, a standard 325i head with a 272 or 285 degree camshaft with vernier pulley, bigger throttle body, 325i injectors and air flow meter plus a later type exhaust manifold with a decent stainless exhaust. Power would be around 200 – 210bhp with a good ECU remap and it would not cost the earth to build it yourself.

2.8-litres and 3-litres – the next stage

Of course, you can never have too much of a good thing. I spent ages on the net trying to find information on a conversion using later M52 internals and found nothing apart from theory and use of the word 'impossible'. As far as I could tell, nobody had actually done it, so armed with an old 2.5 block and a 2.8 engine suffering from the Nikasil bore wear, I set to.

The good news is that with a bit of work, it is possible, although the 2.8 is a reasonably easy job for a machine shop and very worthwhile. Not much work is needed to build this engine and you might as well get that extra 100cc over a 2.7. The M52 crank drops straight into a 325i/Eta block with no modifications at all. The big thing is machining a sleeve for the nose of the crank. This is needed so that the oil seal on the front of the block (the alloy bolt on bit) has something to fit onto. This is very easy to do. Look at the M52 crankshaft damper and you will see that it's actually a two-piece unit. Once the six bolts have been removed, the inner part will tap out of the main damper. This centrepiece is a perfect fit in the M20 oil seal housing and it has a lovely slotted keyway for the woodruff key on the M52 crank. A good machine shop will be able to mill off the excess metal and create a perfect spacer from this seemingly useless lump of steel. The nose of the crank does not need to be shortened and you

This shot shows the raised roof of the 325i combustion chamber - the raised section of the 325i piston matches it. All other M20 heads are flat here.

The stepped part of the M20 crank is shown here

need to fit an M20 gearbox input shaft bearing in the end of the crank because the M52 bearing is too big.

When you come to fit the big front pulley bolt though, you will find that it does not fit. This is because the threads on the M52 crankshaft start about in inch further up the nose of the crankshaft. The way I got around this was to machine down the thrust washer and also machine 20mm from the shoulder of the bolt allowing it to reach further inside the crankshaft. I used some serious thread lock and did the bolt up to 150 lbs/ft.

The connecting rods to use for this conversion are the 130mm 2-litre, 2.3 and Eta rods. The rods used in the M52 are much lighter than the rather stout con rods fitted to the old M20 and they can even be used on an M20 crank because the big end bearing width and diameter are the same. Indeed, the M20, M40, M42, M50 and M52 bearing shells are the same part number from BMW, but the M50/52 2-litre rods are LONGER and cannot be used. If you were building a go-faster 2.5 though, a set of M52 rods would work well.

The pistons used in the M52 are also much lighter, but they will need to be decked by about 3mm and have valve cut outs machined in them. As they stand, they have valve cut-outs for four small valves per cylinder and not two big ones. The answer is to use the 2.8 crank with short 2.0/2.3/Eta con rods and 325i pistons.

Just like the 2.7 build though, you run into problems with the crank webs fouling the bottoms of the pistons if you use the early long skirt type, but using later short skirt pistons should avoid this. Even if the short skirt ones do catch, there are different types from different manufacturers, it is no big deal to machine off the excess. Take 14mm from the bottoms of the early pistons. Using a 2.8 crank, M20 320i con rods and early 325i pistons? It's

*The 325i always had slots in the front
apron for the oil cooler*

almost a perfect fit. The pistons come flush to the top of the block just like they would in a standard 2.5 although I would use a thick head gasket. Why? If you fit 325i pistons into a 2.7 Eta engine with its 81mm stroke, the pistons will be 2mm down in the block. But the 2.8 uses an 84mm stroke which means that the pistons will protrude from the block by 0.4mm and you'd think that it would render the whole thing useless. The thicker head gasket will comfortably take that in its stride.

With some instructions over the phone and the odd e-mail, a colleague of mine built a 2.8-litre engine using a 525e block and a 2.8-litre crankhaft, shorter 2-litre/Eta rods and late 325i pistons. With a standard, overhauled 325i head skimmed 5 thou, the compression worked out at 9.6:1 and a Piper 285 camshaft was used with standard BMW springs. A standard BMW exhaust system was fitted, including manifold, but we used injectors from a 530i M30 (1988-91) allied to a standard 325i air flow meter and throttle body and a remapped ECU. Power on the dynamometer worked out at 212bhp with masses of torque. How does 210 lb/ft at 3500rpm sound? Not only that, but with a standard 3.91:1 LSD it would break traction in the dry in the first three gears and revved round to 6000rpm as sweet as a nut. The sensible compression meant no pinking (detonation) on 95-octane fuel. Further to this, the inlet manifold was modified with a bit of skilled alloy welding to accept the throttle body from an E34 535i manual (the throttle position switch on automatic ones are different) along with a 528i air flow meter. This took a lot of setting up on the dynamometer and although it didn't gain a whole load of torque (230 lb/ft), power shot up to 230bhp and the thing was just an animal, if not quite as nice as before. Fitted with a bigger bore exhaust and a tubular manifold, plus some work on the head, there is no reason why 235+bhp is not achievable. The good news at the moment though is the reasonable availability of scrap 2.8-litre M52 engines. Anything that has gone 'bang' will be covered under warranty and the old units do not always go back to BMW. They did suffer badly from the Nikasil problem and there are a few around. As an alternative to the ubiquitous 2.7, the 2.8 conversion is really worthwhile and you do not have to own a machine shop. Old 2.8 M52s with ruined Nikasil bores are about, and they are cheap too. I have never paid more than £50 for a short engine. The modifications to fit the crank are pretty simple ones, the correct pistons and rods are easily available and thus conducive to a really responsive engine and, best of all, it is an extra 100cc and when it comes to proper grunt, you cannot beat cubic inches! Just check the cost of doing it and weigh it up.

You might think about using M50/M52 lightweight 2-litre con rods in a 2.7 engine build because as everyone knows, the 2-litre rods in the M20 are shorter than the 325i types. Sorry to say, but it cannot be done. The M52 2-litre con rods are actually longer than the 2.8/3-litre rods, these share the same bearing-to-bearing length (135 mm) as the 325i con rod.

Now for the 3-litre and there are two ways of doing this. One is to use an E36 3-litre M3 crank with its 85.9mm stroke and allied to 320i rods and special pistons (nothing factory will really do). You would have about 2850 cc. With a special head gasket and 86mm bores you would have the full 3-litres but we are starting to talk serious money now because M3 cranks do not grow on trees. The 3.2 crankshaft, with its 91mm stroke, is not possible as here you have gone over the ragged edge of what is considered acceptable engine design. As a rule, the connecting rod length centre-to-centre MUST NEVER BE less than the crankshaft stroke multiplied by 1.5. A 525e in standard form is 121.5mm (stroke x 1.5) with a rod length of 130 mm. No problem. The 2.8 conversion is 126mm with 130mm rods; still okay. But the 3.2 M3 crank with its 91mm stroke equals out at 136.5 mm, which, if you used the 325i rods would be too close for comfort and would piston slap like hell. Before long, the pistons, rings and bores would be badly worn on the thrust side. For that reason, the 89mm stroke crank of the 3-litre used in the 330i and 530i cars is also unusable because the M20 block is just not tall enough to accommodate the 325i 135mm rods and any type of piston. Because the 3-litre (not the M3) used the 84mm bore of the 325i and 525e engines, you would think the pistons would fit a treat, but they do not. The reason is the M52 2.8 and 3-litre block is taller than the M20 2.5/Eta block.

Overall, it is a lot of work and in the case of the 3-litre you may not consider it worthwhile, although the 2.8-litre is a really good thing that is cheap and quite simple to achieve. The problem, as ever, is that the complete 24-valve M3 engine will drop in (albeit with a lot of work) and you may well feel that this is a better all round conversion. With 218bhp as standard, the 3.5-litre M30 from an old 535i E34 is a better idea still and this unit will achieve 260bhp on a virtually standard cylinder head. This just makes the expense and complications of a 3-litre M20 too great for what you get in return – 240bhp if you are very lucky. The 3-litre engines built in the 'States are wonderful examples of how to build the ultimate M20 but the law of diminishing returns applies. It's also an answer to a question nobody really asked – exactly who spends this kind of money building an M20 anyway? And why?

Cylinder heads
One of secrets behind getting good power from a modified M20 is the cylinder head although the factory 325i head is pretty good. Tuners (sorry, manufacturers...) like Alpina used inlet valves that were 2mm bigger along with some crafty gas flowing work. With their 210bhp 2.7 motor ten of those horses probably came from the work on the cylinder head. Schnitzer and Hartge also did this sort of thing, although trying to get an original head from one of Germany's 'big three' is very, very expensive. However, Fritz's Bitz in Somerset, England hired an ex-Cosworth employee with cylinder head experience and set him to work on a couple of BMW heads, an M20 and an M30. The results are pretty impressive and probably the equal of anything else, but at rather less cost.

DIY head modifying is really a waste of time because you will not have an expensive flow bench in your draughty lock up with which to equalise flow volumes. Polishing inlet ports looks pretty and suggests hours of work but doesn't always produce results. One school of thought says that a rough-cast or rough-ground inlet port will create turbulence to further mix the fuel and air mixture. For the exhaust ports, it does not matter so much and the smoother the finish of the ports the better. Matching ports to cylinder heads is time consuming and does not really give you much apart from a bit of hard earned satisfaction. It is all very well doing this, but you will need an inlet manifold gasket that is a one hundred per cent perfect fit to gain anything from this exercise.

Ancillaries
Bigger throttle bodies are a nice idea that give up to 10bhp on a full house 2.7, but standard 325i air flow meters and injectors are more than up to the task. However, technology has moved on since the days of early Motronic and the air flow meter is now a pretty outdated piece of equipment. The biggest problem is that its air flowing properties are very poor because there is a big alloy flap right in the air stream. There are also many

Throttle bodies; on the left is the bigger 325i type which is the same bore as a 2.8-litre engine found in something like a 528i. On the right is the Eta, 2-litre and 323i type.

crevices that trap air and, really, you need to be looking at an alternative. This is supposedly taken care of by the air mass meter; a device used on the E36 cars with the 24-valve engine. This was basically a plastic tube with a 'hot wire' in the centre. This wire is heated by electricity and the air being drawn in cools the wire. The faster the air goes through, the cooler the wire gets and it is this temperature information that tells the ECU how much fuel the engine needs; a rudimentary explanation but one that gives you an idea of how clever is the idea. The good news is that a second-hand air mass meter is cheap. Every written-off E36 or E34 24-valve will have one and about £30-£50 is what they cost. The not-so-good news is that they require a lot of work and an inlet air temperature sensor, results can be variable - many owners complained of terrible cold starting and drive-ability. Think long and hard about this conversion!

The M30 air flow meter is another idea, but on a 2.5, no matter what state of tune, it is really bordering on being a waste of time. All that seems to happen is that owners who have fitted one run into fuelling problems and they do not really give any more power. On a 2.7 the M30 air flow meter sometimes works okay, but Alpina used a standard 325i air flow meter on their C2 2.7 and that was good enough for them. You will need an adjustable fuel pressure regulator to set everything up, fuel pressure needs to be set to 3.5 bar, and the unit to use is the 027 from the E34 and 32 cars which are the 530i, 730i, 535i and 735i. Overall though, it's not worth the trouble.

The 325i cast-iron two-part exhaust manifold needs to be replaced with a tubular steel one, Alpina or Hartge style. These are made by companies like Fritz' Bitz in Somerset, England and should be mated to a matching system. However, the later four-bolt single-piece 325i/320i manifold is pretty good and owners of later UK built C2 2.7 cars fitting the Alpina tubular manifold (later RHD Alpinas switched back to the standard iron manifold) did not report great power gains. They do look great though...

Oil coolers? Every 325i had one, and if yours looks at all nasty and second-hand you should fit a new one, along with new pipes and gaskets where the oil filter head fits. They are always oily and horrible, and one school of thought says that with modern fully synthetic oils, you do not need one. There is some mileage in that theory, although if you were really giving the engine some abuse I would continue to use one. Standard 325i radiators and water pumps are fine, and so is the standard gearbox and clutch. Fitting new rubber engine mountings is a good idea though, but the polyurethane ones can transmit too much vibration into the car, especially true with the gearbox mounts.

Radiators are up to the job, but if you live in a very warm climate, such as Southern California, you might want to invest in an alloy radiator from a company such as Ireland Engineering.

Finally, and once the engine has done a couple of thousand miles, you will need to get the car onto a dynamometer and have the ECU remapped to optimise the fuel and timing. Just re-chipping a standard plastic bumper 325i used to release anything up to 9bhp alone so it is worth doing. Use also the pre-1987 type spark plugs as they release a bit more power – a surprising 3 or 4bhp.

At the end of this, you should have a very nice 210bhp engine with strong torque and lots of bite. Many BMW engine builders have built 2.7 engines giving up to 230bhp, but these are very impressive exercises in how to spend money. They are very good engines, of course, but cost more than a second-hand E36 M3 unit. Go figure!

TUNING THE 318iS
As standard, these cars came with 136bhp but they are capable of a lot more. Without getting involved in expensive camshafts (you do not need to), the first stage is to get the ECU remapped to give the car the fuelling it really wants. The standard exhaust manifold is fine and so is the factory exhaust, although a fatter bore pipe with straight through silencers is always a good thing. The other thing to consider is fitting a larger bore throttle body. To do this some owners have adapted 325i units to fit, some have had existing iS bodies bored out with bigger throttle plates. Either way, a 318iS with a re-chipped ECU and a bigger throttle body will give around 155bhp, maybe more. At the end of the day, BMW strangled the iS unit so as not to get too close to the 325i.

TUNING THE M3
Tuning the M3 is expensive. From the factory they already produce between 84bhp and 95bhp per litre. The biggest restriction to these engines is the intake system. With 16 valves and a throttle butterfly per cylinder, the big restriction is the air flow meter. Getting rid of this in favour of a Motec system is a good idea. These aftermarket management systems get rid of the air flow meter and substitute a new ECU with a new throttle position sensor. The Alpha N system is broadly similar and the main aim is to get rid of the air flow meter, they really are restrictive. Again, fitting an air mass meter will improve the car a lot.

M3s tend to benefit a lot from a custom ECU remap, as opposed to a plug-in chip. No two cars are the same, so a custom-made chip set up on a dynamometer is the only way to go. Typically you can expect to find another 8-10bhp from a good standard M3 with marked improvements in torque and driveability. Normally you will see a small improvement in fuel economy too. BMW themselves did a factory upgrade on the 200bhp cars with a different chip, bigger throttle bodies and other detail bits that raised power to 215bhp – these ECUs can be recognised by the corner of the ECU sticker cut off but anyone with a sharp blade can do this. Getting the valve clearances set up can also find inexpensive power.

Going past a remap we have camshafts and all 2.3 cars used the same exhaust cams. The Sport Evo exhaust was the same duration (248 degrees) but with fractionally more lift.

Schrick seem to be flavour of the moment and the results from these are very good. Starting at the bottom is the 274/274 (inlet and exhaust), which will give about 230bhp with an ECU remap. Forget about doing camshafts without ECU work. Next up is the 284/276 arrangement. This will give another 5bhp or more over the 274/274 and it will really bark at the top end. Trouble is, you will lose driveability at the lower end of the scale. Finally there is the 284/284, which gives around 240bhp and over 100bhp per litre. The car will still be road-useable but it will make you quite aware that it would rather be up around 6000+rpm and not driving through road works on the M25.

Exhausts? Well, BMW knew what they were doing and for road use it is reckoned by many that the standard BMW exhaust is the best bet. The trouble is that they are expensive – check out the price of a new Sport Evo system and weep. In cases like this, a custom-made stainless system is the way to go, but only if it is significantly cheaper than a BMW system. The other thing you

An M3 with a works airbox

need to take into consideration is noise. A blaringly loud exhaust system will automatically fail the noise test at most UK race circuits and the standard system is the only one guaranteed to pass. If you have a standard exhaust and are happy with 230/240bhp, stick with the BMW exhaust. Many owners remove the catalytic converter and in many ways it is a good idea. All Sport Evos had them for example and they can rob up to 5bhp. My own Sport Evo had its catalyst removed by a previous owner and it was a very lively car. Indeed, the next owner who already had a pair of Red Sport Evos claimed that my black one was the fastest of the three, and that included a higher mileage car that had seen some action. Removing the catalyst and just putting a straight pipe in its place will probably make the exhaust too noisy. Instead, have a silencer made up to the dimensions of the catalyst. British MOT laws state that any car registered before January 1st 1993 does not require a catalyst so that covers 99.9 percent of all E30 M3s, with just the last dregs of the Convertibles that hung around requiring one.

A similar theory applies to cylinder heads. As they come from BMW the M3 head is superb. The fact that a pair of wild camshafts and an ECU remap can take them up to 230+bhp says all you need to know. Sure, if you have the money you can have the head flowed, three angle valve seats and all the usual expensive modifications but do not be too disappointed when you only gain 6bhp at the top of the rev range. An ultimate specification E30 M3 would be a 2.5 with Alpha N or Motec 284/284 camshafts, remapped ECU, catalyst removed and careful blueprint assembly. From this you could hope to get anything up to 260bhp, and be a track day hero.

TRANSMISSIONS
The old five-speed manual gearboxes do not seem to go wrong, apart from second gear that can die a death after a hard life. There is much talk about the dogleg gearbox and in some ways it is a nice unit. The ratios are close together, allowing the engine to stay on the ball, but against that the gear change pattern is a pain and especially so on right-hand drive cars. On a 2.7 litre E30, one is not really needed as the torque will pull taller ratios anyway. Only the 323i was fitted with this rare option and these cars had a taller 3.25:1 ratio final drive to compensate – the standard ratio was 3.45:1.

FITTING THE GETAG 265 M3 GEARBOX TO AN M20 ENGINE
This is possible too; you need bellhousing part number 21 11 1209 766 (USA spec 528e), clutch plate 21 21 1223 114, the standard M20 228mm flywheel, clutch fork and slave cylinder, release bearing 21 511 223 366, clutch cover 21 21 1223 026 and use the M3 rear mounting and propshaft.

There is talk of the 325i Sport dogleg gearbox but, according to everyone I've spoken with, including BMW factory people, this gearbox does not exist. In fact, BMW state that the 325i was never fitted with a dogleg gearbox and it was not an option. To compensate, BMW fitted a differential with lower ratios like the 3.91:1 or the 3.64:1 as a compromise. Why no dogleg? Because the early chrome bumper 325i has Motronic and a different bell housing is required to take the flywheel TDC sensor. In fact, the 325i gearbox is the very same Getrag 260 unit as the European 525e and 325e manual. Therefore, a dogleg 323i gearbox will not fit without major bell housing welding and to fit one, you'd need to fit a taller final drive as the dogleg's ultra low first gear would be useless. Later 325i cars from the autumn of 1987 (plastic bumpers) went over to a different TDC sensor that ran from the crankshaft front pulley and on these you can fit the dogleg gearbox complete with gear linkage assembly. Look underneath your car and hunt for the two wires running to the bell housing to see what you have. There is also talk of the 325i Sport having different gear ratios from the standard 325i and a look through factory books confirms that the Sport did indeed have closer ratios, but with the conventional H-pattern gear change – the part number is 23001221572. Clutches are very strong and a 200bhp plus 2.7 will be okay with a standard 325i clutch.

The thing with BMW (Getrag) gearboxes is this. Never assume that a standard gearbox in good condition will not take a power increase because it will. I will tell you a quick story about a BMW 2002 Turbo I once saw. With just over 300bhp and 300 lb/ft of torque, you would expect a pretty tough gearbox and it had one – a standard Getrag 240 five speed from an E21 316! Therefore, if you're putting a hot 2.7 into your 320i, do not fret about the gearbox because it will probably be okay with 200bhp and synthetic gear oil. Not the ultimate by any means, but it will do. Stiffer gearbox mounts? You do not need them on a road-going car and standard, new BMW items are more than good enough. You can buy Group N stiffer rubber mounts, but they can transmit an awful lot of vibration into the car. This is okay for a competition car but not for your daily driver.

There are various quick shift gearlevers available, but the cheapest one seems to work the best and it is the lever from the BMW M3 E36 3 litre.

DIFFERENTIALS

When it comes to the differentials you have to be careful because there are so many different types. This does mean that you can gear the car up or down. In the beginning there was one basic unit for four- and six-cylinder cars. When the 325i appeared, it used the bigger and stronger unit with eight bolts for the rear cover that was

first used by the 323i in the latter half of 1984. It is based on the E28 5 Series (1981 to 1988) casing. See the charts for detailed differential information. To check, drain the oil, remove the rear cover and count the teeth on the crown wheel and the pinion, unless the metal tag under one of the rear cover bolts is still legible. An early 320i differential for example has 38 teeth on the crown-wheel and 11 on the pinion – divide 38 by 11 and you have 3.45. Limited slip differentials are rare and well worth having as the more powerful cars have pretty abysmal traction in the wet without it. The trade-off is a more vicious breakaway when the limit of grip is reached.

The E28 CV Joints are bigger than the E30 units - that's why you need to use E30 output shafts with an E28 unit

The "big" differential, and.................
................The "small" unit

Our advice? For road use, stick with the standard ratio differential for each car as a good compromise, but if building a 2.7, a 3.45:1 is a good differential with which to use the greater torque. Finding a 3.45:1 LSD is very hard though. If you're fitting 16-inch wheels to a car built with 14s, then by all means fit a better diff. A 325i with 16-inch wheels replacing the old 14s needs a 3.9:1 to keep it on the boil. A good example of where a differential change can be for the better is the manual transmission 325i Touring. For some reason BMW fitted a 3.9:1 differential with the standard 14-inch wheels and they are just too low geared. Fitting an earlier (chrome bumper) 3.64:1 unit or the 3.7:1 unit from the plastic bumper saloon will improve motorway cruising and fuel economy without harming the performance.

Towards the end of the 323i production run, big differentials were being fitted that were not limited slip. At first, I thought that BMW introduced the big unit with the 150bhp engine in late 1983 but I have now seen enough 150bhp cars made in early 1984 to disprove this and earlier 323i with a limited slip differential use a small differential as well. My 1985 323i Automatic had a big differential and so did my Alpina C1 2.3 built in August 1984. 323i models began using the big differential in around May/June 1984. All 320i models use the small differential and it might surprise you to learn that the LSD on the 320i is the small type – it is also used on the 318iS and any other four-cylinder (non M3) E30, albeit with different ratios. There is much talk of the letter S on the LSD, but this is in fact a letter S stamped into the ID tag on the diff. The letter S was painted on in white paint and most disappeared long ago.

As for the big differential, it is based on the E28 5 Series unit. The rear alloy cover is different and so are the out-

An E28 5 Series LSD. Change the rear cover and output shafts and it will fit an E 30

put shafts, which are bigger. To use an E28 differential in an E30, you need to change the rear cover and also the output shafts. These are removed with two tyre levers and a bit of force to overcome the internal spring clips fitted. E28 LSDs can be bought from a scrap yard for a few quid, whereas E30 ones are quite rare and can be pricey and yes, output shafts from a standard differential will fit an LSD and vice versa. What that means is if you found an E28 limited-slip differential, you can fit the output shafts and rear alloy cover from your standard, non-LSD 323i differential with no problem. Given below is a table of what differentials came from which car. A 524td limited slip differential is the same unit as an M3 Sport Evo and Evo 2. Your only problem is finding one as they were never sold in Britain! Most common E28 LSDs are the ones in the 535i and M535i, and the M5 (or M635CSi) diff will also fit an E30 rear beam. But the output shafts are much bigger and the M5 CV joints will not fit an E30 driveshaft, so these units can't be used.

Now we have the Z3 and the Compacts. In its last dying breath the old E30 differential was dusted off in 1994 and used again in the Compact – in fact, the rear suspension is basically the same. However, all the Compacts, including the LHD-only 323Ti, used the small casing unit and although an LSD was an option, do not hold your breath if you start looking for one. The same goes for the Z3. The 1.8, 1.9 and 2.2 (six-cylinder) cars all used a small casing non-LSD unit. The 2.8 Z3 used a big casing unit, some with LSD and some with traction control, depending on the market where it was sold. All the 3-litre cars though had the LSD and so did the M Coupé and M Roadster. They will fit the E30, but the trouble is that the ratios are not always ideal. They tend to use ratios around the 3.15:1 mark which with an overdrive gearbox is just way too high unless you were building a car with a 230/260bhp M30 3.5 litre engine. These differentials are about, but £50-£70 is about the value of them, although the M differential is worth twice that due to having a lovely finned alloy cover. In comparison, the 3.9:1 ratio LSD from a 325i Sport is still £150/£200 worth because they are so useable. Pay similar money for a 4.1:1 small casing LSD as they are very sought after by 318iS owners.

Oh, the part number for the M Coupé/Roadster finned differential cover is 33 11 2 228 335 but it will only fit the big differentials, such as the late 323i, 325i and M3.

When replacing a small diff with a big unit, the propshaft will be 20 to 25mm too long. To compensate, slacken the propshaft collar nut by the centre bearing and push the rear half prop inwards.

FINAL DRIVES AND ENGINE SPEEDS

Transmission	Tyres	Final drive	Mph/1000rpm in 5th gear
Standard 5 speed	195/65x14	3.64:1	23.5 (100 mph: 4200rpm)
Close ratio 5 speed	195/50x15	3.64:1	20.7 (100 mph: 4830rpm)
Standard 5 speed	195/50x15	3.45:1	25.2 (100 mph: 3960rpm)
Close ratio 5 speed	205/55x15	3.25:1	21.3 (100 mph: 4690rpm)
Close ratio 5 speed	205/55x15	4.1:1	17.04 (100 mph: 5860rpm)
Close ratio 5 speed	195/50x16	3.9:1	19.2 (100 mph: 5200rpm)

FINAL DRIVES – WHAT CAME FROM WHAT?

4.45:1	M40 316i and 318i automatic, plastic bumper models. Plus plastic bumper 320i Auto
4.27:1	M40 316i Manual. Plus some plastic bumper 320i Tourings.
4.1:1(small)	M40 318i/318iS. Post Aug. 85 320i (195/65), 320i (15" BBS).
4.1:1(small)	318iS and 320i with LSD.
4.1:1(big)	USA market M3. Post 1985 320i option with LSD,
3.9:1(small)	Post Aug '85 316/316i and 320i, M10 316/318i auto, 318i 5 speed.
3.9:1(big)	325i Sport auto/ manual. 25% LSD. Also 325iX manual.
3.74:1(big)	325iX automatic, 25% LSD (Not GB).
3.73:1(big)	Plastic bumper 325i.
3.64:1(small)	M10 316, 318i four-speed manual.
3.64:1(big)	325i chrome bumper inc. many 1986/7 Sport (with LSD for Sport).
3.63:1(big)	325i (plastic bumper) and 320iS (optional)
3.46:1(big)	323i (9/84 onwards), 325i Automatic, 320iS (LSD).
3.45:1(big)	324d (Not GB).
3.45:1(small)	320i and early 323i manual with 195/60 tyres.
3.23:1(big)	323i with sports gearbox, most with 25% LSD. 324td, non-LSD
3.25:1(big)	M3, 2.3 cars except Evo II.
3.15:1(big)	M3 Evo II and 2.5 litre M3 Evolution Sport 3. Also Z3 2.8/3.0/M.
2.93:1(big)	325e (Not GB)

E28 and E24 final drives:

3.46:1	528i Auto 9/84 onwards, 525e Auto 12/86 onwards
3.45:1	528i until 9/82, 628CSi
3.25:1	528i 9/82 onwards (manual), 525e manual 12/86 onwards
3.07:1	525e auto 9/85 onwards
2.93:1	525e until 9/85

NOTE: Big differentials are physically bigger casings with eight-bolt rear covers. Small differentials have six-bolt covers. E28 differentials are similar to big E30 units, but the removable rear cover is different. Only later 323i and all 325i cars have the big differentials, although non-LSD 323i from late 1984 use the big unit. The higher the number, the lower the gearing, i.e. a 3.45:1 will give better acceleration than a 2.93:1 but slower top speed. Looking for letter S on an LSD? It's on the metal tag under one of the rear cover bolts – do not bother too much, it is not often there because rust eats it away. LSDs fitted to normally small differential cars (i.e. M40) are also small types, including 320i and 318iS. Diffs used on 3.5 litre with eight bolt side covers are not suitable.

GEAR RATIOS

Standard 320i		323i/325i		325i Sport		323i Dogleg	
1st	3.72	1st	3.83	1st	3.35	1st	3.76
2nd	2.02	2nd	2.20	2nd	2.03	2nd	2.33
3rd	1.32	3rd	1.40	3rd	1.36	3rd	1.61
4th	1.00 (Direct drive)	4th	1.00	4th	1.00	4th	1.23
5th	0.81 (Overdrive)	5th	0.81	5th	0.81	5th	1.00

NOTE: Direct drive (1.00:1) is when the crankshaft and the differential pinion are the same speed. Overdrive is when the pinion is turning faster than the crankshaft. In third or lower gears, the pinion is turning slower than the crankshaft. Thus dogleg gearboxes have the same engine speed in fifth as the standard gearbox in fourth. Automatics all have a 0.73 top gear PLUS converter lock up at 55mph, which is why they are so tall geared.

FITTING THE M30 ENGINE

Alpina started this particular ball rolling back in 1983 with their B6 2.8. You would not want to bother with the 2.8 from a 528i these days because it is nothing special and offers little, if anything, over a lightly modified 325i. But the 3.5 is a different story. In standard form it offers around 215bhp, which is a full 45bhp more than a 325i. It gives 225 lb/ft of torque at 4000rpm, a whopping 61 lb/ft more than a 325i and you should remember that it is torque that accelerates a car, not brake horsepower. There are various ways around this conversion but only one easy way, as outlined in detail by the German E30 club www.e30.de, who are recognised as the experts at this conversion. Their web page is available in English and it really is the definitive guide to this conversion.

Firstly, you need the engine and gearbox from an E34 535i (1988/91), or an E32 735i (1986/92). The older E23 and E28 and 6 Series engines are just too much hassle because the sumps and oil pumps are not suitable – plus they are now very old engines. You can buy a pair of special engine mounting brackets from www.e30.de for around £130, and with these the engine will sit far enough back in the engine bay not to require hammering the bulkhead to death (in fact, you do not have to touch it), but it leaves enough room for an E28 535i or M535i radiator. You will need to discard the viscous fan entirely and cut the threaded fan-coupling mount from the water pump. Use an E30 M3 electric fan, an E23 735i exhaust manifold and down pipe, plus an E30 M3 exhaust system. It will not screw together straight away but with a bit of cutting here and there it goes together nicely. You will also have to modify the floor around the area of the down pipe with that wooden handled special tool to provide clearance.

Use the 3.5 gearbox and an E30 M3 prop-shaft. You may need a prop-shaft specialist to cut 4.5 centimetres from the front half and rebalance it, but some have found that it fits perfectly by juggling the engine position slightly.

Once the engine is sat in there, the E34/32 air box and air flow meter will fit and the rest of the plumbing is simple enough. Starting with a 325i or a Motronic 320i means that the wiring harness is already there and you just plug the air flow meter and the ECU from the 3.5 engine into place. The air flow meter will now go where the washer bottle sits and you can use the bottle from the 324td. These were never sold in Britain, and the part number for a new one is 6166 1385 280. It is the only washer bottle that works.

For a final drive, the LSD from a 325i, M3 or non 535i E28 will fit, as long as you fit the E30 (big differential) output shafts and rear cover on E28 units.

Is it a worthwhile conversion? Well, it is hard work and the arrival of the M50 engine (24 valve 325i/328i) has blunted the appeal because the M50 is such a modern engine. The other problem is the rarity of manual gearbox E34 and E32s, although you can fit a manual 535i E28 gearbox. If you can undertake such a conversion, then building a half decent 2.7 motor and fitting it would be less drama. But the 3.5 conversion is a good one. Ultimately it is up to you.

It looks good, but fitting an M5 or M6 engine is very difficult

You would need to sort the suspension too and a suggested specification is Bilstein Sprint/Sport dampers with a 21mm 320i/325i Convertible front anti-roll bar and Eibach springs. In reality the M30 is not vastly heavier and if Alpina could make it work (the B6S was exceptional), so can the rest of us. Brakes? With 218bhp, standard brakes are just about okay but for anything more you need to be looking at bigger discs and special four-pot calipers to haul it down.

FITTING THE M52 ENGINE

This was BMW's mid-nineties onwards 24-valve unit and it is a good one. Launched in 1990 as the M50, this unit with a cast-iron block was effectively a 24-valve version of the old M20, although the block is completely different and not interchangeable. Initially it was just a 2-litre and a 2.5 (192bhp) but by 1995 the M52 was here. These were alloy blocked and thus quite a lot lighter, with an overall weight around the same as the 2.5 M20 in the 325i E30. The 2.5 unit was mildly detuned to 170bhp whilst the new 2.8 was rated at 192bhp. These engines could suffer from erosion of the Nikasil bore coating. Rather than press steel liners into the alloy block, the bores were instead coated with nickel alloy. Used by Porsche for years, it seemed to be the ideal solution but increasing sulphur in fuels meant that on shorter trips, the sulphur would attack and erode the Nikasil bore coating. What this means is do not buy a 2.8 engine built before March 1998 and check the engine number with BMW.

Even better was to come though – the 3-litre. This is a great engine but as far as I know, nobody has yet fitted one to an E30.

The major problem with the M50/M52 conversion is that the 2.5 engine, the most easily fitted, does not produce much more power than a moderately tuned M20 2.5 and at 4000rpm, the M50 produces less torque, although it gains 10 lb/ft at 4700rpm. An E30 fitted with the 2.5 M50 does drive very nicely though. The 2.8? At around 190bhp it is no more powerful than the 2.5 (a deliberately restricted inlet manifold sees to that) but it does produce more torque, a very handy 207 lb/ft But with the 2.8, you are getting involved in Vanos variable camshaft timing if you want to avoid the Nikasil drama and that involves some extremely complex engine wiring. You also have the EWS anti-theft system to deal with and there is no way around it. You can fit the E36 gearbox or use the M20 unit but if you use the E36 gearbox (a better idea), you can use the front section of the E36 propshaft mated to an E30 rear section. The sump and oil pick up will have to come from an M50 E34 520i/525i engine, but the E36 exhaust front section can be used. The standard front cross member can also be used but

Front springs: 316,325i, M tech 325i and 60mm lowered.

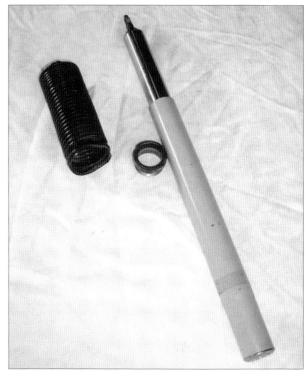

A Bilstein front damper.
This one is for a Hartge application

BMW 320i, 325e, 325i
Front Suspension

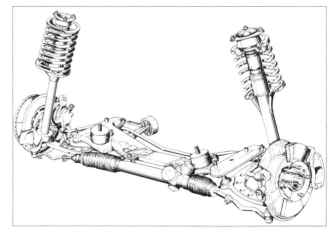

you will run into major clearance problems for the brake master cylinder. The E36 radiator is suitable.

The other thing to consider is expense. To make it worth the bother you need a 2.8 and they do not come cheap. It is a nice idea, but is an enormous amount of work for not much gain unless you find a good early 328i and you're a handy auto electrician. For a 325i, a re-chip, 272-degree camshaft and a better exhaust would give you the same results as a standard E36 2.5. If you are hell-bent on an engine swap, the 3.5-litre M30 is a cheaper, far easier and more effective conversion and it is sobering to think that fitting a 321bhp M3 Evo E36 engine requires little more work than the M52.

SUSPENSION

As standard, the E30 is a good handling car but a little on the soft side after all those miles. Avoid cheap lowering springs – they ruin the car. The ideal combination is Eibach springs with either Koni adjustable dampers or the Bilstein dampers fitted to the metal bumper 325i Sport. Likewise, Koni springs work very well. As a personal preference I absolutely swear by Bilstein dampers and consider them to be the finest dampers available for performance and sheer quality.

E30 front struts come in two types, the 45mm ones as fitted to all non 325i/M3 cars without sports suspension and the 51mm types for all 325i's, M3s and cars with the better dampers. So, if you buy a set of Bilstein M Technic (yellow) front dampers for your standard 318i they will not fit. You will need a pair of 51mm front strut bodies.

The three bushes: Top is standard, Second is the solid version from the E36, lower is M3 offset.

Another good modification is to use BMW Motorsport offset top strut mounts for the M3 E30. They move the top of the strut in towards the engine and increase negative camber. This improves steering feel and the handling is more precise, but do not order standard M3 ones as they are similar to standard E30. The three top studs are always missing, so drift the ones from your old strut tops, press them into the new ones and add a dab of weld as they have a habit of dropping out as you fit the strut. The part number for the offset top mounts is 31 331 139 484. My own personal favourite springs are the Eibach brand and they are not that expensive – about two and a half times that of the bargain springs which you will want to throw in the bin after a week. Combining Eibach springs with some 325i Sport type Bilsteins from BMW or Euro Car Parts will really make a world of difference. Bilstein also make a really special damper called the Bilstein Sprint and this is suitable for cars which are pretty well lowered (more than 25 mm). In the US they are known as Bilstein Sport. Just to confuse issues, Bilstein do a similar damper with the same damping qualities but a longer rod and this is for cars with standard springs or cars with just a minimal lowering job. In Britain these are called Bilstein Sport, in the United States they are called Bilstein H/D. Your Bilstein dealer will know what you want.

BMW M Technic springs? Nice, but too expensive as they are not available as a kit and as good as they are. Alpina, Hartge and Schnitzer stuff are also very expensive and hardly better than the Eibach/Bilstein combination. Schnitzer complete suspension kits are known to be very good though and are not ridiculously expensive either. Some E30 owners swear by Koni dampers and these too are excellent. Springs by Racing Dynamics, Apex and Koni themselves are fine and Spax stuff is pretty good these days too. But for the money and overall performance, Eibach are still number one in my book. And no, I didn't take a bribe!

Changing the front dampers is quite simple, but a couple of pointers. Slacken (but do not remove!!) the top 19mm damper nut before you even jack up the car – with the strut off it can be very difficult, if not impossible, without an air wrench. If the dampers are not going to be re-used, clamp them with some really strong vice grips if you have to. If you are going to re-use them, try to grip the damper shaft as far to the top as you can. If a portion of the damper shaft marked by the vice grips goes past the damper oil seal, it will start leaking and fail very quickly.

Getting the screw collar off the damper body to remove the inserts is not difficult without a simple and cheap tool – Stilson grips. These apply more pressure to the collar the more you twist and for this job they are unbeatable.

Forget about using anything else. You will need to clamp the strut body in a very substantial vice, as these collars are very tight. What I have done is to remove the strut, take the spring off and then refit the top mount and refit the strut to the car. Then you can really get a grip on the collar and get it off. Some are so badly rusted that they have to be removed with a chisel. When fitting the new dampers, do not forget to pour a little neat anti freeze into the strut body before you insert the struts. This cools the damper and is often overlooked. Apply thread lock to the three lower strut bolts as well on M3 cars.

Other modifications? Front strut braces are very effective; those for the rear are a waste of time. There is little else that you can use from the M3, but that car uses solid rubber bushes for the lower arm where it bolts to the chassis rails and not the slotted standard E30 items. M3 bushes resist suspension deflection under braking and are fairly easy to fit.

However, the reason BMW Motorsport fitted these solid (and also offset) front bushes is because they found that the M3 Evo with its 16-inch wheels would often rub the tyre against the front of the sill under full lock. The solid offset bush moved the back of the trailing arm outwards and as a consequence, moved the bottom of the suspension strut forwards. It only moves forward by an inch or so but it increases the castor angle and thus makes the steering a little more sensitive, plus it increases self-centring as well.

Now for the rear end. This is all pretty simple stuff, but even something like changing the rear springs is not as easy as it looks. You need to disconnect the damper from the trailing arm and disconnect the anti roll bar from the trailing arm, get a big solid bar and force the trailing arm down enough to yank the spring out. It is very hard work and mind the brake pipes and hoses. Fitting new, shorter coils can be hard, refitting a standard spring can be a nightmare and sometimes you have to undo the axle mounts and drop the rear axle one side at a time to do it. Greasing the rubber spring gaskets makes it a lot easier, but two people are much better than one, along with a bit of brute force.

As for the various suspension bushes in the rear end, you cannot beat the standard factory rear subframe bushes. You could fit harder ones, but they can transmit too much noise and vibration for a road car. Some people swear by them, but they were comparing this wonder bush against a tired old BMW bush that had been in the car for six years. However, some American BMW tuners produce a rear axle bush made of softer compound polyurethane and these are pretty good. They do not transmit loads of vibration into the car and will locate the rear axle beam a

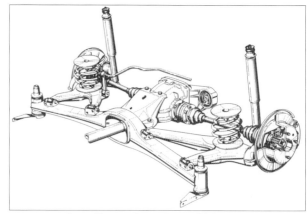

Rear Suspension - BMW 325e, 325i

bit better too. Changing these bushes is not a DIY job unless you have the expensive special tool. The tool costs about the same as a BMW dealer or specialist will charge to supply and fit a pair of new ones so unless you own three E30s and are planning on owning loads more, it might not be worth it. Even with the special tool, it is hard work. Where some inexperienced mechanic, BMW or otherwise, will come unstuck is with the mounting plate. This fits to the rear outer sill area with two Allen bolts. These never like to come undone, and you have to really clean them out inside and find an Allen key that is a good, tight 'hammer' fit. If it still rounds off, hammer a spline drive socket attachment in. The last resort is to drill them out, but forget about using a conventional Allen key because the bolts will just laugh at you.

Trailing arm bushes? Well, if you like you can fit polyurethane bushes, as they are not a bad idea. Unlike the subframe bushes, they will not transmit much noise into the car but it's a good day's work to fit them and they do not make a vast difference to the handling. In fact, you would be hard pressed to find any difference at all. What they can do though is correct the severe negative camber on cars that have been seriously lowered – i.e. 60mm or more. These bushes are available in the States as offset bushings to do just this. What is definitely worth doing is fitting an M3 differential mounting bush. The standard E30s normally used a very flexible 'voided' bush in the rear alloy differential cover where the differential bolts to the boot floor. It allows a surprising amount of movement and fitting the solid M3 bush is recommended. You can either buy the bush from BMW or purchase a Z3 M Coupé/Roadster rear differential cover. The plain bush option is rather cheaper and fitting is simple. You just jack the rear of the car and support it on axle stands, place a jack under the differential and just take the weight of the differential – one pump on the jack handle should do it. Then remove the bolt mounting the differential to the boot floor and let the jack down so that the differential drops about three inches. Now drain the differential oil, remembering to first loosen the refill plug, and remove the rear differential cover. Mount it in a vice, and hacksaw the inner bush sleeve until it drops out. Press the new one in with a vice and reassemble.

The Z3M rear differential cover is a lovely thing with extra cooling fins and it looks just like something Alpina would have made. They come with the bush ready pressed in, and because it is basically an E30 'big' differential, it bolts straight on. But.... it will only fit a 'big' differential, which restricts it to the M3, 325i and those few non-325i/M3 E30s with the big LSD.

However, the M3 bush can be fitted to a small differential car. The result is less axle tramp under hard acceleration and better axle location.

Lowering an E30? Make 50mm (two inches) the absolute limit with an extreme of 60mm on the front only. Any more than that and the car just will not handle properly with weird suspension geometry – the more the rear is lowered, the more negative camber is introduced to the rear wheels that will lower the grip available and wear the tyres out. The steering will feel weird too.

Anti-roll bars are an interesting subject. Four-cylinder cars, like the 316, did not often have rear ones, and the six-cylinder cars had both a rear bar and a thicker front one. They are very easy to fit and make a big difference. Again, Eibach make fairly expensive but very effective up-rated bars as a pair. Front anti-roll bars come from the factory in different thicknesses and I spent a day down at BMW tuner, Fritz's Bits in Wellington, Somerset measuring the anti roll bars on 28 different E30s to produce the definitive guide on what is fitted with what. This also tallies up with what BMW quote for each model.

Fitting a set of second-hand anti-roll bars from a 325i will sharpen up a 318i no end and even on the cars with no rear bar (316), the captive nuts are all there to bolt it straight on.

Eibach list a 16mm rear anti-roll bar for the rear of an E30, but a 20mm for the front. But hang on, a standard 325i front bar is 20 mm. The difference is that the Eibach bar is shorter from the front to back, meaning less leverage and stronger anti-twist properties. They are also made with three tie-rod mounting positions so the strength can be altered.

The chart below tells which car has what bars.

FRONT ANTI ROLL BARS – applications:

18.5 mm: 316, 316i, 318i, 320i, 323i, 325e, 324d, all standard suspension.

19 mm: M3 models (does not fit other E30 models).

20 mm: All 325i, 318iS, all Tourings, cars with M Technic suspension, 324td, 318i Convertible, 320iS.

21 mm: All six-cylinder Convertible models.

REAR ANTI ROLL BARS – applications:

12 mm: 316, 316i, 318i, 324d and 324td, 325e, 320i and 325i Convertible, 320i up to March 1985, 323i up to March 1985.

13.5 mm: Italian market 316i saloon, All Tourings, 325e from September 1986.

14.5 mm: 320i and 323i from March 1985, 325i, 324d and 324td with sports suspension, all standard models with M Technic suspension, M3, 318iS, 320iS, 320i and 325i Convertible with M Technic suspension

NOTE: Baur Convertibles use saloon anti roll bars.

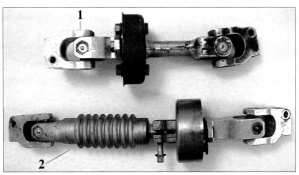

1 - Standard E30 Joint   2 - Standard E26 Joint

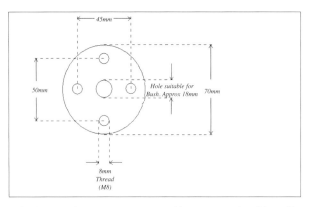

Thickness of spacer is approx. 12mm. You should really measure the required thickness on the car. This will allow for variations from car to car etc.

Remove pinch bolt and separate joint. You don't need the bolt or the top corrugated section. You only need the E36 joint.

1 - Drill out the top of the rivets that secure the pinch bolt section to the rubber donut. They can then be knocked out.
2 - This picture shows one rivet removed and the other has been drilled and is ready to remove.

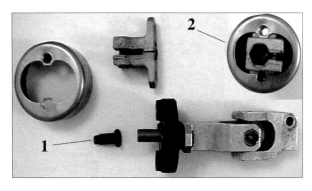

Fitting a rear anti roll bar

This is one of those jobs that are more difficult than they look, but on a car without a rear anti roll bar it is worth doing. The bar bolts onto the rear chassis legs and the captive nuts are all there waiting. The threads are normally pretty rusty by now so it is a very good idea to run the bolts through a couple of times with some penetrating oil. Basically, the anti roll bar fits above the differential and you will notice that the central part of the anti roll bar is raised in the centre to clear the differential housing. If you fit it upside down the bar will foul the top of the differential casing. The bar also threads between the boot floor and the fuel filler neck and to avoid disturbing any of this, there is a way of getting the bar in. You need the back of the car fully jacked up and on axle stands. You do not have to undo and remove the rear 19mm final drive mounting bolt but it will help as back of the differential will then drop down a couple of inches and give you more room. The big thing is removing both rear wheels and dropping down the rear of the exhaust – there is not really any other way. The exhaust does not have to come right off, but support it on a jack, release the rear mountings and drop it down as much as you can without straining the front exhaust to down-pipe connection. The anti roll bar must have its links straightened, and then you can thread it in from the exhaust side, over the differential and in between the floor and the fuel filler neck. Once you have wrestled it into position, lubricate the anti roll bar mounting bushes with washing-up liquid and fit them, followed by the brackets. These hook into a slot on the chassis brackets and a single 13mm bolt tightens them.

STEERING

If the E30 had one downfall it was the rather low geared steering. When something as humble as Morris Minor 1000 had a rack with two-and-a-half turns lock to lock, the E30 with manual, non power-assisted steering was a bit daft at just over four turns. The E30 M3 came as standard with a steering rack with a much tighter lock of three-and-a-half turns. If you have a left-hand drive E30, lucky old you because the choice is simple, fit an M3 steering rack. It goes in without a hitch on the same mountings.

However, if your E30 is right-hand drive, you've got a problem because the E30 M3 was never made as a RHD car and as such, there was never a RHD 'quick rack'. However, it has been found that with a few sly modifications the E36 3 Series power steering rack will go in. The E36 front cross member is very similar to the E30 unit and if you are fitting an M50 or M52 (24 valve) engine, the E36 cross member is the one to use.

British E30 enthusiast, Ian Haynes from the E30 Zone figured out a correct way of doing this conversion, as opposed to some of the horrors that had been done, and I am going to outline his conversion ideas which have been proven to work and looks 'factory'. I saw one car converted to an E36 rack using a different method whose steering coupling was only half an inch onto the steering column splines – the mind boggles.

Fitting the rack

Mounting the rack to the car is really just a straight swap for the E30 rack. You will need to have made up a couple of 14mm spacers because the E36 rack mounting points are not as tall as those of the E30. The hole spacing for the bolts are the same.

The E36 track rod ends fit to the E30's steering arms (on the strut) without a hitch and as for the power steering pipes, you could either modify the existing ones (six-cylinder E36 cars only) with a bit of careful bending or do what Ian Haynes does and fit some custom-made pipes.

The big problem comes from the steering column joint. Ian combined the upper universal joint (UJ) from the E30 with the lower UJ from the E36. He made an alloy spacer to join them together and lengthwise, the standard 275mm long E30 joint needs to be shortened to 250 mm.

The E36 joint is made in two parts. The top half comprises the top joint and a convoluted section. This is connected to the lower UJ and rubber flexible joint by a 13mm pinch bolt. Unscrew this bolt and bin the top section because you do not need it. Now you are faced with the lower section with the flexible joint. Drill or cut the rivets that secure the flexible joint to the joint. Look down the centre of the pinch bolt section; you will see a small securing clip that you will need to remove with a small screwdriver.

Now for the E30 joint. All you need is the upper part that joins to the steering column so split the assembly in two, as you did with the E36 joint.

When you try to mate the E30 joint to the E36 flexible joint, you will find the holes do not line up. The bolt spacing on the E36 joint is 45mm as opposed to 50mm of the E30 part. You will also discover that the overall length is 240mm (10mm short). These two hurdles are easily overcome by making a metal disc 10mm thick with a hole in the centre. Get your machine shop to cut you a disc and drill two holes 45mm apart and the other two at 90 degrees 50mm apart. You will need to use two of the metal spacer tubes from the old E30 flex joint (rubber disc) and fit them into the E36 flexible joint.

As for the hole in the centre of your new steel disc, this is for the centring bush. If you look at the pinch bolt section you removed earlier, you will see a bronze bush in the centre. This is a sod to get out but with accurate cutting work through the side of the joint you can remove

Close up of the rubber donut. You will need to fit 2 of the spacer tubes from the E30 joint in these 2 holes.

This is the E30 joint after it has been dismantled. Mine was bolted together, but yours may be riveted similar to the E36 joint.
1 - This is the joint you will need
2 - You need to remove 2 of these spacer tubes

1 - This is the pinch bolt section. You can see the 4 places that secured the bush in place. Carefully drill these out to allow the bush to be removed.
We need this bush later.
2 - I also cut through this portion of the casing and opened it out with a small chisel.
The bush will drop right out now.

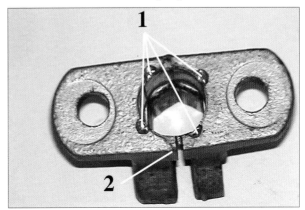

This is the joint after assembly (above) and in position below.

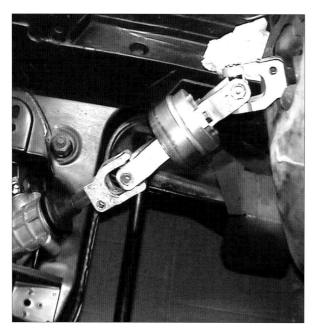

These are the parts you require from the E30 and E36 joints. It's not shown but you will also need the bus that you used from the pinch bolt section.

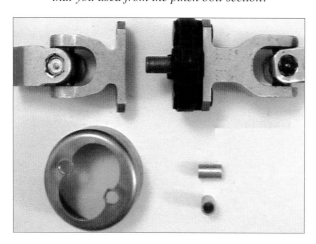

it in one piece. You have to make the hole in the centre of the metal disc the same as the diameter of the rescued bush so that it's a nice snug fit. Use some Loctite bearing fit 'glue'.

Now, this all works fine when it is together, but the clearance between the coupling and the exhaust manifold is very, very tight. During development it was noticed that on sharp left hand corners, the engine would move across slightly and as a result, the exhaust manifold would foul the steering shaft – not good! There are three possible solutions. One is to squash the outer down pipe into an oval but this is not ideal. The better method is to use a pair of E28 M5 left hand engine mounts which, because of their offset mounting pins, will move the engine across slightly. Alternative number three is to support the engine on an engine hoist, remove the mountings altogether and elongate the mounting holes in the cross member by about 20mm – you will need a rotary file in a drill to do this and it will be long, boring work. By doing this you can then move the engine across by up to 20mm but as with using the M5 mounts, you will need to grind the locating lugs off the mounts – using new mounts is absolutely essential anyway as old mounts will be very tired and rather too flexible. The trouble with moving the engine over any great distance is that you will put added strain on the prop-shaft coupling – slackening the bottom mounting nuts on the gearbox and moving that across by 10 or 20mm is a good idea. Last, but not least, consider polyurethane engine mounts that will hold the engine down more securely. The polyurethane gearbox mounts will, however, transmit too much noise into the cabin, but I would still move the engine across 10mm even with the polyurethane mounts.

WHEELS AND TYRES

With wheels and tyres, sixteen inch is as big as you want to go and if you can find them, Alpina, Hartge or Schnitzer wheels are the ultimate. The E30 has now gone past the stage of being plain old fashioned and it's starting to look like a bit of a classic – that is why modern aftermarket alloys always look wrong. The 15-inch cross spoke wheel as fitted to the 325i Sport is an excellent wheel with either 195 or 205 section tyres. All E30s have four-stud wheels, so if you want to convert to five studs you will need a complete suspension set up from an E30 M3. The other way is to use M3 front struts and standard lower wishbones and then fit a complete rear axle from either a Z3 or a Compact E36. Bear in mind that the 1.8, 1.9 and 2.2 Z3s used the small differential without an LSD but sometimes with electronic traction control via the ABS system, but the 3-litre version had a 3.07:1 ratio LSD.

All the Z3 and Compact axles used five-stud rear hubs and the trailing arm angles were reduced to help on-limit handling.

The classic "MiM" wheel.   *A 15-inch king alloy wheel.*
Most need restoring but look superb.

TYRES AND WHEELS - 1983 – 1985 cars

BMW 316: 5 or 5.5-inch wide 14-inch steel wheels with 175/70 R 14 tyres.
         Optional: 5.5 x 14-inch alloys with 195/60 HR 14 tyres.
BMW 318i: 5 or 5.5-inch steel wheels with 175/70 HR 14 tyres.
         Optional: 5.5 x 14-inch alloys with 195/60 HR 14 tyres.
BMW 320i: 5.5-inch steel wheels with 195/60 HR 14 tyres.
         Optional: same size tyres with alloy wheels.
BMW 323i: 5.5-inch steel wheels with 195/60 VR 14 tyres.
         Optional: same tyres but with alloy wheels.
Optional on all cars: Metric 200/60 R365 88H TD. For 323i 200/60 VR 365 TD.

1985 onwards

BMW 316/324d: 5 or 5.5-inch steel wheels with 175/70 R 14 tyres.
         Optional: 195/65 HR 14 tyres on 5.5-inch steel rims or 6-inch alloys.
BMW 318i: 5 or 5.5-inch steel wheels with 175/70 HR14 tyres.
         Optional: 195/65 HR 14 tyres on 5.5-inch steel rims or 6-inch alloys.
BMW 320i and 325e: 5.5-inch steel wheels with 195/65 HR 14 tyres.
         Optional: Same tyres on 6-inch alloys.
BMW 325i/318iS: 5.5-inch steel wheels with 195/65 VR 14 tyres.
         Optional: same tyres on 6-inch alloy wheels.
BMW 325iX: 6-inch steel wheels with 195/65 VR 14 tyres

318iS and 325i Sport: 7 x 15-inch BBS alloy wheels with 205/55 VR 15 tyres.

A rare split rim BBS wheel.   *An original Hartge wheel.*
         The centre caps are no longer available

Grooved disc and better pads improve E30 brakes

Alpina B6 brakes

BRAKES

As standard, the 316, 316i, 318i and 320i cars have front discs and rear drums, the discs being vented on the 320i. Other cars, such as the later ABS 320i, 318iS and the 323i/325i have discs on the back too. Despite having single piston calipers, they are not bad brakes but we would use genuine BMW discs and pads (or Textar pads with Ate discs which is a very close equivalent) for all but the most heated of use. Then you should consider Kevlar pads, grooved or drilled discs and some better brake fluid such as Pagid racing blue.

Early ABS systems were renowned for giving a horrible pedal feel and many owners went blue in the face bleeding the brakes to get rid of what they wrongly thought was air in the system. The problem lies in the excessive length of piping in the engine bay and there is little you can do about it, apart from converting back to a non-ABS system. To do this, you will need a new, non-ABS master cylinder plus the two engine bay brake pipes that go from the master cylinder to each front wheel. The existing front to rear brake pipe is not affected. I have seen a conversion using the existing ABS master cylinder where the single outlet for the front brakes is used. On the non-ABS cylinder there are three outlets, one for the rear brakes (divided in two at the rear axle), one for the right front wheel and one for the front left wheel. On the ABS cars, there are outlets for the front brakes and the back brakes. The pipe for the front brakes goes into the ABS block, where it is separated for each front wheel. What can be done is to use a T-piece on the front brake pipe, but it is a bit inelegant and could lead to problems with front to rear brake bias so avoid going

this route. A new master cylinder is not that expensive from an aftermarket source.

A seemingly good idea is to upgrade the solid brake discs on the 316 and 318 cars to vented discs from a better model. Well, be aware that on a car with the original skinny 5J steel wheels, you will run into caliper clearance problems. Fit the discs and calipers with nice chunky new pads and you will have a few millimetres clearance between the main caliper body and the wheel. But these are sliding calipers; which means that as the pads wear down, the caliper body will move outwards. With just a few thousand miles of wear on the pads, the caliper body will have moved outwards enough to just start touching the wheel. As the pads wear down, the caliper will start eating into the wheel itself and on a long journey in wet weather you might not even hear the noise. So basically, if you want to fit the vented brakes, use the correct wheels.

You want bigger brakes? The standard anchors are 260mm but various companies in the States do bigger brake conversions using discs up to 310mm – but you will need 17-inch wheels to house those. Brembo alloy floating calipers are used and the discs are two-piece jobs with alloy mounting bells. These kits are available for both the four-stud E30 and the M3. A notably good arrangement is the 290mm disc conversion sold by Ireland Engineering in the USA that will fit inside standard 15-inch BBS wheels. This uses Brembo bits, such as the calipers and discs, but Ireland make their own disc mounting bells. If your car has 16-inch wheels, then their 310mm discs are better still, which for a few dollars more can be widened from 20mm to 28mm for some serious brakes. Bigger disc kits are also available for the rear brakes.

On the M3, the brakes do not often need help, even if you drive good and hard. Turner Motorsport in the USA do a few bits starting with Zimmerman drilled discs but they list parts like the ventilated brake back plates that channel air from an intake pipe to the centre of the disc. Sport Evo front apron air ducts can also be added. Brass bushes for the caliper slides also eliminate the flexing from which standard rubber bushes calipers can suffer and once again Brembo big brake kits up to 320mm can be used.

When using high performance calipers, be aware that they do not always come with piston dust seals. In everyday use, the chromed pistons will go rusty and, even with stainless pistons, dirt will get in and damage the seals, leading to fluid loss. To prevent this happening pack the gap between piston and caliper body with copper grease.

For road use though, owners like various different things but the general consensus is that the standard brakes with better pads and fluid are fine. Those everyone seems to like are the original equipment BMW discs but while standard BMW or Textar pads are fine for road use, they were not really designed for pounding around a race circuit with continuous hard braking. The discs are not a bad size and the calipers came from the E28 5 Series, which is a much heavier car. In the case of the 528i it was also a 130mph car. The fluid needs to be changed for arduous use – Castrol SRF and Ate Super Blue are two well-regarded fluids but anything that is a brand name and DOT 4 will be okay. As for pads, the well liked ones are Pagid Blue, Mintex 1155, Hawk HP4 and Ferodo DS2500, with DS3000s being suitable for serious stuff. The only downside with DS3000s are that they make a lot of black dust which can eat into the paint on the wheels.

When buying calipers, the E28 connection is handy because a pair of properly reconditioned units from a company like Budweg (Euro Car Parts) is very inexpensive. At the time of writing on eBay they were just over £100, plus VAT.

Most owners agree that with the right discs, pads and fluid, the stock brakes are fine, even for track day use. The other big thing is cold air – plenty of it needs to be vented into the brakes but we covered that at the beginning.

CONVERTING TO REAR DISCS

As standard, the rear drums on cars like the 316, 318i and 320i without ABS are not bad. But the trouble with drum brakes is that they are a hangover from the fifties and can be a total pain when maintenance is needed.

Therefore, a conversion to rear disc brakes is possible. You will need the complete trailing arms from a disc brake car complete with the brake pipes and the handbrake cables. Fitting the new arms is just simple nuts and bolts job, although it is pretty tedious work. I did this conversion on a 1988 320i over a weekend and this was a car used for everyday use as well as track days. For road use the conversion is just not worth it unless you get the parts for next to nothing. Even then you will find that you need new rear discs and pads and new flexible hoses.

FITTING LATER HEADLAMPS

One problem with the older, metal bumper E30 is that the lamps were not too hot. Well, they were pretty good in 1983 but the world moves on. A nice upgrade is to fit the lamps from a later plastic bumper car – not only do they look nicer but they just work better. The other problem with the older cars is that the chrome in the reflectors goes off with age and there is not a bulb powerful enough to make them work properly when they are that bad.

Fitting the lights is just a straightforward nuts and bolts job – two screws and three spring clips hold each grille in place and then it is just a matter of removing the three screws that hold the headlamp assembly in place. These can be very tight so a nice big crosshead screwdriver and a pair old vice grips on the shaft are often needed. When buying the replacement lamps, be aware that you need the whole lot, including as well the backing plates. You should also cut the wires a few inches past the connectors because early and late type plug connectors are different. It is then a simple case of cutting the old connectors off your old headlamp wiring loom and soldering on the new ones. Plastic bumper type headlamps come in two forms – the early ones from September 1987 ran for about a year but the later ones had the 'smiley' cut outs in the outer lamps.

FITTING E30 FOGLAMPS

1.) First you will need to remove the foglight blanking covers. These can be removed by giving them a good thump and they will pop out. They are held in by plastic clips and some may be left behind in the front panel. Grovel underneath the car and pick them out with a small screwdriver. Removing the front undertray makes this easier.

2.) Now you will need to fit the 8 new plastic clips into the holes where the previous clips came from. They just press fit into the holes.

3.) Now fit the fog lamps using the 8mm bolts supplied. You will see the wiring plugs hidden away under the inner wing. Give these a dose of WD40 and plug them in.

4.) Go inside the car, now remove the lower steering

A pair of original front foglamps

*Good used M3 fogs are hard to find -
as are pre '88 E30 units*

*All the bits to fit headlamp wash wipe.
Seized motors are all too common.*

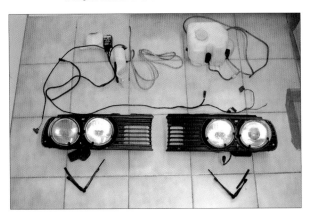

column/dash cover - 3 or 4 plastic twist screws and it drops down. From behind, push the old single button foglamp switch out, unplug it from the wiring socket and fit the new twin button switch. Quite often, this switch will need dismantling and the internal contacts cleaning. Don't refit the lower dash cover just yet ....

5.) Under the bonnet, fit relay K8 as well as fuses in positions 29 and 30. The fuses are 7.5 AMP. Relay K8 is marked on the fuse box lid.

6). Now try the foglamps. Non functioning could be corroded connector or a faulty bulb so test with a 12v test lamp. Make sure the extra green lamp comes on the dash for the front foglamps. Some E30's without front fogs were fitted with the dash bulb, most were not.

FITTING THE DASH BULB
1.) You will need to remove the instrument cluster for this. With the dash undertray removed, feel up behind the dash for the two aluminum knurled nuts that secure that plastic panel between the instruments and the steering column - using a lead light peer under the dash and you will see them.

2.) With that panel removed, you will see four screws along the lower edge of the instrument panel surround. The outer two are long black ones, the inner two are short silver ones. Remove these along with the two at the top of the plastic instrument surround and remove the surround.

3.) Now you will have just two screws left holding the body of the instrument cluster to the dash at the top. Remove the steering wheel (straighten it first) with a 22mm socket. Pull the instruments forward and disconnect the 2 or 3 multiplugs (white, blue and yellow). Only cars with and OBC have the centre yellow plug and getting these plugs out and in again is a swine.

4.) Pull the cluster out, hold it up to the light and you will see where the bulb goes, one place to the left of the rear foglight lamp. Fit the bulb by twisting it in.

5.) Reassembling is a reversal of dismantling but test the fog light bulb before refitting all the trim. Refit the cluster in this order. Cluster in, two top screws, surround in, two long screws on outer edge, two short chrome screws in inner positions and two top ones.

FITTING AN ON-BOARD COMPUTER (OBC)
This is the procedure for fitting an E30 OBC as outlined by Adam Patchton on www.e30zone. It is a good guide and using it, I have fitted an OBC myself so I know it works. Even if your OBC comes as a box of loose bits, it is pretty clear where it all fits.

The 13-button OBC was an option on all six-cylinder cars and M3s and standard on the 320i SE and 325i SE. Despite the factory excluding the four-cylinder cars, E30 Zone tested a 325i OBC with a 318i instrument cluster and it all seemed to work with accurate readings.

Functions of the OBC:
Time
Date average speed
Fuel consumption
User selectable speed limit (gong)
Fuel range on remaining fuel
Stopwatch timer
Outside temperature
Code function (anti theft)

Parts you will need:
Main OBC unit
Wiring loom
Relay control module (above ECU mounting plate)
With just the above bits the OBC will function but without outside temperature.
Outside temp sensor (in nearside brake duct)
OBC horn (just above temp sensor)
Temp sensor and horn loom (follows back from the temperature sensor and joins to main loom shortly after entering bulkhead)
Audible gong (mounted in trim panel above pedals)
Remote indicator stalk (replaces standard indicator stalk for remote OBC access)
Tools needed: Nothing special – crosshead screwdriver and another with a short stubby head, a flat blade screwdriver, pliers and a 10mm socket with ratchet and extension.
Connections: These are the connections so you know what goes where:

Main loom:
Large yellow connector – back of instrument cluster
Larger green connector – back of OBC main unit
2 x small green connectors – relay control module
Small black – audible gong
Small blue – remote indicator stalk
Brown wire with circular ring connector – earth point behind glove box
2 x small white connectors – control box behind glove box
Black circular connector – connects to temp loom

Temp sensor loom:
Blue plug – horn
Black circular plug – temp sensor

FITTING
Before you think about fitting an OBC, you will need to remove certain bits. First remove your stereo and remove the lower dash trim panel from above the pedals.

The OBC computer - You will need a whole kit of parts, ideally removed from another car.

Now drop the glove box down – remove the plastic push in pins from the two hang down straps and it will flop down and rest on the floor – three more screws at the hinge and you can remove it altogether if you want. Then remove the upper glove box trim panel – it is a single crosshead screw and a couple of the plastic twist clips that need a quarter turn before being pulled out.

Next, remove the instrument cluster as detailed elsewhere. Also remove the clock because this is where the OBC unit will fit. To do this, prise the plastic clock surround out with a small flat blade screwdriver. This will reveal the two spring tags on the white clock body – just prise these up and the clock will come out.

Now you have room to start fitting the OBC bits. Start by threading the loom through the dashboard with each connector in the right place and you may want to tie-wrap the loom in place. Now start connecting the bits to it – OBC unit first, but the screws that hold it in from behind are a pain to get in and are easily dropped and lost forever. It is often better to remove the heater control panel. To do this, remove the centre console. The back half comes out first and the retaining nut is hidden under the ashtray. Removing the gearlever gaiter will reveal the others and it is also attached by screws at the front. Removing the push switches above the radio will reveal the screws that hold the panel to the top of the dash. Two more screws go in at the bottom edge.

With the OBC unit fitted and plugged in, now to fit the relay control module. You need to undo the four 10mm bolts that hold the ECU in place and then remove the plate above the ECU. The ECU is under the dash between the steering column and the door on RHD cars, above the glove box on LHD. The relay control module is attached to the ECU mounting plate by a couple of crosshead screws. Fit the module, plug it into the loom and refit the ECU.

At this point, check to see if the OBC is working. Plug in the yellow connector and the other two into the back of the cluster, switch on the ignition and see if the OBC lights up with 'UHR' (Hour) flashing. If it does, all is well.

Now swap over the indicator stalks by removing the lower column cowling (four screws), unplug the existing stalk wiring and fit the new one. Tie-wrap the wiring back in place and do not forget the brown earth wire!

Now fit the temperature sensor to the left hand front brake cooling duct and you will see where it plugs in. You will also need to bolt on the OBC horn and cover – it goes above where the fog light would sit but if you removed the bits from another car you will know where it goes.

Plug the temperature sensor and horn wring loom into both components, feed it back along the side of the engine bay, clipping it in with the rest of the car's loom. You will see a rubber grommet under the brake servo, so push the loom through the hole in the grommet (you might have to make your own) and into the car. From inside the car, plug the two looms together behind the glove box. You will see the main earth point where all the brown wires meet – remove the nut, fit the new brown wire on top of the others and refit the nut.

You should now be left with two spare wires, a green one and a red wire with a white tracer. These wires plug into the main control box and they only fit one way. Now refit the radio and the bits of trim you removed and off you go! If it does not work (you should have checked it before removing it from the donor, fitting a battery if you had to), the bulb pack in the back of the unit has failed. It is the white plastic unit that slides in from the right.

Fitting heated seats
It is a very rare option in Britain, and heated seats are more common on European market cars. But you can easily fit heated seats to a car that left the factory without them. The only way to buy these is second-hand but do not buy them without testing them first. You want to see these seats in a car where you can try them out. Either that or test them with a 12 volt supply. To remove them, the first job is to remove the seats themselves – just four

A rare Recaro interior. Note the bolsters are much bigger than BMW sports seats.

17mm nuts and bolts. You will see the connector where the heated seat loom plugs in so just disconnect these. The next job is to remove the carpet entirely. This will take you about half an hour but it is easier than trying do it with the loom in. With the carpet out, you will see the loom running under both seats and up to the power pick-up under the glove box. It either runs along the transmission tunnel of along the inner sill. The earth attaches to the main earth point under the glove box, and the power point plugs into the loom power connection nearby. You will need a 15-amp fuse in location 16 in the main fuse box plus the relay in location K5 that can be identified on the fuse box lid. Refitting is as simple as removing it.

Fitting opening rear side windows
Many of the older and cheaper E30s didn't have these and unless you carry rear seat passengers all the time there is no real reason to need them – but if you are a die-hard E30 nut case, it is another string in your bow. The best source of these is another car. To take them off you will need to remove the seat belt anchorage on the B post and then the plastic B post trim itself. This will reveal a couple of holes drilled in the B post and down here are the two nuts that hold the front hinge to the body. The only trouble is that the holes are too small to take a conventional 10mm socket. Instead you will need a 10mm box spanner (a tube with 10mm hex end) to reach them. Sure, you can butcher the holes on the scrap car to get them out, and you can always use a big drill to open up the holes in your car, but the box spanner is the best way of doing it. That apart, it is a nuts and bolts job getting it apart and back together. When removing the old sealed side windows, use a Stanley knife to cut the rubber – that way the rear window will pop out without risk of glass breakage. Okay so they were only going in the bin anyway but glass gets everywhere.

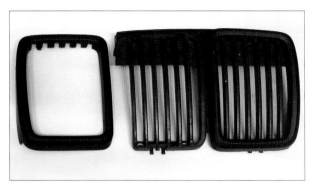

The black centre grille is popular. The chrome rings will come off, but they need aggressive sanding and plastic primer. They will need to be glued back on too.

Fitting BMW factory body kits and styling parts

For many, the 1989/91 325i Sport M Technic body kit is the one to have and they do look good. However, there are many nasty fibreglass copies about and they are normally pretty lousy. The better ones (go on recommendations with these) look okay and are possibly easier to fit than the real thing. The genuine BMW parts are fairly hard work to fit because the mounting lugs on the side panels require not only fixing holes, but small depressions in the door and rear quarter panels as well. The front and rear bumpers are a straight swap for the standard bits, but if you're buying used, you need to buy everything with all the mounting brackets, clips etc. A good used M Technic II body kit in good condition is also expensive.

Later SE models had plastic sill covers that look quite good. These were also fitted to the six cylinder Tourings

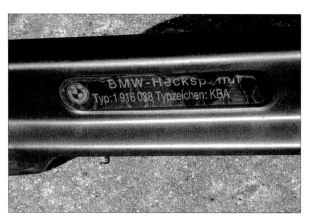

An original BMW bootspoiler

and are quite easy to fit, requiring a couple of holes to be drilled – remember to paint the edges of the holes though.

ANY OTHER BUSINESS

Standard E30 seats are not the best for serious motoring. E30 Recaro seats are about but expect to pay £200 for a decent pair – a complete leather interior is at least £450 with black interiors selling for around £600 in decent condition. If your car is a four-door or Touring, bear in mind that Recaro seats from the E28 M535i will fit. Like the seats, the standard four-spoke E30 steering wheel is a horrid thing that needs binning. Any E30 leather wheel will fit, as will the wheel from an E30 M3. Sport steering wheels from a post 1986 E28 will fit too.

There are two sizes for the M Technic I steering wheel. The earlier cars used a wheel of 365mm diameter but the later ones as used on the E28 are 380 mm. The leather three-spoke SE steering wheel is also 380 mm.

M Technic I wheel

An M Technic II steering wheel

Restoration Notes

Chapter 15

THE E30 IN SOUTH AFRICA

BMW South Africa started building cars in the sixties in CKD kits, CKD standing for complete knock down and meaning cars built from kits of parts. Many parts were made locally though; the glass was a slightly darker green tint and is stamped "Armourplate" as opposed to "Sekurit" on European cars. The South African market cars were different in other ways too. Most had air conditioning, long range fuel tanks, front sumpguards and all cars used the Type 188 final drive which is the big one used in the 325i....even the basic 316 used this stronger item. Later cars with plastic bumpers did not use the black plastic panel in between the rear lamps and all cars used a km/h speedo and econometer as well as a litres fuel gauge although carburettor 316 cars used a clock with built-in econometer which was unique to the South African market. The bodyshells often used the inner wing reinforcing plates from the Convertibles that were welded in between the strut top and the inner wing. Convertibles, Tourings and M3's were not built in South Africa.

Production started in 1983 with the 2- and 4-door 318i, 320i and 323i. The 316 arrived along with the 325i in 1985 and the car had a facelift, with the plastic bumpers, colour coded door mirrors and bigger tail lamps in January 1988. The 325i Sport arrived in January 1988 and is virtually the same spec as the English version with the bodykit, M Technic suspension, 15-inch BBS wheels and limited slip diff. The engine however has a better camshaft than the regular South African 325i; it is reckoned to be an Alpina cam but it isn't. Its part number from BMW is 1131 1706 655 and it does indeed translate into the Alpina parts catalogue as the cam for a Catalyst equipped C2 2.7 (later rebadged as B3 2.7). This cam is the exact same item as fitted to every standard production non-catalyst European 325i! South African BMWs are an odd spec compared to European cars. For example, there was an Executive Pack which was an option that replaced vinyl trim with cloth, added air conditioning, alloy wheels, front foglamps, power steering and a check control panel and electric mirrors. In South Africa the M10 engine continued in limited production next to the M40 until 1990.

The BMW 333i

This was a project cooked up after hours by BMW SA employees Vic Doolan (a British ex-pat) and head of engineering, Berndt Pischetsrieder and it was basically a 2-door 323i fitted with the engine from the E23 732i saloon. 204 or 215 (depending on who you talk to....) cars were made between 1985 and 1987 at the Rosslyn

The Evo Sport style spoiler lower lip used on the 325iS Evo

Note: SA E30's it didn't have a black plastic panel between the rear lamps

Interior shot of 325iS

factory and the car used a lot of Alpina parts; engine mounts, radiator, inlet manifold (to reposition the throttle body and airflow meter to the passenger side) and Alpina 7 x 16 inch wheels with BMW centre badges. The exhaust was a locally made special with a tubular manifold as Alpina did not make a right hand drive E30 with the M30 big six engine. Suspension was all from the B6 3.5 as were the 11.6 inch front discs with ABS and bigger callipers. The gearbox was the dogleg 5-speed unit from the M535i and there were two diff ratios available, a 2.97 or a 3.07. Externally, the 333i used the chrome bumpers with the M Technic I bodykit made by Metzeler, a special 333i boot badge with a triple colour Motorsport flash behind it and colour coded mirrors. Inside it had BMW sports seats in leather, the M Technic I steering wheel, Alpina red needle instruments but oddly no air conditioning. BMW SA said there wasn't room for a power steering pump and an air con pump - Alpina managed this okay. Another detail was the Alpina digital dashboard auxiliary display which took the place of the right hand centre air vent - it monitored the engine oil pressure and temperature, manifold vacuum and rear axle oil temperature. Colours for the 333i were Henna Red (A European BMW colour used from 1978 until 1986), Charcoal (Diamond) Black metallic, Ice White and Aero Silver which is a pale metallic silvery blue not unlike Sapphire Blue. Power was 197 bhp at 5500 rpm with 211 lb.ft. torque at 4300 rpm.

BMW 325iS

This looks the same as a 325i Sport; under the skin though it's a very different car indeed. BMW South Africa needed a weapon to race in Group N and as there was no M3, a highly modified and lightweight 325i was the answer, a kind of 325i CSL if you like. Basis of the 325iS (built in March 1990) was a regular 325i shell with the M Technic II bodykit......but the bonnet, front wings and doorskins were pressed from a high grade imported aluminium resulting in a car that weighed 1147 kg fully loaded with power steering, sunroof, electric windows and air conditioning. The suspension was straight from

the E30 M3 including the five bolt hubs and the wheels were standard 7 x 15 inch M3 BBS cross spokes with 205/60 tyres. The steering rack was standard RHD 325i. The final drive was the regular 3.7:1 ratio diff from a non-Sport 325i with an LSD unit fitted, but the interesting bit was the engine which was built in Germany by BMW using the Alpina C2 2.7 head and a cam which was a unique grind - it's not the same 268 degree Alpina cam but something slightly more tame and power is reduced from the Alpina's 210 bhp to 197 at just 5800 rpm. Torque is 196 lb.ft. Following this car came the 325iS Evo which was built in two batches, March 1991 and June 1991. This car reverted to steel skinned doors but the engine was the proper Alpina C2 2.7 unit with gas-flowed ports in the head plus a higher compression along with an Alpina ECU and an E34 535i air flow meter, specially tuned to the engine to give 204 bhp. It also used the forged steel crank from the 524td that all C2 2.7 engines used and a bored out throttle body with the throttle disc from the E32/E34 3 litre and 3.5 litre engines. Like the first iS, the shocks are Japanese spec M3 Boge items but with Alpina anti roll bars and the final drive was lowered to 3.9:1. Common colours for South African E30's are Brilliant Red, Astral Silver (similar to Polaris), Aero Silver (bluey silver) and Ice White. Interior trim was "Uberkaro cloth" meaning "large squares" or check pattern and the same cloth used on the European 318iS and later model South African 318i saloons; black leather was a popular extra. An electric sunroof was an optional extra but air conditioning and power steering were standard, as was an on-board computer. Only 2-door cars were produced but it's not known how many; we're talking low hundreds. Don't confuse this highly specialised car with the USA market 325iS which is merely a very high spec standard 2-door 325i. The chassis numbers don't often provide conclusive proof; the OAF 44492 series code is for the original 325iS and the Evo cars were OEJ 94000 series or AF45408/AF45355. If in doubt, you must contact BMW South Africa who can confirm its true identity particularly in the case of the later steel panelled cars which are relatively easy to fake.

333i Engine bay: Note Repositioned Throttle Body

1985 BMW 333i

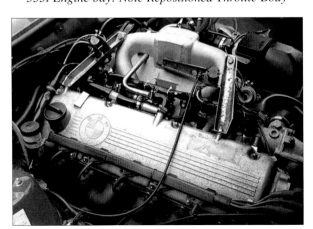

Chapter 16

E30 STANDARD SPECS

E30 STANDARD SPECIFICATIONS

BMW 316 1983 to 1988 (two- & four-door saloons + Baur Cabriolet)

ENGINE: BMW M10 four cylinder, iron block, alloy head with chain driven camshaft, 71mm stroke and 89mm bore, 1766cc, 9.5:1 compression ratio. Power output is 90bhp at 5500rpm, 103 lb/ft torque at 4000rpm. Solex Pierburg 2B carburettor until September 1983, electronic control Solex Pierburg 2BE September 1983 onwards. 8-blade fan.

MANUAL GEARBOX:
Four speed Getrag 242 gearbox as standard, ratios:
1st = 3.764:1
2nd = 2.04:1
3rd = 1.320:1
4th = 1:1

Five speed Getrag 240 or 242/5, ratios:
1st = 3.72:1
2nd = 2.02:1
3rd = 1.32:1
4th = 1:1
5th = 0.81:1

AUTOMATIC GEARBOX: ZF 3HP22 (three-speed) or ZF 4HP 22 (four-speed).

DIFFERENTIAL: 3.64 ratio until approx. 8/85. 3.9:1 ratio fitted from 8/85 and to four-speed automatics.

SUSPENSION: Independent front and rear suspension, front Macpherson struts with oil dampers and anti roll bar, rear semi-trailing arms swept back at 15 degrees, separate springs and dampers and no rear anti roll bar unless fitted with optional M Technic suspension.

STEERING: Standard: non-power assisted rack. 21.4:1 pinion to rack ratio (4.4 turns lock to lock). Optional power steering with 20.5:1 pinion to rack ratio (4 turns lock to lock).

Manual steering rack with steering hydraulic damper. (Also 318i)

BRAKES: 10-inch servo assisting front solid 255mm discs and 250mm rear drums, ABS optional for 1986 model year with rear discs.

WHEELS: Earlier cars have 5-inch steel wheels with 175/70 profile tyres, post September 1985 with 5.5-inch wide steels. 6-inch wide Bottle top alloys with 195/60 tyres optional (195/65 from September 1985). BBS 6 x 14-inch cross-spoke alloy wheels optional from 1986, 15 x 7-inch BBS cross-spoke alloy wheels with 205/55 tyres optional from 1987.

DIMENSIONS: Length (chrome bumper) 4325mm, (plastic bumper) 4318mm. Track 1407mm. Wheelbase 2570mm. Width 1645mm. Height (standard suspension) 1380mm. Unladen weight (standard car) 1000kg. (4 door cars weigh 20kg more) Cars with automatic transmission weigh 30kg more.

PERFORMANCE: (5 speed manual)

0 – 30mph	3.4 secs
0 – 40mph	5.4 secs
0 – 50mph	7.7 secs
0 – 60mph	11.9 secs
0 – 70mph	15.7 secs
0 – 80mph	22.3 secs
0 – 90mph	35 secs
30 – 50mph (4th gear)	9.7 secs
50 – 70mph (4th gear)	10.3 secs

Maximum speed: 106mph
Overall fuel consumption: 25mpg.

Battery: 44ah

Note: 316S: 75bhp/5800rpm, 81 lb/ft torque/3200rpm, Pierburg 1B2 carburettor.

BMW 316i 1987 to 1988:

As for 316 but with Bosch LE Jetronic fuel injection, power 102bhp at 5800rpm, torque 103 lb/ft at 4500rpm, 8.2:1 compression ratio.

Notes: M10 engined 316i not imported into Britain.

BMW 316i 1988 to 1991: (two- & four- saloons, Baur cabriolet & Touring)

ENGINE: BMW M40 engine, iron block, alloy head with hydraulic tappets, Bosch Motronic engine management, belt driven camshaft. 84mm bore and 72mm stroke, 1596cc, 9:1 compression (8.8 with catalyst). Power 102bhp at 5500rpm, torque 105 lb ft at 4250rpm.

MANUAL GEARBOX: Getrag 240/5 five-speed, ratios as for 316 with Getrag 240/5.

AUTOMATIC GEARBOX: ZF 4 HP 22 as for 316.

DIFFERENTIAL: 4.27:1 (manual), 4.45:1 (automatic)
.
SUSPENSION: As for 316.

BRAKES: As for 316.

WHEELS AND TYRES: As for 316 but 5.5 inch steel wheel standard.

DIMENSIONS: As for 316 but unladen weight 1109kg (4 door. 2 door car 20kg less).

PERFORMANCE: (5 speed manual)

0 – 30mph	3.1 secs
0 – 40mph	4.8 secs
0 – 50mph	7.1 secs
0 – 60mph	10.1 secs
0 – 70mph	13.8 secs
0 – 80mph	18.5 secs
0 – 90mph	25.3 secs
30 – 50mph (4th gear)	9 secs
50 – 70mph (3rd gear)	7 secs

Maximum speed: 112 mph.

Overall fuel consumption: 25.3mpg.

Notes: Lux models feature 62-litre fuel tank.

BMW 318i 1982 to 1987 (two & four door saloons, Baur Cabriolet)

ENGINE: BMW M10 1766cc as for 316 but with Bosch K Jetronic electro/mechanical fuel injection (11/82 until 9/83) and Bosch LE Jetronic fuel injection thereafter. Compression ratio 10:1 (K Jetronic cars) or 9.5:1 (LE Jetronic cars). Power 105bhp at 5800rpm (All cars), torque 107 lb/ft at 4500rpm (K Jetronic cars), 105 lb/ft at 4500 (LE Jetronic cars).

MANUAL AND AUTOMATIC GEARBOXES: As for 1982 – 1988 316.

DIFFERENTIAL: 3.64 (4 speed cars), 3.91 (5 speed and Automatic cars).

SUSPENSION: As for 316.

STEERING: As for 316.

BRAKES: As for 316.

WHEELS AND TYRES: As for 316 but with HR rated tyres.

DIMENSIONS: As for 316 but unladen weight 1010kg (1030 for four-door).

PERFORMANCE:

	K-Jetronic	LE Jetronic
0 – 30mph	3.3 secs	3.1 secs
0 – 40mph	5 secs	5.3 secs
0 – 50mph	7.1 secs	7.4 secs
0 – 60mph	9.8 secs	10.7 secs
0 – 70mph	13.6 secs	14.5 secs
0 – 80mph	18.1 secs	18.9 secs
0 – 90mph	24 secs	26.4 secs
30 – 50mph (3rd gear)	7.2 secs	(7.5 secs).
50 – 70mph (4th gear)	10.5 secs	(12.1 secs).

Maximum speed: 112mph.

Overall fuel consumption: 28.5mpg.

Notes: Right hand drive K Jetronic 318i cars were built for the Australian and New Zealand markets. U.S cars weigh 1071kg, and all have Bosch LE Jetronic, a catalyst with oxygen sensor and power is down to 101bhp at 5800rpm with torque at 103 lb/ft at 4500rpm. All US models come with the 5.5-inch alloy wheels. Vinyl trim is a no cost option. Early cars have a pod on top of the dash with seat belt and oxygen sensor warning lights. Air conditioning is also is standard on US cars.

BMW 318i 9/1987 on (two- & four- saloons, Baur Cabriolet, Convertible & Touring)

ENGINE: BMW M40 engine as for 316i but with 81mm stroke, 1795cc. 8.8:1 compression ratio. Power 115bhp at 5500rpm, torque 119 lb/ft at 4250rpm.

MANUAL AND AUTOMATIC GEARBOXES: As for 316i.

DIFFERENTIAL: 4.1 (manual) or 4.45 (automatic).

SUSPENSION: As for 316i.

STEERING: As for 316i.

BRAKES: As for 316i.

WHEELS AND TYRES: As for 316i.

DIMENSIONS: As for 316i, weight 1089kg (4 door).

PERFORMANCE:

0 – 30mph	3.4 secs
0 – 40mph	5 secs
0 – 50mph	7 secs
0 – 60mph	10 secs
0 – 70mph	13.2 secs
0 – 80mph	17.8 secs
0 – 90mph	23.5 secs
30 – 50 (4th gear)	11.2 secs.
50 – 70 (5th gear)	12.3 secs.

Maximum speed: 115mph.

Overall fuel economy 30mpg.

Notes: M40 engined 318i not sold in U.S but reintroduced the 318i into Australia.

BMW 318iS 1989 onwards (two-door saloon and Baur Cabriolet)

ENGINE: BMW M42 1795cc engine, bore and stroke as for 318i M40 but with 16 valves and twin chain driven camshafts, Bosch DME Motronic engine management with separate coil ignition. 10:1 compression ratio, power 136bhp at 6000rpm, torque 127 lb ft at 4600rpm.

MANUAL GEARBOX: As for 318i M40 (early), or special unit shared with E34 528i.

DIFFERENTIAL: 4.1 ratio as for 318i, limited slip differential with 25% lock up optional.

SUSPENSION: As for 318i but with M Technic suspension, gas dampers, up-rated front anti roll bar and rear anti roll bar fitted.

STEERING: Power steering standard.

BRAKES: 260mm vented front discs. 258mm solid rear discs.

WHEELS AND TYRES: 195/65 HR 14 tyres on 5.5 x 14 steel wheels, options as for 316, 316i.

DIMENSIONS: As for 316, weight 1160 kg.

PERFORMANCE:

0 – 30mph	3.3 secs
0 – 40mph	4.8 secs
0 – 50mph	6.5 secs
0 – 60mph	9.3 secs
0 – 70mph	12.2 secs
0 – 80mph	15.6 secs
0 – 90mph	20.7 secs
30 – 50mph (2nd gear)	3.6 secs.
50 – 70mph (3rd gear)	5.7 secs.

Maximum speed: 125 mph.

Overall fuel consumption: 28mpg.

Notes: Sold in the US as a 318iS in very similar trim to European models also as 4 door and basic 318iC. Standard features include airbag steering wheel, leather trim, air conditioning and catalyst. Power 134bhp at 6000rpm, torque 127 lb/ft at 4600rpm.

BMW 320i 1982 to 1991 (two- & four-door saloon, Baur Cabriolet, Touring and Convertible)

ENGINE: BMW M20 six cylinder, 80mm bore and 66mm stroke, 1990cc. 9.8:1 compression ratio, belt driven camshaft, Bosch LE Jetronic fuel injection, power 125bhp at 5800rpm, torque 123 lb/ft at 4000rpm. From 9/87: As for earlier model but with 9.4:1 compression ratio (8.8 on catalyst equipped cars), Bosch Motronic engine management. Power 129bhp (see notes) at 6000rpm, torque 128 lb/ft at 4000rpm. Dual exhaust pipes from mid 1988. 9 blade cooling fan.

All catalyst equipped cars from late 1985 use Motronic.

MANUAL GEARBOX:
ZF S19 or Getrag 240 5 speed gearbox, ratios:
1st = 3.72
2nd = 2.02
3rd = 1.32
4th = 1.00
5th = 0.81

AUTOMATIC GEARBOX: ZF 3HP 22 (three-speed) or ZF 4HP 22 (four-speed).

DIFFERENTIAL: 3.45 until August 1985, 3.91 September 1985 onwards along with 4.1 option (normally with LSD and 15-inch BBS wheels). From September 1987: 4.1 and 4.45 auto. 4.27 on some manuals Tourings.

SUSPENSION: As for 316 but with gas dampers and stronger front anti roll bar.

STEERING: As for 316.

BRAKES: As for 316 but with vented front discs.

WHEELS AND TYRES: Standard wheels 5.5-inch steels with 195/60 tyres. After August 1985 fitted with 195/65 tyres. 14 and 15-inch alloy wheel options as for 316. All 320i tyres HR rated.

DIMENSIONS: As for 316, unladen weight 1272kg (1983 2 door).

PERFORMANCE:

0 – 30mph	2.7 secs
0 – 40mph	4.4 secs
0 – 50mph	6.2 secs
0 – 60mph	9 secs
0 – 70mph	11.5 secs
0 – 80mph	14.4 secs
0 – 90mph	18.9 secs
30 – 50mph (2nd Gear)	3.5 secs.
50 – 70mph (3rd Gear)	6.1 secs.

Maximum speed: 121mph (4th gear, early car with 3.45 diff), 118 in 5th, later cars.

Overall fuel consumption: 26mpg.

Battery: 50 ah

NOTES: Rear anti roll bar was fitted as standard is some markets. Power increased to 129bhp from 9/1985.

BMW 323i 1982 to 1985 (two- & four-door saloon, Baur Cabriolet)

ENGINE: As for pre 1988 320i with LE Jetronic but stroke 77mm. Compression 9.8:1, power 139bhp at 5300rpm and torque 151 lb/ft at 4000rpm. 1984 onwards models 150bhp at 6000rpm, torque unchanged.

MANUAL GEARBOX: Getrag 260 five speed, ratios:
1st = 3.83
2nd = 2.20
3rd = 1.40
4th = 1.00
5th = 0.81

323i with Sport (dogleg) gearbox:. Getrag 245, ratios:
1st = 3.76
2nd = 2.33
3rd = 1.61
4th = 1.23
5th = 1.00

AUTOMATIC GEARBOX: As for 320i.

DIFFERENTIAL: Standard car 3.45, when fitted with sport gearbox 3.23. 150bhp cars use 3.23 differential in some markets; some Baur cars use 3.64 from 318i.

SUSPENSION: As 320i but with rear anti roll bar and with option of Bilstein sport suspension.

STEERING: As for 320i.

BRAKES: As for 320i but with rear disc brakes.

WHEELS AND TYRES: As for 320i but with VR rated tyres.

DIMENSIONS: As for 316 – 320i, weight 1090kg (std) – 1135kg (4 door automatic).

PERFORMANCE:

0 – 30mph	2.5 secs
0 – 40mph	4 secs
0 – 50mph	5.8 secs
0 – 60mph	8.1 secs
0 – 70mph	10.7 secs
0 – 80mph	13.7 secs
0 – 90mph	17.6 secs
30 – 50mph (4th gear)	9.1 secs.
50 – 70mph (4th gear)	9 secs.

Maximum speed: 125 mph.

Overall fuel consumption: 23.8mpg.

BMW 325e 1984 to 1987 (2 and 4 door saloon, Baur Cabriolet)

ENGINE: BMW M20, 84mm bore and 81mm stroke, 11.1 compression (10:1 from mid 1985 and 9.7:1 on European catalyst equipped cars), Bosch Motronic engine management, 4 bearing camshaft, power 122bhp at 4250rpm, torque 170 lb/ft at 3250rpm.

MANUAL GEARBOX: Getrag 260 five-speed, ratios as for 323i.

AUTOMATIC GEARBOX: Unique ZF 4 HP22 from 525e saloon, optional switchable sport/economy settings.

DIFFERENTIAL: 2.93 ratio.

SUSPENSION: As for 320i.

STEERING: As for 320i.

BRAKES: As for 323i (4 discs) with optional ABS.

WHEELS AND TYRES: As for 320i.

DIMENSIONS: As for 320i, weight 1120kg (automatics 20kg more).

PERFORMANCE: (early 11:1 compression model with manual gearbox)

0 – 30mph	3.1 secs
0 – 40mph	4.8 secs
0 – 50mph	6.6 secs
0 – 60mph	9.6 secs
0 – 70mph	12 secs
0 – 80mph	15.8 secs
0 – 90mph	20.1 secs
30 – 50mph (5th gear)	11.9 secs.
50 – 70mph (5th gear)	13.2 secs.

Maximum speed: 116 mph.

Overall fuel consumption: 28mpg.

Battery: 66 ah

Notes: Late European cars may well have used the 325i cylinder head like the USA "Super Eta"

BMW 325i and 325 ix 1985 to 1992 (two- & four- door saloons, Baur Cabriolet, Convertible and Touring)

ENGINE: BMW M20, as for 325e but with 75mm stroke, lower compression; 9.7:1 on metal bumper cars, 9.4:1 on later cars and 8.8:1 on catalyst cars. Bigger valves and ports, power 171bhp at 5800rpm, torque 167 lb/ft at 4000rpm.

MANUAL GEARBOX: Getrag 260 as for 325e. 325i Sport uses the same Getrag 260 gearbox but with closer ratios:

1st = 3.35
2nd = 2.03
3rd = 1.36
4th = 1.00
5th = 0.81

AUTOMATIC GEARBOX: ZF 4HP 22 four-speed automatic, optional switchable sport/ economy settings.

DIFFERENTIAL: 3.64, and 3.73 on metal bumper cars including Sport LSD, later Sport uses 3.91 ratio LSD, Tourings and 325 ix use 3.91 standard diff. 3.74 on 325 ix Automatic. 3.63 used on standard plastic bumper 325i 2wd manual.

Transfer box and power distribution of 37% front wheels and 63% rear wheels on 325 ix.

SUSPENSION: As for 323i but with gas filled dampers front and rear, thicker front and rear anti roll bars. Sport model has Bilstein M Tech suspension, Bilstein damper on metal bumper cars, Boge on later cars.

STEERING: As for 320i.

BRAKES: As for 325e and 323i, standard ABS on Tourings and plastic bumper cars.

WHEELS AND TYRES: Standard 195/ 65 VR rated tyres on 5.5 inch steel of 6 inch alloy wheels, 205/55 VR 15 tyres and 15 x 7 inch BBS alloy wheels optional, standard on Sport model.

DIMENSIONS: As for 316 – 325e, weight 1180kg (two -door manual saloon, 1988) 1330kg (Automatic Convertible) 1270kg (Manual Touring) 1285kg (325 ix).

PERFORMANCE: (1986 325i Manual 4 door).

0 – 30mph	2.2 secs
0 – 40mph	3.6 secs
0 – 50mph	5 secs
0 – 60mph	7.2 secs
0 – 70mph	9.3 secs
0 – 80mph	12 secs
0 – 90mph	16 secs
30 – 50mph (4th gear)	7.2 secs.
50 – 70mph (5th gear)	11 secs.

Maximum speed: 132 mph.

Overall fuel consumption: 22.8mpg .

Battery: 66 ah

Notes: Late Sports from 89/90 use Boge dampers as opposed to Bilsteins. 325i "Motorsport" convertibles have type number "798".

BMW 324d and 324td (four-door saloon)

ENGINE: BMW M21 Diesel, 80mm bore, 81mm stroke, 2443cc with 22:1 compression ratio, power 86bhp at 4600rpm (324d), 115bhp at 4800rpm (324td), torque 112 lb/ft at 2500rpm (324d), 162 lb/ft at 2400 (324td). Bosch mechanical diesel injection with six piston pump, Garrett T-03 turbocharger on 324td.

MANUAL GEARBOX: Getrag 240 as for BMW 320i. 324td uses 325e/325i Getrag 260 gearbox.

AUTOMATIC GEARBOX: As for BMW 320i (324d) or 325e (324td).

DIFFERENTIAL: 3.45, small casing unit manual and auto. 3.23 large casing unit for 324td.

SUSPENSION: As for 320i (324d) or 325e (324td).

STEERING: As for 316 – 325i.

BRAKES: As for 316 and 318i (324d), As for 325e (324td).

WHEELS AND TYRES: 195/65 HR 14 (324d and 324td).

DIMENSIONS: As for 316 – 325i, weight 1195 kg, 324d manual, 1280kg 324td automatic.

PERFORMANCE:

	324d	324td
0 – 30mph	5 secs	3.9 secs
0 – 50mph	11 secs	8 secs
0 – 60mph	16 secs	12 secs
50 – 70 (4th gear)	15 secs	10 secs
Maximum speed:	100mph	116 mph

Overall fuel consumption: 32.5mpg (324d) and 40mpg (324td)

BMW 320iS (two- & four-door saloon)

ENGINE: BMW Motorsport S14 engine as for M3 2.3 Evo 11 but with 72.6mm stroke, 1990cc. Standard 2.3 cylinder head, camshafts, valves and inlet manifold, 10.8:1 compression ratio, power 192bhp at 6900rpm, torque 123 lb/ft at 4600rpm.

MANUAL GEARBOX: As for M3.

DIFFERENTIAL: 3.45 ratio LSD, 25% lock up.

SUSPENSION: Boge gas suspension as for 325i or Bilstein M Tech suspension as for 325i Sport.

BRAKES: Standard 325i.

STEERING: Standard E30 power steering.

WHEELS AND TYRES: As for 325i including 7 x 15-inch BBS.

DIMENSIONS: As for 316 – 325i.

PERFORMANCE:

0 – 30mph	2.8 secs
0 – 40mph	4.5 secs
0 – 50mph	5.8 secs
0 – 60mph	7.1 secs
0 – 70mph	9.3 secs
0 – 80mph	11.5 secs
0 – 90mph	14.3 secs

Maximum speed: 141 mph

Overall fuel consumption: 25mpg

Notes: 2 door model fitted with full M Tech body kit (as for the 325i Sport). Four-door model uses standard 320i body. All cars use plastic bumpers.

BMW M3 (two-door saloon, Convertible)

ENGINE: BMW Motorsport S14, 4-cylinder twin camshaft 16 valve, all 2.3 litre except Sport Evolution with 2.5-litres. Bore 93.4mm, stroke 84mm. Compression ratio 10.5:1 (11:1 Evolution I) Sport Evolution; Bore 95mm, stroke 87mm. Compression ratio 10.2:1.

Power: 195bhp at 6750rpm (Catalyst cars), 200bhp at 6750 (early cars and Convertible), 215bhp at 6750rpm (late saloons), 220bhp at 6750rpm (Evolution II), 238bhp at 7000rpm (Sport Evolution),

Torque: 169 lb/ft at 4750rpm (catalyst cars), 176 lb/ft at 4750rpm (200bhp early cars and Convertibles), 170 lb/ft at 4600rpm (late 215bhp saloons), 181 lb/ft at 4750 (Evolution II), 177 lb/ft (Sport Evolution).

All cars except U.S market models have an electric fan, U.S cars use viscous fan.

MANUAL GEARBOX: Getrag 265 Sport gearbox (dogleg pattern except U.S cars), ratios:

1st = 3.72
2nd = 2.40
3rd = 1.77
4th = 1.26
5th = 1:1

U.S market cars:
1st = 3.83
2nd = 2.20
3rd = 1.40
4th = 1:1
5th = 0.81

DIFFERENTIAL: 3.25 Evo II and Sport Evo that have 3.15. U.S cars have 4.1.

SUSPENSION: Special suspension with Boge gas dampers and revised mounting and pick up points, revised anti roll bar mounting points.

STEERING: LHD only and with quick ratio steering rack with 19.6:1 pinion to rack ratio and 3.6 turns lock to lock.

BRAKES: 280mm vented front discs with E28 5 Series brake calipers, 282mm rear discs and ABS.

WHEELS AND TYRES: Five stud BBS alloy wheels as standard, 7 x 15-inch on standard cars with 205/55 VR 15 tyres. Evolution II and Sport Evolution cars use 7.5 x 16-inch BBS alloy wheels with 225/45 VR or ZR tyres.

DIMENSIONS: Length 4325mm, width 1645mm, wheelbase 2570mm, track 1407 (front) and 1415 (rear). Weight: 1241kg (1986 base car), 1274kg (Evolution II).

PERFORMANCE: (Evolution II, 220bhp)

0 – 30mph	2.5 secs
0 – 40mph	3.6 secs
0 – 50mph	5.1 secs
0 – 60mph	6.6 secs
0 – 70mph	8.8 secs
0 – 80mph	11 secs
0 – 90mph	13.9 secs
30 – 50mph (2nd gear)	2.5 secs
50 – 70mph (3rd gear)	4.2 secs

Maximum speed: 148 mph

Overall fuel economy: 26mpg

NOTES: 215bhp cars used bigger throttle bodies than 195 and 200bhp cars.

The E30 enjoys good club support

USEFUL NAMES AND ADRESSES

AC Schnitzer: (0049) 241 56 88130. www.acschnitzer.de

Active Autowerke (USA): BMW Tuning
001 305 233 9300. www.activeautowerke.com

All Gear: BMW, ZF & Getrag gearbox specialist.
01909 478581

A – Trim: Specialist in all BMW interior retrimming, North West London. 01923 228070, www.atrim.co.uk

Alpina GmbH: (0049) 8241 50050. www.alpina.de

Alpina United Kingdom: (Sytner Nottingham)
0115 934 1444

Bentley Manuals: www.bentleypublishers.com

Bexley Motor Works: E30 and M3 specialist, Kent.
0208 304 9797. www.bmsport.com

BMW Car Club GB: Officially BMW recognised BMW club, part of BMW Club Europa 01225 709009

BMW GB: BMW AG owned British importer.
01344 426565

BMW Owners Club: 6, Uplands, Walditch, Bridport, Dorset. DT6 4LE

BMW Mobile Tradition: D-80788 Munich, Germany (0049) 89 382 20028

Bilstein UK: 0208 956 5049. www.eurocarparts.com

Bridgegate BMW: E30 friendly BMW Main Dealer, Chesterfield 01246 208681

Brooklands Books: for Bentley Manuals and E30 road test books. 01932 865051. www.brooklands-books.com

Chipped UK: ECU remapping 07815 501867

C3: London based E30 M3 parts specialist,
0208 676 8667

CPC Autos (instrument specialists): 07960 280953

Dickhaut Specials: E30 and M3 used parts and new stainless steel brake pipes, Central Germany (Kassel) 0049 562492 6966 / 0049 160 268 0491

E30 Zone: Internet based E30 club. www.e30zone.co.uk

E30.de: German E30 internet club, www.e30.de

Eta Motorsport: E30 serving, repairs and race car preparation, Kent. 01474 328777, 07974 912139

Fritz Bits: Tuning, parts and service for pre 1988 BMW's in Somerset. 01823 669425

Hadrian Panels: 01373 865684 www.carpanels.co.uk

Hartlake: BMW Specialist, East London/Kent area 01474 326626

Ireland Engineering: USA based BMW performance specialist in California. 001 626 359 7674, e-mail jireland@earthlink.net

Lepsons: Kent based alloy wheel restoration specialist, Gillingham, Kent. 01634 580582

MJF Engineering: Surrey based BMW Mechanic, all E30s and M3 cars. 01306713232

Moseley Motorsport: Specialist in M3's, Telford. 01952 503992. www.moseleymotorsport.com

Parkside Garage (Worksop): M3 and M50 conversions 01909 506555

PMW: Mechanic for all E30 especially M3. West London /Bucks/Berks area 07970 645599

Quarry Motors: BMW parts and service in Sheffield. 01142 769076

Rossiters: Specialist for E30 and M3 AC Schnitzer tuning parts both current and obscure. 01485 542000. www.rossiters.ltd.uk

Turner Motorsport: USA E30 performance specialist. 001 978 388 7769

171

THE 'ROAD TEST' BOOKS BELOW REPORT ON ALL E30 MODELS, WITH VIEWS DRAWN FROM EUROPE, AUSTRALIA, SOUTH AFRICA AND THE US

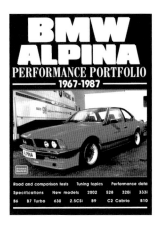

BMW 3- Series (E30)
Official Service Manual 1984-1990

This workshop manual is produced by Bentley Publishers in the US. It is recommended by Andrew Everett and covers the 318i, 325, 325e, 325es, 325i, 325is and 325i convertible. 528 pages, 825 illustrations/diagrams.
Soft Bound (B390)

BMW 3 Series
Enthusiasts Companion

The complete production & sporting story of BMW's 3 Series from 1975 into 2000 has been meticulously researched & carefully written. A full account is given of the sales & motorsport accomplishments of the various models plus detailed spotter's & buyer's guides. 300 pages, over 350 black & white photos & illustrations.
Soft Bound.

For further information on these and other titles please refer to our web-site: **www.brooklands-books.com**

From specialist booksellers or, in case of difficulty, direct from the distributors:

Brooklands Books Ltd., P.O. Box 146, Cobham, Surrey, KT11 1LG, England Phone: 01932 865051
E-mail us at info@brooklands-books.com or visit our website www.brooklands-books.com
Brooklands Books Australia, 3/37-39 Green Street, Banksmeadow, NSW 2019, Australia. Phone: 2 9695 7055
CarTech, 39966 Grand Avenue, North Branch, MN 55056, USA Phone: 800 551 4754 & 651 277 1200
Motorbooks International, P.O. Box 1, Osceola, Wisconsin 54020, USA Phone: 800 826 6600 & 715 294 3345

Further reading on BMW cars

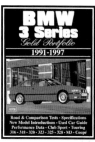
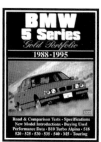

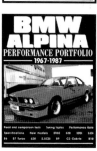
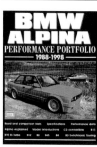

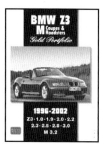
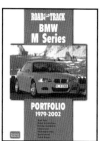
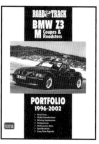